A Help for using

The Psalms

in personal and family worship

A Help for using

The Psalms

in personal and family worship

by C.W.H. Griffiths, M.A.

pearlpublications.co.uk

Contact: info@pearlpublications.co.uk

A Help for using The Psalms in Personal and Family Worship

Paperback: ISBN 978-1-901397-03-1

Hardback: ISBN 978-1-901397-04-8

E Book: ISBN 978-1-901397-05-5

First published 2023.

The moral rights of the author are asserted.

British Library CIP Data available.

BISAC: REL006120; REL006770; REL055020

We acknowledge with thanks permission from Christian Focus Publications to quote Alec Motyer, *Psalms by the Day* and also Alec Motyer, *Journey: Psalms for Pilgrim People*.

The help of David Legg and Margaret Maclean in the completion of this book is gratefully acknowledged.

CONTENTS

PREFACE

This book was born out of trouble and trial.

I turned to the Psalms as I sought my personal blessing and guidance. With the work of the ministry closed to me, I committed my thoughts to writing. What I have written was therefore intended firstly for my own use, and maybe for the use of my family. If others are helped by what has been written, I will be so thankful. To God alone will be the glory.

Howell Harris wrote on the progress of the eighteenth century revival in Wales 'A door was opened to me to speak and to pray through a man who went about teaching people to sing Psalms'.[1]   May the Lord be pleased to revive and bless his people as a result of this encouragement to sing Psalms.

My desire is that, through God's personal dealings with me, a fragrance of Christ will be spread abroad

Awake, O north wind,
and come, thou south!
Blow upon my garden,
that the spices thereof may flow out.
Let my Beloved come into his garden
and eat its pleasant fruits.

Song of Solomon 4:16.

---

[1] Richard Bennett, *The Early Life of Howell Harris*. Banner of Truth Trust.   A translation of *Blynyddoedd Cyntaf Methodistiaeth*.

INTRODUCTION

This book is a help and encouragement to sing God's praise daily. Scripture repeatedly encourages - indeed requires - his people to sing praise. For many reasons, that is more important now than ever. This book highlights the value of the Psalms and the importance of singing them.

The custom of Calvin's Church in Geneva, and of the French Huguenots, was to sing the entire book of Psalms, singing each consecutively. Robert Murray McCheyne urged that the Scottish Metrical Psalter should be read or sung through at least once every year. We hope that, through daily use of the Psalms, readers will reclaim this book of Scripture as their very own 'Book of Praises'.

For some, it is hard to know where to begin in singing the Psalms. In this book, the Psalms have been divided into 365 manageable portions. The sections are based on natural breaks in the structure or meaning of the Psalms. These short sections enable the whole book of Psalms to be sung in a year.

Short devotional thoughts and expository notes are given for each day of the year. One or more leading thoughts are given daily. This is not a comprehensive exposition. References are given that can be the basis of further study. 1 Cor. 14:15 instructs us to 'sing with understanding'. It is hoped that these notes may assist the singer to achieve that.

We have followed the plan of Charles Bridges, 'The composition of this work has been diversified with as much variety as the nature of the subject would allow. The descriptive character of the book will be found to be interspersed with matter of discussion, personal address, hints for self-inquiry, and occasional supplication'.[1] We trust that we have not neglected to highlight important doctrinal truths that are present in the pages of the Book of Psalms, nor their prophetic application.

Whilst this book is a help to using the Psalms in personal and family worship, it does not aim to be a child-friendly book that enables the understanding of the Psalms by all ages. Such a book would be well-nigh impossible to produce, and we suggest its value would thereby be limited for the adults of a family.

Many Christians who have been brought up with worship-songs and hymns are unaware of resources which enable the entire Book of Psalms to be sung. In Appendix 9 we set out some of the materials available.

Why should we sing the Psalms?

The Psalms were written to be sung. The Lord 'inhabits', or 'is enthroned upon', our songs of praise (Ps. 22:3). Singing to the Lord should be a constant part of our daily walk with God. 'So will I sing-Psalms[2] to your name for ever, that I may daily perform my vows' (Ps. 61:8). 'While I live, I will praise the LORD; I will sing-Psalms to my God while I have any being' (Ps. 146:2).

When should we sing the Psalms?

David said, 'I will bless the LORD at all times, his praise shall continually be in my mouth' (Ps. 37:1). So it was

---

[1] Charles Bridges, *Exposition of Psalm 119: As Illustrative of the Character and Exercises of Christian Experience.*

[2] 'Sing' here is Hebrew *zamar*, the root of *mizmor*, a Psalm. Calvin and others translate "sing-Psalms" when this word is used. We have adopted this translation throughout.

in the early Church. Everywhere, in private and in public, at home and at work, in the town and in the countryside, the Psalms were sung[1].

The Westminster Standards express this clearly: 'God is to be worshipped everywhere, in spirit and truth; as in private families daily, and in secret each one by himself; so, more solemnly in the public assemblies'[2]; 'It is the duty of Christians to praise God publicly, by singing of Psalms together in the congregation and also privately in the family'[3].

Where should we sing Psalms?

In Personal Worship. Christians are accustomed to refer to their private devotions as a 'Quiet Times', but should we not sing to God in our times of personal prayer and worship? Is it not our duty, privilege, and responsibility to sing to the LORD? 'Sing-Psalms to the LORD, O you his saints' is the exhortation of King David (Ps. 30:4). In the New Testament, James says, 'Is any merry? Let him sing Psalms'[4]. Billy Bray, the converted Cornish tin miner, used to say 'God made the crow as well as the nightingale, and he likes to hear them both sing'!

In Family Worship. Even where families do worship together today, they rarely sing. Douglas Conin writes, 'It is truly a joy and a privilege for families to join together in the singing of praise. Here is where a singable version of God's own songs – the Psalms of

---

[1] *See* Michael Bushell, *Songs of Zion*; A.F. Kirkpatrick, *Cambridge Bible – Psalms*.

[2] *Westminster Confession of Faith, Chapter 21, Section 6.*

[3] *The Directory for Public Worship* (approved by the Westminster Assembly).

[4] James 5:13. Merry = cheerful, in good spirits.

the Bible – can provide a rich blessing for the whole family. Children are thus encouraged to memorise God's Word through one of the most proven techniques of memorisation, namely the combination of words with music'[1]. See Appendix 10 for more comment on Family Worship.

In Church. The New Testament instructs us to sing Psalms when we gather together[2].

Until the eighteenth century the majority of Protestant Churches sang the Biblical Psalms and little else. In the Greek Orthodox Church, the entire Psalter is sung every week, and there are similar customs in all the ancient Churches of Christendom. The 1662 Book of Common Prayer of the Church of England took worshippers through the whole Book of Psalms each month.

In our day, a Psalm is hardly ever sung in Church, and even when a handful of Psalms are listed in hymn books or worship books, they usually bear little resemblance to the Biblical text.

We have included a select reading list in Appendix 11 - The Psalms in Congregational Worship, as we believe that the nature of what we sing in Church worship deserves serious reconsideration by Christians.

What will be the effect of singing the Psalms?

It has frequently been said that Christians learn their

---

[1] *Returning to the Family Altar. A Commentary and Study Guide on The Directory for Family Worship adopted by the General Assembly of the Church of Scotland in 1647.* Douglas W. Conin. (James Begg Society).

[2] Eph. 5:19, Col. 3:16.

theology from what they sing in worship. Singing together embeds the words in our memory. In singing the Psalms we have our thoughts and understanding of God moulded by Scripture itself.

As we use the Psalms in worship, we 'sing and make melody in our hearts unto the Lord' (Eph. 5:19). We are built up and edified. The Psalms are 'the word of Christ' that can 'dwell in us richly' and give us instruction and warning (Col. 3:16). They declare Biblical truth and God's revealed will. They are fitted for our personal use and for the use of the Church (Eph. 5:19, 20; Col. 3:16; James 5:13; 2 Tim. 3:16).

By singing your way through the Psalms, we believe that you will find 'the Psalms tend to produce a distinctive type of piety that is thoroughly God-centred and experimental in a balanced way, as one would expect from using materials of Divine inspiration'[1]. Your walk with God, in obedience to his Word, will be blessed.

---

[1] John Keddie, *Sing the Lord's Song*.

HOW TO USE THIS BOOK

We recommend reading the Appendices as a preparation to the use of this book.

The daily portions can be used to read the Psalms through in a year. This book could therefore simply be used as an aid to personal Bible Study.

However, the primary intention is that each portion should be sung. The daily notes are for devotional use, or for use in family worship. They are intended to help understand one or two key points of each portion, rather than providing a detailed exposition.

You will need to obtain a Psalter that you can use for singing. If you do not already have a version of the Psalms for singing, the companion volume to this book – *Every Psalm for Easy Singing* might be the best option, as it is divided into the same 365 portions. However, see *Appendix 9 - Resources for Psalm Singing*, particularly if you belong to the Scottish, Anglican, or Genevan Psalm-singing traditions.

The following procedure is suggested

- Read the Bible portion.
- Read and think about these daily notes
- Sing the portion.
- Use the 'thinking points' at the end of this book in a family worship context.
- Pray over what you have learned from the portion.

Book 1

Psalms 1 – 41

Day 1   Psalm 1

The Perfect Man

This first Psalm sets themes for the whole book. It describes two pathways, two types of people. It speaks of judgment and blessing. A person is righteous or wicked, godly or ungodly, a believer or an unbeliever, blessed or cursed. There is no middle ground.

Who then is the blessed and perfect man described in verses 1 and 2? Surely, 'all have sinned and fall short of the glory of God' (Rom. 3:23)? In speaking of the blessed and righteous one, the Psalms tell of the Lord Jesus Christ, who fulfilled all things, so that in him we might be blessed (Rom. 5:19).

He who keeps separate, and delights in God's ways, will be like a fruitful tree, continually watered. The wicked are the opposite of this. They are like the chaff of the threshing floor which the wind blows away. The chaff is unwanted. It is worthless and useless.

We do not yet see outward prosperity for God's people, although, in times of drought, the green leaf and fruitfulness of the righteous is more apparent. But in the Judgment (v5) all will be recompensed, and the way that seemed right to unconverted men will perish (v6).

May our roots go deep, to draw upon God for all our needs. May we follow in our Saviour's steps to the blessing that this Psalm promises.

Day 2   Psalm 2:1-6

Two Governments

Psalm 1 describes the two ways for individuals; Psalm 2 speaks of two ways for nations.

David expresses dismay that the rulers and kings of the Gentile nations have set themselves against the LORD and his Christ, determined to throw off their restraint. Acts 4:23-31 shows how this has ever been true. We learn from that passage that raging against God's people is rebelling against God. This state of affairs worsens as the end of this age draws near, and will be fully manifested (see Rev. 16:13, 14; 19:17-19).

Awesome and powerful as the confederacy of evil seems, David looks up, and sees it in the light of God's power. The LORD views it with utter contempt. He waits for his appointed time to destroy the perpetrators and vindicate himself. When Satan has done his worst; when all the demons and powers of evil have armed themselves, and think they have the victory (as they did at Calvary) – then the LORD will triumph.

What a comfort this is to the suffering Church in a world that is groaning (Rom. 8:22).

The break of day, when the King, even our blessed Jesus, is introduced (v6) will follow the darkest hour. He will then rule and reign as King of kings and Lord of Lords.

Day 3   Psalm 2:7-12

The King will reign

Having introduced his King in verse 6, the LORD describes Messiah's reign in verses 7-9. Warning and counsel to kings and rulers is then given in verses 10-12.

Christ's kingship is here particularly in view. God calls him 'My King'. He is not one of 'the kings of the earth' (v2). He is the King of Kings and Lord of Lords (Rev. 17:14, 19:16). By the decree of heaven, his Eternal Sonship is proclaimed (v7, compare Luke 3:22; 9:35; 2 Pet. 1:17, 18). He rules with a rod of iron (v9; Rev. 19:15).

However, the LORD's 'King upon Mount Zion' (v6) represents a change from the previous state of affairs. Our King, the Son of David, does not yet reign from Mount Zion (Ezek. 21:26, 27; Mark 11:10; Luke 19:38; Matt. 23:37-39). The LORD here makes 'the decree', which results in dominion over earth's widest bounds (v8; Ps. 72:7, 8; Isa. 11:9, 10; Zech. 9:10; Rev. 11:15).

The description of Mount Zion as the LORD's 'holy hill' (or, literally, 'hill of my holiness') also represents a changed condition. Jerusalem will be distinguished by Divine holiness (see Ezek. 43:1-6; Zech. 14:20, 21).

The closing words are to all those who hold authority in Government. They speak of the goodness and severity of God (Rom. 11:22). Would that our rulers and judges would act in the fear of God, and 'kiss the Son' (v12)!

Day 4   Psalm 3

Fleeing from Absalom

Believers are engaged in warfare (Eph. 6:10-18). David here was under threat, with tens of thousands set against him. Just as the Devil used Job's wife to attack Job's faith (compare v2 with Job 2 verses 5 and 9), here David faces his own son Absalom (so the title of the Psalm).

This 'fiery dart' left David in confusion and turmoil. We know how he doted on Absalom (2 Sam. 13:37-39). When Absalom died, he was overwhelmed with grief (2 Sam. 18:32, 33). How must he have felt at this time when Absalom sought to remove and destroy him?

Family troubles cut deep. It is difficult to keep our balance and perspective in them. When other people, or our own hearts, tell us that God cannot, or will not, deliver us (v2, 3) we must defend ourselves with the shield of faith. We must continually seek help from the LORD (v4), and count our mercies as well as our difficulties (v5).

May the Lord give us grace and trust in the conflict. May we be faithful to him, even in difficult family matters, for they will come (Mark 13:12, 13). The Lord even sends them lest we should set our hope of joy and peace in this passing world. We must depend upon God alone for deliverance and blessing.

Day 5   Psalm 4

Peace in perplexity

The best way to understand this Psalm is David 'musing' – or as we might say 'puzzling things out' – laying on his bed and thinking (v.4). He cries out to God. He rebukes the strength and greatness of the natural man (*'ish* in Hebrew) (v.2). He encourages himself and other believers v3-7. After this he rests in God, and goes to sleep v8.

We are not told what his former distress was (v.1). It is left as a blank into which we can write the name of our personal trial. We are told: (1) It has in some ways still continued v.2; (2) His prayers have not yet been fully answered v.6; (3) He is confident that God will eventually bless - in a way, his trial is 'his glory', he is 'set apart for the Lord' v.2, 3; (4) His eventual joy will exceed the present carnal joys that others experience now v7 (compare Hab. 3:17-19).

His walk as a believer is in some ways a lonely walk. He is 'set apart' from others v3. He communes 'with his own heart' v.4. Yet, though he is solitary and alone, he is protected by God v.8. Calvin considers the meaning of v.8 to be that God alone (and no-one else) gives him security, which almost amounts to the same thing.

Pray this Psalm when you go to bed tonight.

Day 6   Psalm 5:1-6

Light in a time of darkness

How do we respond to the increasing evil around us? Do we despair? Have we become desensitised to blasphemy and immorality? Or do these things drive us to prayer for God to intervene?

In this Psalm David speaks of a time of great wickedness. Verse 5 speaks of those who are 'foolish' and boastful even 'before the eyes' of God. Such 'workers of iniquity' are hated by God. The psalmist's faith is tested by those who speak lies, who are violent, bloodthirsty, and deceitful (v6). He knows that God, the true GOD (Hebrew *El*) will not tolerate evil in his presence (v4).

Vile and filthy things are happening in the professing Church. When will the Lord Jesus gather out of his kingdom all things that offend, and those who do iniquity Matt. 13; 49-50?

David's response was not one of despair. He cried to God with increasing earnestness. There is progression in the words that he uses at the start of the Psalm. 'give ear', 'consider', 'attend to' (AV 'hearken'). His prayer develops from 'words' to 'inner thoughts' ('meditation' AV), and then to a 'cry' to God. He rises up early in the morning to bring his concerns before God, expecting Lord's answer (verse 3).

May the growing darkness likewise cause us to 'look up' and pray.

Day 7   Psalm 5: 7-12

Shielded by the LORD's favour

There are three parts to this section.

1. (v7, 8) David dedicates himself to the worship and service of God and looks to the LORD to lead and, make his way plain and straight. He is unworthy. His prayer is based on God's loving-kindness alone.

2. (v9, 10) He desires God to justly judge and punish rebel sinners. Our desire for the salvation of the lost should not be at the expense of inadequate views of God's holiness and justice. In Revelation 8 the prayers of the saints finally bring judgment down. Delitzsch considers this Psalm to be the key to all the Psalms containing prayers against one's enemies.

3. (v11, 12) He desires joy, blessing, and protection for all those who put their trust in the LORD.

The thoughts of de Burgh upon these words are helpful – 'The prayers of Scripture are prophecies, and their repetition hastens their fulfilment'[1]. So, as we use this Psalm in personal, family, and corporate worship, our voice hastens the day. It is as the voice of 'the Spirit and the Bride' – 'Come, Lord Jesus. Come quickly'

May he shield you this day and this night with his 'favour' – his delight and acceptance. May he keep you 'as the apple of his eye' and give you a straight path.

---

[1] William de Burgh, *A Commentary on the Book of* Psalms.

Day 8   Psalm 6:1-5

The LORD returning in mercy

In this Psalm David desires the return of former blessings (v4). From this we see that it is possible for believers to lose that sense of God's favour for a time, and to feel under the LORD's wrath and anger. We may seem to grope in darkness, anguish of spirit, and torment of conscience. This prayer turns to God as the only refuge, the only hope in such dark times. God's loving-kindness, known and experienced previously, is the longing of a soul in such a condition (v4).

This is the first of the Penitential Psalms. David feels under both the persecution of men and, yet worse, under the chastisement of God. It is the language of the saint in trouble, whether of physical suffering or distress of mind (v2, 3). The writer longs for this time to pass, as he has gloomy forebodings of death, when the light of his testimony will be put out. In such a situation, let us remind ourselves that if we should die we shall be with Christ, 'which is far better' (Phil. 1:23).

Dear brother and sister, if these words echo the experience of your heart at this time, make this prayer fully your own, and place all your dependence on God's mercy. Then, at length, you shall rise from your knees, knowing that he has returned to you with mercies.

Day 9   Psalm 6:6-10

Weary, weeping, but heard by the LORD

We have in these verses the truth that 'weeping may endure for a night, but joy comes in the morning' (Ps. 30:5).

David's experience was not pleasant. He felt utterly crushed, 'every night' or 'all through the night' (v6). Yet tears of grief and anguish are very effectual in bringing the answer from the LORD (Ps. 126:6; James 5:16-18). Although the answer may not come as quickly as *we* desire, be sure that he keeps all our prayers in remembrance (Ps. 56:8).

The Psalm began with David conscious that he was under God's displeasure and chastening for his sin. It closes with his faith rising. He knows that God has heard his tearful cry - 'the voice of his weeping' and his plea for mercy.

We know too that our prayers will be heard, not for our merits, because we have an Advocate with the Father, Jesus Christ the righteous (1 John 2:1). By faith David too can declare that all those who hated him will be finally and suddenly turned back.

If your sorrow is like David's sorrow, I pray that in his words in verses 8-10 you will find a ray of sunlight that will keep your faith looking upwards until his answer is given.

Day 10   Psalm 7:1-8

In God we trust

We have in this Psalm an excellent example of how to bring our trials and troubles to the throne of grace. We need really say no more than the opening words, 'O LORD, my God, in you do I put my trust'. If only we could stop and ponder upon those words, all our anxieties would cease.

This is the prayer of David, persecuted despite his kindness. 'Cush', in the Psalm title, is not known to us. This demonstrates the antiquity of the titles, as it shows a knowledge of the history of David outside the Bible record. He was someone who must have shown bitter hatred against David.

The person speaking in this Psalm most closely fits the Lord Jesus himself, as he alone could plead his complete innocence (v3-5; John 8:46; 10:32). He forgave his murderers; but a time of judgment must come ('the judgment appointed', v6). Then the LORD's wrath, held back by the dam of his mercy for so long, will finally break upon the wicked.

The Lord Jesus promised his blessing to those of us who are persecuted for righteousness' sake (Matt. 5:10; 1 Pet. 2:19-23). We may safely leave our cause in the hand of him who judges justly. We can say to our persecutors, 'The LORD rebuke you' (Jude 9). He will at length come to our aid.

Day 11   Psalm 7:9-17

God is outraged every day

This Psalm is an appeal to the Judge who always does right (Gen. 18:25). It is the cry for vindication, not just of the oppressed believer, but of God himself. The conclusion of the Psalm shows the confidence and faith of David. He does not sink into doubt or accusation against God, despite all the contradictions of his own experience. He raises his voice in praise to the LORD – God in all his perfections. He desires to offer praise worthy of, and answering to, God's great righteousness. He declares him to be the Most High God, a Judge to all the oppressing powers of man, and the Devil.

What fearful words we have in verses 11-13! Jonathan Edwards' great Gospel sermon[1] says it well, 'So it is not because God is unmindful of their wickedness and does not resent it that he does not let loose his hand and cut them off. God is not altogether such an one as themselves, although they may imagine him to be so. The wrath of God burns against them, their damnation does not slumber; the pit is prepared, the fire is made ready, the fire is now hot, ready to receive them; the flames do now rage and glow. The glittering sword is whet and held over them, and the pit has opened its mouth under them'.

May we sound an alarm to the ungodly in this day of God's mercy.

---

[1] Jonathan Edwards sermon, *Sinners in the Hands of an Angry God*.

Day 12   Psalm 8

All things under his feet

This Psalm returns to the theme of Psalm 1 – the perfect man. Some consider these first eight Psalms a distinct section.

In the first and last verses of this Psalm we see the fulfilment of the prayer 'Thy kingdom come, thy will be done on earth, as it is in heaven'. It cannot refer to the glory of Adam, whose enemies were not stilled (v2). It refers to the incarnate Son of God. We see no reason for making the words figurative or mystical. Hebrews 2:8 shows that some of these things are yet future.

Our Jesus is now glorified and wears the victor's crown of glory and honour. He is seated at the right hand of the Father (Heb. 2:9; Ps. 110:1). All authority is given to him in heaven and earth (Matt. 28:18), and yet..., and yet... there is a greater day coming; when his heavenly glory will be seen (v1); when the 'weak things' which God has chosen will triumph (v2; 1 Cor. 1:26-29); when all things are put under his feet in deed, not just in title (v6); and when the groan of creation shall cease (v7,8; Rom. 8:22).

If we long for the vindication of God's perfection and justice (Psalm 7), how much more do we long to see all the sweet and gracious promises of Scripture fulfilled to the letter; and to behold him who is the fairest of ten thousand, crowned with glory and honour.

Day 13   Psalm 9:1-10

Marvellous works of the LORD

Although the circumstances described here may have reference to his present experiences, David speaks as a prophet of things to come. He refers to:

- The nations or Gentiles (v5, 15, 17 'heathen' AV).
- The 'wicked one' (v5) and the 'enemy' (v6), whose destructions are come to a 'perpetual end' (compare 2 Thess. 2:8 and Isa. 14:4-6).
- The reign of the LORD in righteousness that follows. It is over the world – 'the habitable earth' (Heb. v7, 8; Isa. 14:7).

This points to the return of our Lord Jesus.

Well may David praise the LORD with his whole heart and show forth all his marvellous works (v1). A.A. Bonar notes the similarity of the things referred to in the opening part of this Psalm and Isaiah 25:1-5. He observes that all is spoken in the past tense (v4-6), 'because the future is to the Lord as sure as if already come and gone'[1]. It is certain. 'God is not a man, that He should lie, nor a son of man, that He should repent. Has He said, and shall He not do? Or has He spoken, and shall He not make it good?' Numb. 23:19.

How good it will be when you and I, and all God's saints, shall join together in these words of thanksgiving.

---

[1] A.A. Bonar, *Christ and his Church in the Book of Psalms*.

Day 14   Psalm 9:11-20

The needy will not always be forgotten

This Psalm gives assurance and consolation in times of abounding iniquity, and severe trial. It is prophetic. It speaks of the ultimate vindication of the saints, of the just judgment of the wicked, and the fulfilment of the promises of blessing. In doing so it offers comfort to those who rest in its truths by faith, although they are suffering now.

The call of verse 11 is for universal praise, because the LORD has answered the prayers of his people. He dwells in Zion. The psalmist's confident cry for relief is given in verse 13 and 14. The final answer is assured in verses 15-17, with not just the destruction of all ungodly nations (compare Zechariah 12-14), but of the Wicked One himself (see v.16 – singular).

The words *higgaion selah* (v16), although uncertain in meaning, seem to have been inserted here to underline the need to pause for meditation on these things.

Let us write verses 18 and 19 across our newspaper front pages. The Lord will return when the nations are distressed, men's hears failing them for fear and looking after those things which are coming on the world' (Luke 21:26).

Today is man's day – mortal, frail, feeble and arrogant man – but God's day is hastening on, day when the meek shall inherit the earth.

Day 15   Psalm 10:1-11

A portrait of the Wicked One

This Psalm continues Psalm 9.[1]

We have here the groaning of the psalmist in the face of persistent wickedness and oppression. It seems a hopeless and awful situation.

De Burgh refers this rebellion to the time of Antichrist. He considers the actions described here as the actions of that 'vile person' who will act as a God-despiser (v3, 4; 2 Thess. 2:4); arrogantly self-confident (v5, 6; Rev. 13:4), a deceiver (v7-10; 2 Thess. 2:10, 11); and a persecutor of the poor (also v7-10; Matt. 24:21, 22).

It seems to the psalmist that God is far off and inaccessible (v1). He almost seems to believe the wicked person who says just that (v11) - but 'the needy will not always be forgotten' (Ps. 9:18).

Luke describes the time before the coming of the Lord as 'men's hearts failing them for fear and for the expectation of those things which are coming on the (inhabited) earth, for the powers of the heavens will be shaken', but goes on to say 'Now when these things begin to happen, look up and lift up your heads, because your redemption draws near' (Luke 21:26-28). Let us look up, if we find ourselves in such dark times.

---

[1] Psalms 9 and 10 are linked together alphabetically. Lines begin in the sequence of the letters of the Hebrew alphabet. The two Psalms are one in the Old Greek version.

Day 16   Psalm 10:12-18

The destruction of the wicked

We have a judicial scene in these verses. It is as though the case for the prosecution has been made by the psalmist and he calls upon the Judge to rise, to still the courtroom, and to give sentence (v12). The defendant thinks that his actions will escape the Judge's inquisition (v13). However, the Judge will requite with his own hand; he will demand payment (v14).

In this Psalm we have stern, exact justice – He will break the arm of the wicked man, and will seek out his wickedness until none is found. There will be no debt that is not paid in full.

This is not a purifying of the wicked person, but a removal of both him and his wickedness (compare Isa. 41:12). For what purpose? It is to bring in the Kingdom of peace and righteousness (v16; compare Matt. 13:41). It is to give justice to the fatherless and the afflicted and 'that the man of earth[1] may no more oppress (or, 'cause terror and fear')' (v18).

As noted yesterday, we are dealing particularly with that day of mature evil 'when transgressors are come to the full' (Dan. 8:23). May we stand, and endure to the end, if we are called to witness when that day at last comes.

---

[1] We may translate the Hebrew as 'the weak and earthbound man'.

Day 17   Psalm 11

The watchful eyes of the LORD

'If the foundations be destroyed, what can the righteous do?' (v3). When wickedness, lawlessness, and injustice over-whelm a land, those who stand for righteousness are hard pressed. Of God's coming judgment, A.A. Bonar comments[1], 'all that came upon Sodom and Gomorrah shall be realised at the Lord's appearing 'in flaming fire' (2 Thess. 1:8: compare v1 with Gen. 19:17 and v6 with Gen. 19:24)'.

Whatever happens to us, we must always remind ourselves of the truth of v4; 'The LORD is in his holy Temple. The LORD's throne is forever. His eyes behold, his eyelids try'. Delitzsch comments, 'when we observe a thing closely or ponder over it, we draw the eyelids together, in order that our vision may be more concentrated and direct'. God in heaven likewise scrutinises not just the deeds, but every thought and purpose of men upon earth'

Therefore, 'Let no temptation decoy me from my duty. Let no danger deter me from it. While JEHOVAH, my reconciled God and Father, manages and judges the world, my safest course is to commit myself to him in well-doing'.[2]

---

[1] A.A. Bonar, *Christ and his Church in the Book of* Psalms.

[2] John Brown of Haddington *The Psalms of David in Metre, with Notes*.

Day 18   Psalm 12

When vileness is exalted

This is yet another of the 'persecution Psalms'. The first four verses are the prayer of David in days when the ungodly prosper, and the godly are under pressure. Verse 5 gives the LORD's answer. The remaining verses express dependence and trust.

How the words used here resonate with the conditions around us now! – vanity and emptiness fill our television screens, our cinemas and everyday conversation (v2) – flattery and the cult of celebrity (v3) - the national leadership is dominated by people who can manipulate the media to their advantage ('with our tongue will we prevail' v4) - the demand for freedom of speech and 'artistic expression' that knows no limitation by decency, morality, or the fear of God (v4). 'The wicked walk on every side, when the vilest men[1] are exalted' (v8, AV).

As we might expect, at such a time the poor are oppressed, and the needy groan (v5). Such mourning should be our response too.

But the LORD will in his time, in the fulness of time, rise up to deal with these things (v5). His word is certain. It is without any deceit or dissimulation (v6). It is utterly sure to come to pass. 'Amen. Even so, Come Lord Jesus!' (Rev. 22:20).

---

[1] Or the vilest things – Hebrew 'vilenesses'.

Day 19   Psalm 13

How long?

Martin Luther knew the trials of the psalmist and commented, 'Hope despairs, and yet despair hopes'. Such Psalms as this teach us how to pray, and how to deal with discouragement. It is a dialogue between the writer and his God, and a dialogue with his own soul, to stir up greater faith and trust.

We find the cry 'How long?' seventeen times in the Psalms, and three times in this Psalm. Suffering and trial would be softened if only we knew when we would get relief - but we rarely know.

The darkest thing about David's trial was that God appeared to be hiding his face from him during it. He appeared to be forgetting him. David then did what we often do - he schemed (v2). But this gave no relief from his sorrow.

His doubts and forebodings are, in the end, removed by his affirmation of trust and faith –'I have trusted' – 'my heart shall rejoice' – 'I will sing' – 'because the LORD has dealt bountifully with me'. When he has finished his work in us, when he has purged us, we will come forth as gold (Job 23:10).

As we use these inspired words in our worship today, may sunbeams of hope shine into our hearts through the darkness.

Day 20   Psalm 14

Foolish, filthy, and soon to be fearful

This Psalm is almost identical to Psalm 53. The best explanation is that Psalm 53 in Book 2 of the Psalter was adapted for a different use. Here the oppressors of Israel are addressed and in Psalm 53 Israel is addressed (compare Psalms 14:5 and 53:5).

The 'fool' in verse 1 is not one who is mentally deficient, but a person whose mind is darkened (compare Ps. 10:4). What is described is not an up-front, declared atheism, but a practical denial of the God of the Bible. Alas, how often we see this today when men in the world and the Church fashion God after their own imagination, rather than know him according to the Scriptures.

This is a teaching Psalm. God is not addressed directly in prayer or appeal. It nevertheless expresses a deep longing for the LORD to intervene in the affairs of men. In verses 5 and 6 it is as though the psalmist sees God beginning to intervene. The last verse gives words of an aching, yearning heart that wants God to change things without any further delay. Note that the yearning is not for God's salvation to come to Zion, but to come out of it. There Messiah will reign and his law shall go forth from Mount Zion (see Isa. 2:3; Mic. 4:2; Rom. 11:26). Israel's joy, and Jacob's gladness, shall then be ours also. These things are certain. Let us give thanks to our God.

Day 21   Psalm 15

Who will dwell with God?

Luther comments that, just as Psalm 14 is a description of the ungodly, Psalm 15 is a description of the righteous. It is essentially a description of the Golden Rule that we should love our neighbour as ourselves.

The opening verse asks who will dwell with God, and who is fit to worship him. The answers are paralleled in the book of James.

1. He who walks uprightly and works righteousness (v2a - James 1:19-27).

2. He who guards and controls his tongue (v2b, 3 - James 1:26; 3:2-12).

3. He who does not show respect of persons, and rejects the vile person whatever his status (v4a - James 2:1-7).

4. He who speaks the truth at whatever cost (v4b - James 5:10-12).

5. He who shuns covetousness and the love of money (v5a - James 1:9-11; 2:5, 6; 5:1).

Ps. 24:3 also asks a similar question, and gives the same answer. We should be those who 'have clean hands and a pure heart'.

May we seek to be Christ-like in all we do. Then we will not be moved - as a tree planted by the waters (Ps. 1:3). This is not salvation by works, but a description of those who are truly saved.

Day 22   Psalm 16:1-6

Our Inheritance

The title is 'a Michtam of David'. The exact meaning of this Hebrew word *michtam* is unknown, but many think it means 'golden'. If the LORD is our portion this is indeed a golden Psalm!

David first commits himself to God (v1, 2). He then declares his love for God's people – holy in the sight of God (v3). His determination is to only worship the true God (v4). That separation to the LORD means a total separation from false gods. He will not even utter their names.

With joy he claims God to be his portion and his inheritance (v5-6). As believers, chosen from the foundation of the world, the LORD is our portion. He is also our cup – he makes daily provision for us. He '*maintains* our lot' – he takes good care of what he has given us (John 14:2, 3). His (measuring) lines have secured a pleasant inheritance (v6). Compare Zech. 1:16; 2:1-4, which speaks of Jerusalem's future blessing.

It is very easy to get frustrated and disappointed when things do not turn out for us in life as we expect, or as we think they should. We must keep a spiritual view of all that happens. Our God and his people are our portion. They are everything to us. In the end, nothing else matters.

Day 23   Psalm 16: 7-11

The life pathway of the believer

This section is the sweet testimony of the psalmist. He is totally committed and therefore enjoys the blessings that come from setting the LORD before him (in front of him, living in his presence) continually, constantly – compare this section with Deut. 6:1-19.

He blesses the LORD for his counsel, his guidance, his instruction, because he makes known 'the path of life'. But he also looks forward to the time when there will be 'fullness of joy' and 'pleasures for evermore' (v7-11). Have you tasted the joy of the LORD and the pleasures (sweet and delightful things) that he gives even now? Then what will it be like when he gives them in their fullness and without ceasing, for evermore?

Peter quoted verses 8-11 on the day of Pentecost (Acts 2:24-32) and said that David prophesied here of Christ's resurrection. The verses speak of the Father's care and protection of him, but also speak of us. For three days Christ's body lay in the place of death, but the LORD kept his promise. Bless God! Death could not hold our Saviour. He declared 'I am he who lives, and was dead; and, behold, I am alive for evermore' (Rev. 1:18). And, if he lives, we shall live also.

Dear Christian, he who cared for his Son, 'how shall he not also with him also freely give us all things?'

Day 24   Psalm 17:1-7

Upheld by the LORD

This Psalm, and particularly these opening verses, is again concerned with God's justice and with the writer's integrity. There is strong connection between Psalm 16 and Psalm 17. This points to the same author and speaker (compare 16:7 and 17:3; 16:8, 11 and 17:5; 16:1 and 17:7; 16:5 and 17:14, 15).

As the New Testament clearly shows Christ speaking prophetically in Psalm 16, we naturally see the words of Psalm 17 as those of the Saviour as well. Indeed, no one else could make his claim to blamelessness and integrity.

Only he could challenge his accusers with 'Which of you convicts me of sin?' (v3; John 8:46). He was 'without sin' before God (Heb. 4:15). The Prince of this world had nothing in him (John 14:30). His heart is pure (v3). His words are pure (v1, 3). His ways are pure (v4, 5).

Through Christ we too may have 'clean hands and a pure heart' (Ps. 24:3, 4) that will make our worship acceptable, that will open his ear to our prayers (v1, 6) and that will fit us to dwell in his presence (Ps. 15:1, 2). This is not through our good works though. We could translate the first prat of verse 7 'display the wonder of your loving-kindnesses'. As the LORD makes known to us the vastness of his mercy, so we will be drawn to follow his ways in love and thanksgiving.

Day 25   Psalm 17:8-15

The apple of God's eye

David calls upon God for the safety that comes from being near to God – as the pupil of his eye, and as one under the shadow of his wings (v8). He is importunate and urgent in his prayer throughout his Psalm. 'Hear... attend to my cry... give ear... I have called upon you... you will answer me... incline your ear... hear my speech...' (v1 and v6). 'Keep me!', 'Hide me!' (v8), 'Arise!', 'Save!' (v13). He is desperate for God to act.

It is the darkness, hostility, and wickedness he sees all around that drives him to this prayer. Wicked men are a deadly enemy to the believer (v9). They are prosperous and proud (v10). They desire his overthrow (v11). They stalk him as a lion (v12 - compare 1 Pet. 5:8). They are worldly, and seek their satisfaction in material things (v14).

And would you make this world and the unregenerate your friends, dear believer? Is this vain world a friend to grace? As time goes on, we must expect evildoers to grow worse and worse (2 Tim. 3:13). Therefore, let us cling ever closer to our God.

We seek those things that are above. Verse 15 has every element of 1 John 3:2 – supreme satisfaction, a great transformation, and an enlarged vision[1]. It will soon be ours.

---

[1] E. Bendor Samuel, *The Prophetic Character of the Psalms*.

Day 26   Psalm 18:1-6

The day of deliverance

After so many Psalms in which David cried out 'how long?' under oppression from his enemies, we have here 'the words of this song in the day that the LORD delivered him from the hand of all his enemies' [Psalm title].

We may take comfort from this as we sigh about the condition of things in this world. We, like David, sometimes cry out 'How long?' Be sure: the deliverance, and the full answer of our prayers, will come at last.

These verses simply state that David called, and the LORD answered. The distress, the delay, and the spiritual impatience are scarcely remembered.

In verse 2 the writer bubbles over with grateful affection to his God. The words used for God may be translated in different ways. Several of them refer to the sort of rocky fastnesses where David sought refuge from Saul: 'my Strength (craggy rock) … my [cleft in the] Rock… my Fortress… my Deliverer… my God… my [strong] Rock of refuge… my Shield… the Horn of my salvation… my Strong Tower (literally, 'high stronghold').

Make God your only refuge and security.

God's answer will come fully and certainly. Our tongues will be loosened to praise our God in that day - the day that the Lord delivers us from the hand of all our enemies.

Day 27   Psalm 18:7-15

David's last words

With minor alterations, this Psalm is a repeat of 2 Samuel 22. It bears the marks of thankful remembrance in old age. It is followed in 2 Samuel by 'these are the last words of David' (2 Sam. 23:1).

These verses describe a direct intervention by the LORD. The language is symbolic, but nevertheless, the events presented here clearly go far beyond David's deliverance from the hand of Saul and from all his earthly enemies.

The interpretation of these verses cannot be limited to David's time. The description goes beyond anything the world has yet seen. The events described foreshadow the final consummation, when the LORD shall arise as a man of war (Isa. 42:13) and shall shake terribly the earth.

This is the 'Day of the LORD', when our Saviour returns. Compare verse 7 with Zech. 14:4 and Isa. 2:17-22. Compare verse 10 with Rev. 1:7 and 14:14. What a fearful day that will be for the ungodly

Although he may have been inspired by his own deliverance and by God's faithfulness to him personally, David prophesied. 'The Spirit of the LORD spoke by me, and his word was in my tongue' (2 Sam. 23:2).

Day 28   Psalm 18:16-19

Personal deliverance

David suddenly returns from the big picture of the LORD's mighty intervention in the Day of the LORD to his personal deliverance. On a battlefield, the general has in mind only the overall victory. The foot soldiers, whether they live or die, are deployed to that end. They are dispensable in the achievement of the big plan. It is not so with God. We are 'as the apple of his eye' (Ps. 17:8). In the conflict that is this life, everything he does is for the good of each and every believer.

David describes his predicament. He was like a drowning man (v16); he was confronted by his strong enemy (v17); he was exposed to the malice of many who hated him and who were too strong for him (v17); it was the day of his calamity and distress (v18).

Look at what the LORD did for him – he sent forth – he took me – he drew me – he delivered me – he was my support and stay – he brought me forth – he rescued me – he delighted in me. This is a personal faith of a man who knows his God.

Can we speak in such personal terms of what the LORD has done for us? Does the LORD not also delight in us each one? Or do we imagine in all the noise of the battle that he has forgotten us?

Day 29   Psalm 18:20-26

Reward and recompense

In this portion David links the LORD's delight in him with his personal righteousness, obedience, and sincerity. This is difficult for us. It sounds at first like the voice of the Pharisee (Luke 18:11, 12). But David knew his sin (Psalm 51). These cannot be the words of a self-righteous hypocrite.

Let us consider this in three ways.

Firstly, despite his failings, David was exceptional in his integrity and obedience. The inspired Scriptures confirm this (1 Kgs. 11:33-38; 14:8; 15:5).

Secondly, the New Testament once, and possibly twice, makes Christ the speaker of this Psalm (v49 – Rom. 15:9 and v2 – Heb. 2:13). As Dr Gill comments, there are many things that relate to Christ in this Psalm. He is David, the LORD's anointed (v50). There is no difficulty in Christ using these words, for in him the Father is well pleased.

Thirdly, because we are 'in Christ' we can use these words too. The Father also delights in us. Our sin is covered, and, if we confess our sins, we are given a clean heart (Ps. 51:6-10; 1 John 1:9). This goes beyond mere cleansing. His righteousness is imputed to us (Rom. 5:19). He promises to 'reward' our subsequent obedience and service (1 Cor. 3:8-15; Rev. 22:12). So, by sovereign grace, we too can take these words upon our lips.

Day 30   Psalm 18:27-36

Armed and ready for battle

The imagery of most of this passage is once again that of the battle, and of the LORD equipping and enabling David for his part in it. The LORD is his shield (v30); his rock of refuge (v31); he is accoutred with strength (v32); swift (v33); skilled for battle (v34); given the shield of salvation (v35). He is strong in the LORD even though his true condition is one of weakness and darkness (v27, 28).

There are many gems in this passage, and there is much benefit in meditating upon its words. Here are examples, 'You will light my lamp. The LORD my God will enlighten my darkness' (v28); 'Your gentleness has made me great' (v35). Verses 29-35 can be read profitably in connection with Ephesians 6 – the Christian's armour – and with other passages that refer to the Christian life as a warfare.

Let us commit ourselves to the LORD's service. Let us fight the good fight, putting on the whole armour of God that we may be able to stand against the wiles of the Devil.

Matthew Henry writes, 'Let them that walk in darkness, and labour under many discouragements, in singing these verses, encourage themselves, that God himself will be a light to them'.

Day 31   Psalm 18:37-45

Complete victory

This part of the Psalm gives thanks for victory over the enemies of the king – those who were his personal enemies (v37); those who rose up against him (v39); those who hate him (v40).

So shall King Jesus conquer and reign. All peoples shall be subdued under him (v43, 47). He will be given 'dominion and glory and a kingdom, that all the people, nations, and languages should serve him' (Dan. 7:14).

His Church can take these words to heart. Often, we may feel, as David in Ps. 13:2, perplexed and sorrowful: our enemy Satan exulting over us: the constant pressure of temptation and failing. Yet, does not the Scripture say that, 'the God of peace shall bruise Satan under your feet shortly'? (Rom. 16:20). Shall the saints not judge the world? (Rom. 3:6; 1 Cor. 6:2). Shall we not soon be 'as the angels of God in heaven'? (Matt. 22:30).

The irresistible power of Christ to put down his enemies is shown in these verses.

At present he sits at the Father's right hand awaiting the time when his enemies shall be made his footstool – waiting until the word goes out to him - 'Rule in the midst of your adversaries' (Ps. 110:1,2). That day will surely come.

Day 32   Psalm 18:46-50

Great deliverances

The words of this last part of the Psalm are sure words of victory. Here is the universal dominion, the time when the kingdoms of this world shall become the kingdoms of our God and of his Christ (Rev. 11:15). Verse 50 speaks of 'great deliverance' (literally, 'salvations' or 'victories'), which the LORD gives to his King. He shows loving-kindness, steadfast love (Hebrew - ḥesed), to his Anointed – to David, and to his offspring for evermore.

The words of this Psalm are echoed by the Apostle Paul. He says 'if God be for us, who shall be against us?' (Rom. 8:31) In v 47, David uses a special word for God – he is 'the El' – the great transcendent God.

In Corinthians Paul urges us to thank 'God, who gives us the victory through our Lord Jesus Christ' (1 Cor. 15:57). 'The God of peace shall bruise Satan under your feet shortly' (Rom. 16:20). This Christ shall rule the nations with a rod of iron (Rev. 19:15), so too shall we (Rev. 2:27).

Christ rules now in the hearts of Christians, but a time is coming when every knee shall bow, and every tongue shall confess that he is Lord.

Day 33   Psalm 19:1-6

Visible speech

After a series of Psalms focussed on personal circumstances, we have here one in which the writer simply stands to worship.

It is a Psalm of two halves. Two apparently separate poems are put together in a beautiful balanced statement of the greatness and glory of God in nature (v1-6) and in the Scriptures (v7-14).

What God proclaimed 'very good' still declares the glory of God despite the Fall (v1, Rom. 1:19, 20). Each new day pours out more of the glory of God in his creation (v2). Each night reveals the knowledge of God. Astronomers return to their task endlessly, with more to marvel at, and more to learn.

Yet the 'speech' of God's handiwork is not in anything we can hear (v3). We must take time to 'consider the heavens' (Ps. 8:3); otherwise its message will be lost in the hubbub of human voices. Yet, truly, there is nowhere in this world without testimony to God's greatness (v4), just as there is nothing hid from the heat of the sun (v7), which is resplendent as a bridegroom in happiness and as a warrior eager for the battle (v5).

'In like manner, the Gospel of Christ preaches to all nations ... while it reveals his mercy, concerning which the works of Creation are silent' (Rom. 10:18)[1].

---

[1]Robert Haldane, *Exposition of the Epistle to the Romans*.

Day 34   Psalm 19:7-14

The LORD's perfect law

In verses 7-11, the psalmist is overwhelmed with the awesome instruction provided by the Scriptures. It is in many forms - the law; the testimony; the statutes (or precepts); the commandments; the fear and the judgments of the LORD.

He declares their beneficial effects – they convert (or restore); they are reliable (sure); they make wise; they are right (or straight); they rejoice the heart; they are pure; they enlighten; they are clean; they endure forever; they are truth; they are righteous; they warn; they promise great reward. He piles up metaphors and similes to make his description even more graphic – they are like gold, better than much fine gold; like honey, and even the drippings of the honeycomb.

And yet... the psalmist has a problem. In the light of all this, why does he fall into errors (sins of accident or ignorance, Lev. 4:14); secret and hidden faults; presumptuous, planned, and wilful sins (v13); sins of word and sins of thought (v14)? He pleads that they may not have dominion over him (v13).

Let us thank the Lord for the Gospel (Rom. 6:14) which magnifies God and his law, and gives deliverance through Christ. In the Gospel may indeed pass from our experience of the bondage of sin, expressed in Romans 7, to the glorious assurance of Romans 8:1.

Day 35   Psalm 20

Hope in the day of trouble

The first four verses of this portion are prayer on behalf of a dear friend. This rises to a confident expectation of the answer in verses 5-8. The last verse provides a summary.

We can apply this Psalm in several ways. For example, we may take this prayer and offer it on behalf of some struggling brother or sister in the thick of the fight. We then act in the LORD's Name. He is the God of weak and failing Jacob (v1). We stand for the honour of his name (v5, 7). We represent him in the fight. We should pray for each other in this way.

Yet again, this reminds us of the intercession of Christ. This is a Psalm of David, and does not our David, our Anointed One, plead over us in our weakness (Luke 22:31, 32; Heb. 7:25; 8:1)? Does he not intercede for us as Moses on the hilltop, when Joshua battled with Amalek (Exod. 17)? Our faltering human prayers may fail. We may 'ask amiss' (James 4:3), but his mighty, prevailing mediation with the Father never will. The LORD will fulfil all his petitions (v5).

Take heart, dear believer, you do not battle alone. We look to Jesus, the Author and Finisher of our faith, who will keep us in our day of trouble, and to the end.

Day 36   Psalm 21:1-7

The King's joy

This follows on from and links with the previous Psalm. The prayer of Ps. 20:4 has been answered and we are called to give thanks (Ps. 21:13). It is, as Bishop Horsley entitles it, 'A Thanksgiving of the Church for Messiah's Victory'.

In these verses we have the answer to the Lord Jesus's prayer in John 17. 'And now, O Father, glorify me'. Verse 5 of this Psalm reads, 'His glory is great in your salvation: honour and majesty you bestow on him'.

This is heartfelt thanksgiving for the joy that has been poured upon Messiah. He 'for the joy that was set before him' (Heb. 12:2) endured the cross. Now we find him 'exceeding glad' (v6 – literally, 'to rejoice with joy', 'to gladden with joy'. Compare Ps. 4:7; 16:11). 'You have loved righteousness, and hated iniquity; therefore God, even your God, has anointed you with the oil of gladness above your fellows' (Ps. 45:7; Heb. 1:9). He was the Man of Sorrows, but he is no longer. The dreary figure knocking at the door in Holman Hunt's painting is little short of blasphemy.

We do not yet see all things put under him, but a time is coming when every knee shall bow at the name of Jesus and every tongue shall confess that he is Lord. Let us join our voices in the Saviour's prayer, 'Father, glorify the Son!'

Day 37 Psalm 21:8-13

The fires of judgment

This portion deals with the utter destruction of the King's enemies. Although it is written of King David, the application is clearly to Christ triumphant.

The rebels described here planned and devised evil against the king himself (v11). They were rebels, traitors. In the day of his wrath there will be no place of escape for them (v8; Josh. 10:17ff; Isa. 2:19-21; Rev. 6:15-17).

Their fate will be unimaginable. Commenting on v10, Dickson[1] writes, 'There is no possibility to apprehend the horrible punishment of Christ's enemies: for after their casting into a fiery oven, they are set down here as fuel, to suffer what God's being incensed in anger, as a consuming fire swallowing them up, and devouring them in his incomprehensible wrath, importeth'. So shall the righteous be separated from the wicked (Matt. 13:40-43).

Let us, indeed, 'kiss the Son' (Ps. 2:12), while his mercy may be found, and let us respond to the awful danger of those who are yet 'children of wrath' (Eph. 2:3) by prayer and by doing the work of an evangelist.

Let us gladly, but soberly, 'sing and praise *God's* power' (v13).

---

[1] David Dickson, *A Brief Explication of the Psalms*

Day 38   Psalm 22:1-5

Forsaken by God

As we approach this Psalm, we need to remove the shoes from our feet, for we stand on hallowed ground.

We have here the spiritual history of the cross, with at least eleven allusions to the Lord's Passion. The inner three disciples witnessed Gethsemane, and then beheld his wounds and excruciating death on the cross. The silent majesty of his Person hid the inner agonies of his soul. Here, in this Psalm, as nowhere else, we are shown the inner breathings of his spirit under the awful load. Only here are we shown the true character and intensity of his sufferings.

The opening five verses are spoken when forsaken in the silence of God the Father. They are a prayer like no other. They contain no petition, for there could be no answer, no lightening of the load. They make no confession of sin or guilt, but they are free from any bitterness. They are spoken when the sun was darkened at noonday, and when the Father had turned his face away from the Sin-bearer.

Dear child of God, by his obedience and death he has discharged all your debt; he bore your sins, and satisfied the justice of God. Yet more than this, he obtained for you the favour of God, righteousness, and eternal life. Would you complain about *your* troubles when he has done so much for you?

Day 39   Psalm 22: 6-13

Contempt for the Sufferer

His hope and trust, though cruelly derided, is plain in verses 6-10 as he hangs there upon the cross. He is in subjection to the Father's will, still holding fast to his hope and trust through the floods and torrents of Divine wrath, the assaults of devils, and the mockery of wicked men.

The malice and force of all Satan's fiery darts are felt by the Redeemer – 'dogs', 'piercing', 'the power of the dog', 'the lion's mouth', 'the horns of wild oxen'. There is no hiding, or protection – enclosed, encompassed, looked at, and stared upon.

In this Psalm we are taught how to pray.

When he pleads for relief, the speaker describes his circumstances to the LORD. This is common in Bible prayers (e.g. 2 Kgs. 19:9-19; Neh. 9 esp. v36, 37). God is omniscient. He knows all things; but he desires that we make our needs known. The Lord Jesus knew Bartimaeus was blind, but the blind man needed to acknowledge his condition and declare his need (Luke 18:41).

In the Bible, prayer lays the case of the suppliant before the LORD. It confesses his need. It then pleads on the grounds of God's character and promises. That is the true nature of effective intercession

Day 40   Psalm 22:14-21

Wounded for our transgressions

In these verses, bodily suffering, and groaning lead to prayer for deliverance.

The sufferer sees God's hand in all his circumstances (v15) 'You have brought me to the dust of death'. It was the time for Zechariah's prophecy to be fulfilled, 'Awake, O sword, against my shepherd, and against the man that is my fellow' (Zech. 13:7).

Satan, and wicked men, bear responsibility and blame, and will receive their punishment. We must always see God in control. They were, and are, the mere instruments he uses when he brings affliction.

Our Saviour's physical agony – bones, heart, bowels, strength, tongue, hands, and feet - is described here. He is utterly despised. Men haggle unfeelingly, and cast lots for his sole possessions, even in the face of his utter desolation,

In verses 20 and 21 there is a prayer for deliverance from the malice and hurtful power of his enemies. His deliverance came at length. He was not taken out of the trial. He was sustained through it. Perhaps that will also be our experience, and we will need to bear our present difficulties. He who was his Strength (v19) is our Strength too, and he will deliver.

Day 41   Psalm 22:22-31

Mission accomplished

We may write Isaiah 53:10 over this Psalm, 'Yet it pleased the LORD to bruise him; he has put him to grief. When you will make his soul an offering for sin, he will see his seed, he will prolong his days, and the pleasure of the LORD shall prosper in his hand'. In these remaining verses, he passes from the darkness of the separation from the Father to the peace and assurance of his mission completed.

However, the remarkable thing in these verses is that the triumph is not expressed as a personal one. It is a victory shared. Its joys and its benefits are not his alone, but they are the treasured possession of ... 'my brethren', 'the congregation', 'those who fear the LORD', 'all the seed of Jacob/Israel', 'the great congregation', 'the meek', 'those who seek him', 'all the ends of the earth', 'all the kindreds of the nations', 'the LORD's kingdom', 'the nations', 'all those that prosper', 'every mortal man', 'a seed', 'a generation', 'a people'.

We owe him a debt beyond measure, 'For, as by one man's disobedience many were made sinners, so by the obedience of one shall many be made righteous', (Rom. 5:19). We share with Christ this glorious, glorious victory.

Day 42   Psalm 23

The LORD is my shepherd

The Shepherd Psalm is intensely personal. 'I', 'my' and 'me' are in every line. This is strange, for sheep are gregarious creatures and shepherds deal with them in flocks. Yet there is no 'we', 'our' or 'us' in these verses. The believer's walk with God must be a communion of two hearts. The believer, as 'the beloved' of the Song of Songs, is enthralled and wholly transfixed by the one who leads and guides him. He is always drawn to where he feeds his flock (Song 1:7, 8).

De Burgh unfolds the pattern of this Psalm very clearly. The first two verses are a parable; the remainder is an interpretation of it. The interpretation starts with restoration or conversion of the sinner and traces his journey, till at length the believer reaches the everlasting and eternal rest.

Here we see our blessed Saviour, the Good Shepherd (John 10); even he who sought the one sheep that was lost (Luke 15); the Great Shepherd of the sheep (Heb. 13:10); the Shepherd and bishop of our souls (1 Pet. 2:25).

We know his voice and we follow him, for by his choosing we are his sheep. We are in a covenant relationship with him, and he is the one who has brought us into that covenant with himself.

Day 43   Psalm 24

He is the King of Glory

We have in this Psalm a joyous celebration of the LORD's power. The earth is the LORD's. This world is his by creation. The thing someone makes is uniquely his.

This Psalm speaks of the ownership rights of the Lord Jesus. Through him the Father made the worlds, and he is the Heir of all things (Heb. 1:2).

But since man's fall, and his sin in the Garden of Eden, another power has claimed dominion. Satan could, with some truth, offer the kingdoms of this world to the Lord Jesus (Matt. 4:8-10), for he is 'the Prince of this world' (John 16:11). The day is coming, though, when our Saviour, strong and mighty, strong in battle, shall come 'conquering and to conquer' and when the cry shall go up 'The kingdoms of this world are the kingdoms of our God and of his Christ' (Rev. 6:2; 11:15).

Once, as he entered the gates of Jerusalem, the Jews hailed him Son of David. He shall come to that city again as Israel's King (Zech. 9:9; Matt. 21:5), as the Son of David (Mark 11:9, 10). This cry will then go up, 'Who is this King of glory?' They will answer, 'the LORD strong and mighty'; 'Blessed is he who comes in the name of the LORD' (Matt. 23:39).

May the cry of our hearts be that the gates may open, and that he may soon come forth in all his glory.

Day 44   Psalm 25:1-7

Margaret Wilson's Psalm

This is an alphabetical Psalm[1]. Each pair of lines brings a fresh thought. The general theme is deliverance from sin and trial.

This Psalm was sung by the younger of 'the two Margarets' in the 'killing times' endured by the Scottish Covenanters. The two women were martyred by being tied to stakes fixed in the waters of the Solway Firth in 1685. Having watched the older woman in deeper water drown when the tide came in, the eighteen-year-old sang out the words of this metrical Psalm when her turn came to seal her testimony with her death[2].

The Psalm starts in the shadow of enemies, and those who do evil without a cause (v1-3). The psalmist then cries out (O that the words were on the lips of our children and our young people) 'show me your ways...teach me your paths...lead me in your truth and teach me...on you do I wait all the day' (v4,5). There is then a request for God to 'remember' his tender mercies and loving-kindnesses; 'not to remember' the sins of youth; and to 'remember'...me (v6, 7).

May LORD remember us and our families.

---

[1] See Psalm 10, 34 etc

[2] For the history, see Jock Purves, *Fair Sunshine*. She probably sang a tune from the original (Anglo-Genevan) Scottish Psalter of 1564. See Millar Patrick, *Four Centuries of Scottish Psalmody*, p.112.

Day 45   Psalm 25:8-14

An unexpected 'therefore'

In these verses the writer meditates upon God, and what God does for men. David has a deep confidence in, and knowledge of, the heart of God. He declares him to be 'good and upright' and '*therefore* he will teach sinners his way'! (v8). We might expect the opposite - an impatient and harsh response - but God loves the sinner, though he hates his sin.

Even David's great iniquity (v11) does not destroy his hope; he trusts God to pardon 'for your name's sake'. God's 'name' is all his revealed nature. He is mercy as well as judgment. His love and wisdom can be appealed to, whatever our predicament, and however great our sin.

There are no requests in verses 12-14. How different from our prayers! We come with our shopping list of requests to God, and then hurry back to the business of the day. Should we not learn to pray in a way which builds our confidence that God will answer? The psalmist does. He reminds himself of how that God deals with men; that he directs those who fear him (12); that he gives rest and prosperity to their souls (v13); that he confides in them regarding his fixed counsel or design; and causes them to enter into covenant with himself (v14). This the Lord Jesus promised to his disciples (John 11:15).

Day 46   Psalm 25:15-22

Complete dependence

Strengthened by his meditation in verses 8-14, David renews his prayer. He recognises his utter dependence upon God for deliverance in verse 15. 'My eyes are ever towards the LORD'. His feet are in a net and only the LORD can free him. He does not plead his own merit or his own strength. A.W. Pink was once asked how he was keeping. He replied, 'I am not keeping, I am being kept'! The psalmist too feels the need of this, and prays in verse 20 that his soul may be 'kept'.

His prayer is intensely personal. He is not conscious of others until he reaches the end of the Psalm. He is pleading his own need and communing with God. The phrases are full of 'I', 'my', and 'me'. This is not selfishness. Unless our own walk with God is strong and vibrant, our intercession for others will fail.

The summary of these verses, indeed of the whole Psalm, is found in the closing verse. 'Redeem Israel, O God, out of all his troubles!' What he has desired for himself (v17) he also desires for all God's people - that all their afflictions, tribulations, and restrictions should be relieved.

He no doubt saw answers for himself. However, we still long for the final deliverance and consolation of Israel, and of the Church.

Day 47   Psalm 26:1-7

Compassing the altar

'If we say that we have no sin, we deceive ourselves, and the truth is not in us' (1 John 1:8). How then do we understand this Psalm, where the writer calls upon God to vindicate him because of his innocence? (v1).

Some take these to be the words of the Lord Jesus. In the fullest sense they can only be his words. And yet, these are the words of David. De Burgh sees the Psalm as an assertion of 'faithfulness in the midst of abounding error and infidelity'. May we not aspire to such a testimony and seek God's blessing upon it?

The writer's separation is a determined stand (v4, 5). He is motivated by God's mercy (v3). He declares that he will go about, or 'compass' God's altar (v6). We too may walk round the altar of sacrifice, surveying the redemption work of Christ, meditating on what is 'our only comfort in life and death'. We must be separate from the world, knowing 'that I am not my own, but belong body and soul, both in life and death to my faithful Saviour Jesus Christ. He has fully paid for all my sins with his precious blood.[1]

Such a view of Christ will surely stir us to be separate. We will then want to proclaim God's praise, and tell of all his wonderful deeds (v7).

---

[1] *Heidelberg Catechism*, Lord's Day 1, Q1

Day 48   Psalm 26:8-12

Staying in the right place

The pathway of faithfulness to God is one of personal obedience. Notice in these verses how often the words 'I', 'my' and 'me' occur. David does not speak of his wife, his children, or even his friends. His focus is wholly upon God and his personal walk with him.

The psalmist wants to be where God is, and so loves the Tabernacle, where God was pleased to meet with his people (v8). He again desires to be separate from sinners (v9, 10). This time it is as though he fears to be with them lest God's hand of judgment should fall upon them and him together. 'Gather not [or 'do not remove'] my soul with sinners'.

Is the threat of God's wrath as real as this to us – are we conscious that they walk over the pit of hell on a rotten covering that in many places cannot bear their weight?[1] Can we walk with them?

The writer prefers the sure foothold – the even place. Bishop Horne comments 'the law of God is that "even place", that plain and direct path'. Though for now that may seem lonely and isolated, there will come a time when David's (and our) feet shall stand in the congregations of the righteous and there bless the LORD forever (v12).

---

[1] Jonathan Edwards, *Sinners in the Hands of an Angry God*.

Day 49   Psalm 27:1-6

One desire

The first half of Psalm 27 follows on so closely from the previous Psalm that Bishop Horsley considers these verses to have been 'very improperly' divided from Psalm 26. In Ps. 26:12 the writer promises himself the protection and fellowship for which he longed. In these verses he triumphs in the certainty of that hope. Verses 1-3 read like an Old Testament equivalent of Paul's triumphant certainty in Rom. 8:31-39.

The psalmist's love of the house of the LORD (Ps. 26:8) leads to the 'one thing' that he desires - 'that he may dwell in the house of the LORD all the days of his life' (Ps. 27:4). There alone is his peace and his protection (Ps. 27:5).

Whilst he 'compassed' the altar of atonement with devotion (Ps. 26:6), he here finds himself shouting for joy as he offers sacrifices upon the same altar (Ps. 27:6). Whilst he encouraged himself with the thought that he would, at length, bless the LORD in the gatherings of his people (Ps. 26:12), he here commits himself to sing, to sing psalms[1] to the Lord (Ps. 27:6).

Dear believer, hope in God, for you will yet praise him (Ps. 42:6).

---

[1] Hebrew *zamar*

Day 50   Psalm 27:7-14

A plain path

Verse 7 marks a change from confident hope to pleading for God's mercies. How dependent we are on God for his presence and blessing.

Every believer may expect to know times when the Lord appears to hide his face. The Song of Solomon is wonderful parable of the Lord's dealings with us, and how by such experiences he stirs us up to treasure his nearness and seek him more earnestly (S of S chapter 5).

Even our nearest and dearest may fail us (v10). The LORD alone is our unfailing comfort in life and in death. We need the certain hope that he will see us through – 'unless I had believed to see the goodness of the LORD in the land of the living…!' (v13).

Let us seek the LORD's path for our lives. May it be plain and straight for us (v11). However, this will never be if we walk aimlessly on the King's highway and wander off into bypath meadow. Bunyan saw this clearly and set out his warning in *Pilgrim's Progress*.

We will only find that straight and sure way as we are obedient to the final verse of this Psalm – 'Wait on the LORD: be of good courage, and he shall strengthen your heart: Wait, I say, on the LORD' (v14). We have here the psalmist talking to his unbelieving heart. Dr Martyn Lloyd Jones, in his book *Spiritual Depression*, encourages us to reason with ourselves in this way.

Day 51   Psalm 28

God's speaking place

David continues the supplications he began in Psalm 27. He is fearful that the LORD will not reply to his pleadings (v1). From these words it is plain that he knows the LORD hears, and he expects to receive an answer.

In the second half of the Psalm David is able to bless God (v6) that he has heard his supplications.

He uses an interesting word in verse 2. Most older commentators and lexicons link it to the common Hebrew verb 'to speak'. He lifts up his hands toward God's 'holy oracle' (AV). The word is used of the Holy of Holies (1 Kgs. 6:5, and elsewhere). It is God's 'speaking place' or 'audience chamber', as promised in Exod. 25:22. It was here that Moses, and Aaron and the High Priests that followed, spoke with God and received his answer (see Numb. 27:21; Josh. 9:14 etc).

Dear reader, we have a Great High Priest. We have the privilege of drawing near to the innermost sanctuary through him. Therefore, 'let us draw near with a true heart in full assurance of faith, having our hearts sprinkled from an evil conscience, and our bodies washed with pure water' (Heb. 10:21, 22). He is 'the God who answers' (1 Kgs. 18:24).

Day 52   Psalm 29

The voice of the LORD

We again have a clear sequence in the Psalms. David had pleaded that the LORD should not be silent. He looked to God's 'speaking place' (Ps. 28:2). He desired a blessing upon his people (Ps. 28:10). In this Psalm we hear the mighty 'voice of the LORD' seven times, and the great closing promise is that he will give strength and peace to his people (Ps. 29:11).

Some see this Psalm in terms of a storm. The Book of Psalms describes thunder as 'the voice of the LORD' (Ps. 18:14; compare John 12:28-30). The Hebrew word translated 'voice' in v3 is translated 'thunder' in Exod. 20:18 and 1 Sam. 12:17, 18.

How awesome it will be when God speaks in power, answering the prayer of his people for vindication, and quelling the tumult of the nations. Did not even a sanctified and prepared Israel tremble when God appeared? (Exod. 19:16; compare Joel 3:16 and Rev. 10:1-3).

When the final thunders have sounded, and when the mystery of God shall be finished (Rev. 10:7) the cry will go up, 'the kingdoms of this world are become the Kingdoms of our Lord and of his Christ, and he shall reign for ever and ever' (Rev. 11:15) - or in the words of this Psalm - 'Yea, the LORD sits as King for ever' (v10). For in his Temple everything shall speak of his glory (v9).

Day 53   Psalm 30:1-5[1]

Joy after weeping

We have here the rejoicing and encouragements of a man who walks with God. Here is a real, living, personal experience of God and a recognition of his hand, both in times of darkness, and when the darkness gives way to joy. Dear believer, can you express your walk with God in such words as these? Or is your prayer but an intellectual exercise -formal prayers from a cold heart?

There is another way in which these words can move our hearts. A.A. Bonar wrote, 'Our David could take up these strains and adopt them as his own. There was a time when his sacrifice was offered, and *the temple of his body* accepted by the Father. He too had been low, and had been lifted up (v1); had cried, and been healed (v2); had been brought up from among the dead (v3). Who could call on men so well as He to sing to JEHOVAH (v4a), and *celebrate the memorial of his holiness?* (v4b)'.

Take these words on your lips if you have ever been brought out of the darkness into God's marvellous light and known your heart warmed by the message of the Gospel. 'Weeping may lodge for a night, but joy comes in the morning'.

---

[1] The title of the Psalm is better rendered '... Dedication of the House. [A Psalm] of David' i.e. it refers to God's house, not David's. See Ps. 29:9; 1 Chr. 22:1, de Burgh, and *David, King of Israel* by B.W. Newton, p154.

Day 54   Psalm 30:6-12

Sunshine and Showers

David reflects on his experiences in life. In verses 6 and 7 he recalls a time when he took for granted his rest and his strength. We often imagine that our trials, like David's, will never end. Then, when God gives a time of prosperity and rest, we think it will never cease. We forget that this life is a pilgrimage. The Shepherd leads us by the still waters, but we must also pass through the dark valley.

When God hid his face, all David's false security vanished. He was driven to prayer (v8). This is the way that the LORD deals with us to remind us of our dependence upon him. We then ask ourselves afresh, 'What shall it profit a man if he gains the whole world, but loses his own soul' (Mark 8:36).

Trouble, and the hiding of God's face, changes our view of the landscape of our lives (v8-10), just as the sun passing behind clouds changes our view over the countryside. Likewise, the renewal of our fellowship with him changes everything (v11-12).

There is a time to mourn, and a time to rejoice. Sorrow can come in midst of a summer's day, and situations of impossible gloom can be transformed in a moment. We must serve and please God to the best of our ability and opportunity, but there will be changes for good or ill that we do not expect (2 Kgs. 4:18-37).

Day 55   Psalm 31:1-8

Into your hands I commit my spirit

'Into your hands I commit my spirit' (v5) were supremely words of the Lord Jesus Christ as he hung on the cross (Luke 23:46). He alone had power to lay down his life and take it up again. Yet these have also been the dying words of the martyr Stephen (Acts 7:59), of John Huss, Martin Luther, and John Knox. The Covenanter martyr Hugh McKail sang the Psalm. He then climbed the scaffold with the words 'every step of this ladder is a degree nearer heaven'.

As words of the Lord Jesus[1], the first four verses give his strong pleading under the assaults of the evil one. It is a prayer for deliverance and defence, for leading and releasing. Verses 5-8 show confident faith – trust, gladness, and assurance. God has seen all his adversities and trials.

The Lord Jesus only gave us one pattern prayer, but there are many pattern prayers in the Psalms, as this which the Master used. Note the grounds for each of the petitions. They relate to the character of God – his righteousness, his invincible strength, his truth, his mercy – or (the inclusive term) 'his Name' (v3).

---

[1] Interpreting this of the Lord Jesus, de Burgh suggests translating "delivered" rather than "redeemed" in (v5) as in the AV of Ps. 55:18 and 119:134. He likewise translates "have mercy" (v9) as "be gracious". Again, "iniquity" (v10) signifies the punishment as a result of sin here *imputed* to the sinless Saviour (see Gen. 4:13, etc)

Day 56   Psalm 31:9-15

My times are in your hand

Whether David writes as an old man here or not, he is conscious of the aging process, and that he is rapidly coming to the end of his days.

For some this can be a time for blessed reflection and fulfilment, as Bunyan spoke of 'the delectable mountains' near the end of the pilgrim's journey.

For others, it can seem a place of sorrow and disappointment. So it was for Jacob (Gen. 37:35), and thus it seemed to David here. He speaks of his life ending in grief and weakness: of his strength draining away (v10): of people forgetting him as someone already dead: as being like a thrown-away broken dish (v12): He is Fear-all-around[1] (v13).

Dear brother or sister, do these dark thoughts come upon you? Do you allow them to cause you to doubt or despair? Or do you cast yourself upon God's mercy (v9)?

In the end, Jacob found his doubts and fears unwarranted (Gen. 45:26-28; 47:11). So here, David comes to trust, even when in the darkness (v14). He sees that our times of prosperity and adversity, of life and death, are all in God's hands (v15). May we do so too.

---

[1] Fear-all-around: The name Jeremiah that gave to Pashur in Jer. 20:3 = *Magor-missabib*, (מָגוֹר מִסָּבִיב).

Day 57 Psalm 31:16-20

Hidden and kept by the LORD

In the land of Goshen the LORD made a difference between his people and the people of Egypt (Exod. 8:22; 9:26). The purpose was 'in order that you may know that I am the LORD in the midst of the land'. Although we may not discern it, the Lord always deals in this way. Even in the case of outward judgments, Abraham was right to argue that God would not punish the righteous with the wicked (Gen. 18:23-25). It is the constant prayer of the believer in Scripture that the LORD will openly vindicate him before the ungodly (v17). Without this, the wicked will say 'all things continue as they were from the beginning of the creation' (2 Pet. 3:4), and become bold in their rebellion.

There needs to be an evident distinction: the one ashamed: the other not ashamed (v17). Today we see the reverse. The godly are oppressed by unjust laws which, in the name of 'equality' and 'human rights', frequently encourage the wicked, who do unspeakable things (Eph. 5:12).

David longed for the light of God's face to shine upon him (v16; compare Exod. 10:22, 23), and he expected this in hope. He could rejoice in his heart and cry out 'Oh how great is your goodness, which you have laid up for them that fear you' (v19). Our future blessings are secure, for we are hidden and kept by our God (v20).

Day 58   Psalm 31:21-24

Marvellous mercy

David has been rejoicing over the blessings common to all the elect in the previous verses. He now turns to his personal testimony. The LORD has shown his great loving-kindness to him! In verse 21 the word means 'extraordinarily and wonderfully worked'.

We are reminded of the words of the Apostle Paul, 'O the depth of the riches both of the wisdom and knowledge of God! How unsearchable are his judgments, and his ways past finding out!' (Rom. 11:33). The Church can say, and Israel will too, 'We have a strong city; salvation will God appoint for walls and bulwarks' (Isa. 26:1 compare v21).

In our trials we may be brought to apparent despair. The Lord Jesus on the cross cried out 'my God, my God why have you forsaken me?' He knows our hearts and will not allow us to be tested past our breaking point (1 Cor. 10:13).

In the second half of verse 22 David can testify, 'God heard… when I cried'. If you can say this too, tell others, as David did, and call them to love the LORD and 'strengthen their heart' in all their trials. Turn your eyes from the evil-doer. God will deal with him for all his wickedness (v23). Do not let the prosperity or the spite of evil men disturb you. God keeps his promises.

Day 59   Psalm 32:1-6

Transgression forgiven and sin covered

This was Augustine's favourite Psalm, and one of the four that Luther called 'Paul's Psalms', because of their emphasis on free grace[1]. The Psalm is also the second of the so-called Penitential Psalms. David fell into awful sin, but his repentance and broken-heartedness are a lesson to us all. In Ps. 51:13, even when the smart of his sin and chastisement was still overwhelming him, he looked forward to a day when 'I will teach transgressors your ways'. This Psalm fulfils that desire.

There is a blessedness when sin is at last confessed and dealt with (v3-5). A burden is lifted. David finds that joy in his own experience: the open heart towards God; the intense sorrow over sin; the clearing out of all the hidden dirty things by true repentance. That is the experience of every sincere believer.

But we are not to sin and presume upon God's forgiveness and justification. '*Today* if you will hear his voice, harden not your hearts'. Only in a day when God may be found will you be heard (v6).

Give thanks, if you know the experience of which David speaks. If you do, go and teach transgressors his ways.

---

[1] See Martin Luther's *Table Talk*, Comments on Psalm 32 in C.H. Spurgeon's *Treasury of David*.

Day 60   Psalm 32:7-11

Stubborn as a mule

Rich people sometimes have a country home where they can escape the pressures of workaday life. Those under threat from violent men are sometimes provided with a 'safe house'. How good it is that we do not need to be rich or under the protection of the Government to know a place of safety and rest with God. David could say, 'You are my hiding place, you will preserve me from trouble' (v7). He expected this in Ps. 31:20, and here he proves it.

But God does not just provide a place to hide. He promises to guide and instruct in the way in which we should go (v8). His eye is upon us. As we look to him, we see him indicating the direction that we should take.

How strange that we often resist his guidance and direction! Why do we think we know a better way than God? Why should the LORD ever need to bridle and chasten us to ensure that we go in the correct way (v9)? Even an untamed animal knew to yield to the Master (Mark 11:2, 7) – should we resist?

Let us not imagine that believers can go in the way of the world, or that we shall be happy in it. Better to know sorrow here and joy forever than to know the sinner's rejoicing now and then his sorrow for all eternity (v10, 11).

Day 61   Psalm 33:1-6

The joy of the upright in heart

This Psalm takes up and expands the last verse of the preceding Psalm, which calls upon the saints to praise God. It suits those who are upright that they should offer praise! The joy found in the worship of God is remarkable in the Book of Psalms. It is not a cold, dead, and legalistic religion. This Psalm begins and ends with the joy of praise. The first three verses give six calls to joy and singing.

In verse 2, the writer encourages the cheerfulness that musical instruments can bring, but we need to heed the warning of John Calvin, that the name of God can only be properly extolled with the voice; 'When they [believers] frequent their sacred assemblies, musical instruments in celebrating the praises of God would be no more suitable than the burning of incense, the lighting up of lamps, and the restoration of the other shadows of the law'. Let us carefully consider what God desires of us in our congregational worship.

Our new song (v3) is a renewed song, telling again with freshness all that God is and has done. So the following verses encourage us to praise God for his word and his work (v4), for his character and providence (v5) and for his creation (v6). This is but a summary. We begin to extol the LORD now, but will never complete, even in eternity.

Day 62   Psalm 33:7-11

A heap of water

The opening verses of this Psalm have spoken of God's character and acts generally. These verses are more specific.

Although we see a link between verse 7 and creation (Gen. 1:9), the gathering of the waters of 'the sea' into a heap surely speaks of the miracles at the Red Sea and the Jordan (Exod. 15:8 and Josh. 3:13).

Taking David Baron's thought that his Psalm is appropriate for restored Israel to sing[1], it seems also to point to the latter-day exodus, when the LORD shall bring his people back to his land (Isa. 11:15; Zech. 10:10,11).

If we consider this portion prophetic, verse 8 is not the writer's hopeful wish. It will surely happen by God's intervention, described in verse 9. No longer will scoffers say, 'Where is the promise of his coming?' They will see at last that he speaks, and it is done. The nations may say, 'Let us break their bands asunder, and cast away their cords from us' (Ps. 2:3), but truly, 'The LORD brings the counsel of the heathen to nought: he makes the plans of the people of no effect' (v10).

Nothing is too hard for our God. He will do it.

---

[1] David Baron, *Types, Psalms and Prophecies.*

Day 63   Psalm 33:12-17

He shapes and moulds the hearts of men

This Psalm speaks of two peoples - his chosen people, 'the nation' (v12) - and 'the nations' (v10, 13-17). The Church is 'a people for his own possession' (1 Pet. 2:9 'a peculiar people' AV) and we may gain personal benefit from these verses, but this is not the primary meaning.

Israel was 'a nation whose God is the LORD', not because they had found him by searching; nor because they had unilaterally committed themselves to him. He was not merely their national deity. The LORD is their God because *he* has chosen them for his inheritance and possession (v11 see Deut. 4:20; 9:29; 14:2; 26:18; 32:8, 9). By this all the boasting and pride of man is excluded.   He has yet kept 'a remnant according to promise' and, in the end, the Lord will 'turn ungodliness away from Jacob' (Rom. 11:5, 26).

All the nations are under God's watchful eye (v14). The verb that the Authorised Version translates 'fashions' in verse 15 is also used of the way that a potter moulds clay. How foolish that men should rely on kings and armies, human strength, and horses (v16, 17).   All the might of apostate mankind in rebellion cannot thwart God or destroy his people (Ps. 2:1-5; Zech. 14:1-15; Rev. 19:11-21).

Let us not trust in man, but look to the LORD alone.

Day 64 Psalm 33:18-22

The eye of the LORD

These verses describe the loving relationship between the LORD and his people.

'The eye of the LORD is upon them that fear him, upon them that wait for his loving-kindness' (v18. Compare Ps. 34:15). This is a wonderful statement. He is a God who neither slumbers nor sleeps. Nothing is hidden from his watchful eye. He may be hidden from our view, but we are not hidden from his view. We should walk before our all-seeing God with reverent fear, and yet with expectation that his hand is full of mercies, ready to bestow upon us.

Waiting on, or trusting in, the LORD is a theme of verses 18 to 22. In verses 18 and 22 'long patient waiting' (AV 'hope') is meant (Hebrew *yahal*, as Ps. 69:3). Another word, meaning 'earnest longing', 'eager, expectant waiting' (Hebrew *hakâ*, as Hab. 2:3) is found in verse 20.

Let us continue to trust and call upon the Lord in faith, until he shows his grace and mercy. 'For our heart shall rejoice in him because we have trusted in his holy name'. His mercy will be 'according to' (and go far beyond) our hopes and expectations. It rests upon as the blood on the doorposts of the Israelites in Egypt (v22). We are marked out as recipients of his loving-kindness.

Day 65   Psalm 34:1-6

Praise at all times

The title relates this Psalm to the bizarre events of 1 Samuel 21:10-15. The Psalm encourages the believer to bless the LORD at all times, even when circumstances seem to run against him, or her. It is hard to praise God in the face of adversity.

In the opening words, David expresses the determination of his heart. When he had lost everything, Job's determined response was 'Blessed be the name of the LORD' (Job 1:21). How precious when the humble and poor (v2 and v6) and those beset with infirmities of sickness or old age can lift a Psalm of praise to their God, despite all their discouragement.

Note the emphasis in these verses. How often 'me' and 'my' are used! His praise is personal, 'at all times'; in every season; 'continually'; 'in his mouth' – not just in his mind or his heart. His 'soul' – his whole being – wants to spend time glorying in the LORD's greatness. There is a glow, a radiance, on such as will do this, as if a reflection from being in the LORD's presence (Exod. 34:29, 2 Cor. 3:7-9, 18).

Are we poor? Are we destitute? Let us simply bless God. The LORD will hear. He will rescue from all our troubles (v6). O for the determination and faith that can see the smile of the Father through grey skies, and in the darkness of night.

Day 66   Psalm 34:7-15

The Unseen Angel

This Psalm is an alphabetical Psalm[1]. As with the other alphabetic Psalms, this has the effect of producing a 'string of pearls' with individual gems, rather than long sections on a theme. Perhaps (using the metaphor of v10) we should say that this is a banquet with many different courses!

As Elisha calmed his doubting servant by opening his eyes (2 Kgs. 6:15-17) so we should walk in the light of God's unseen protection. 'The angel of the LORD encamps round about them that fear him, and delivers them' (v7). Who is this 'Angel', but our Jesus? (Josh. 5:14; Isa. 63:9; Zech. 3:1-7).

David, like the Lord Jesus, has care for children (v11). He encourages them to turn aside from their sports and recreation to consider, and learn to reverently fear the LORD. And not just children, those who aspire to a long and happy life are also instructed (v12-14). Filial, disciplined obedience in both cases is what is needed. We need to discipline our tongue (v13) and our social life (v14). Turning from evil, we should pursue peace – peace with God, peace in the Church of God, peace with our fellow man, and peace in our own heart – and all this from the God of peace (Heb. 13:20 and 21), whose eyes and ears are open to us (v15; 1 Pet. 3:12).

---

[1] As Psalm 25, it omits one letter of the Hebrew alphabet and doubles another.

Day 67   Psalm 34:16-22

Deliverance from all afflictions

The key verse of this section is verse 19, 'Many are the afflictions of the righteous, but the LORD delivers him out of them all'.

Consider what this tells us about the man who walks with God. One of the marks of the believer is that he gets chastening and affliction (2 Tim. 3:12). Difficulties mental, physical, spiritual, marital, and social will be the experience of the believer. It is said of Moses that he chose 'to suffer affliction with the people of God'. Affliction will follow the saint like a shadow when he walks in the light. It is this that causes the believer to 'cry' to God for deliverance (v17). It is a midwife to true prayer. It is these experiences, rightly used, that give to the believer 'the broken heart' and 'the contrite spirit'[1] that are so precious to the LORD (v18). Without this heart attitude, a man is self-righteous.

This passage is quoted in the New Testament in reference to the sufferings and afflictions of the Messiah (v20; John 19:36). We should therefore take time to ponder the verses and to apply them to him – who alone is truly righteous [singular in v19, 21 – 'the Righteous One'], and yet was 'a man of sorrows and acquainted with grief' (Isa. 53:3, 4, 11).

---

[1] Literally, 'crushed of spirit'

Day 68   Psalm 35:1-8

As chaff before the wind

This is one of the so-called imprecatory Psalms, in which judgment and punishment are sought upon those who wickedly persecute the writer.

The call for God to intervene and judge comes from the psalmist's exalted view of God's holiness - his desire that God might be glorified. When wickedness is unchecked, God's glory is hidden.

These evildoers are not mere enemies of David. They are enemies of God himself. It has been said that verses 11-16 apply more exactly to Christ than to any other person. His afflictions and harassment are described here. Christ therefore speaks in this Psalm. He knows every heart, and has the right to seek vindication and retribution.

In verses 1-3 David calls on God to arise, as a man of war, on behalf of his people (see Exod. 15:3 and Isa. 42:13). Human nature, equipped with the armour of God, strives valiantly against principalities and powers, but how different it will be when God himself shall arise with his shield, buckler, and spear. Who shall then withstand his power (v1-3)? Who shall escape when pursued by the angel of the LORD?

Day 69   Psalm 35:9-16

Talking bones

David, in words fitting to Christ, firstly exults in God in the midst of his darkest night (v9). He then recounts the awful cruelty and spite of men against him (v10-16). In his anguish it is as if his whole body speaks (v10; compare Psalm 22). The strange interpretation of this verse by the rabbis has led Jews to rock to and fro whilst reciting prayers (davening).

We see the Lord Jesus in these verses. He is accused by malicious lying witnesses (v11; Matt. 26:60). They repay his good with evil (v12a; John 10:32). He is left bereft of human affection (v12b); one whom he treated 'as a brother and a friend' betrays him. He bears the abuse of the religious leaders, the soldiers' contempt, the mockery of Pilate's trial, and the derision thrown at him on the cross.

He was the Friend of sinners, the Joy of the widow of Nain, the Light of blind men, and the Solace of demoniacs. Yet all seemed to rejoice at his betrayal (v15a) and destruction. The religious leaders hit him and laughed (v15[1], Luke 22:64). Their slanders did not cease (v15 - until he yielded up his spirit to God; Mark 15:29-33). Their mockery, rage, and hate against him was extreme (v16, as with Stephen - Acts 7:54).

And yet his soul rejoiced in the LORD! v9. How great was his love for us! Let us exalt him.

---

[1] For AV "abjects" read "smiters" as de Burgh and Perowne.

Day 70   Psalm 35:17-23

My Lord!

The continued reference of these words to the Lord Jesus is confirmed by the Apostle John's statement on their fulfilment (v19; John 15:25).

In this section (v17,22, 23), the psalmist addresses God not by his covenant name, LORD (JEHOVAH), but as My Lord (*Adonay*) – the unique name only used of God, which emphasises the personal relation of the speaker. This is the essence of all his pleading for vindication. The Servant makes himself of no reputation. His cause is his Master's cause.

The Servant's request is for God's active response and engagement. It seems, as in that awful abandonment on the cross:

- that God simply looks on impassively (v17a).

- that the servant will certainly be destroyed (v17b).

- that his enemies can rejoice over him with impunity (v19).

- that they are able to deceive God and man (v20).

- that God is silent and remote from the sufferer (v22).

- that God is slow in his judgments (v23).

None of these things are true, and the speaker knows that they are not true, but he pleads to God to act for the vindication of his own name. We should pray likewise.

Day 71   Psalm 35:24-28

Restraint, recompense, and rejoicing

We have in this portion a prayer for restraint of the wicked, for recompense, and for rejoicing. It concludes with an expectation of renewal.

It is an evil day when the wicked rejoice in triumph over the godly (v24). Evil men long to have their own way, unhindered by the people of God. In relation to Christ, their words were 'we will not have this man to rule over us' (Luke 19:14). We need to pray that evil people will be restrained.

Linked with this is the need for recompense to be paid to the wicked. Instead of their unrighteous pride and arrogant confidence, they should have shame and confusion. It should be apparent to all – they should be *clothed* with their shame (v25, 26).

When the godly are in honour, the LORD is magnified. The LORD's people should then shout for joy (v27). We are reminded of the story of Esther and the establishment of the feast of Purim (Esther 9:20-22).

Pray that God would grant a clear line between good and evil in society, either by his direct intervention, or through governments (1 Pet. 2:14). One day these things will be. We will then speak of his righteousness, and will praise God all the day long (v28; Mathew 6:10).

Day 72   Psalm 36:1-4

Plotting mischief in bed

The title again identifies David as 'the servant'.

The Holy Spirit enables us to recognise godlessness (v1), even when it is glossed over with taste and beauty.

These verses refer to 'the wicked one' (singular) and look ahead (as Psalm 10) to the development of evil in the person of Antichrist (2 Thess. 2:8); consequently verses 1-4 describe antichristianism - the spirit of this age.

The thoughts and actions of this wicked one are made without reference to God. He has no respect for God (v1). He is proud and does not see his own faults (v2). As his heart is, so he speaks. He is lawless and deceived. He therefore speaks as though there is no law, and deceives others (v3). As 'the fear of the LORD is the beginning of wisdom' (Ps. 111:10), so by disregarding God he has no real wisdom. He is so busy with his godless schemes that even the quiet rest of sleep is taken from him, and he is consumed with planning and plotting through the night (v4).

What a description of the great ones of our age!

The eight uses of the word 'bed' (AV) in the Book of Psalms make a very profitable study. Here it is misused. May the Lord teach us to sanctify the place where we spend a third of our day.

Day 73   Psalm 36:5-12

David is almost lost for words

Here David looks up from his pressures and persecutions and rejoices in God. He struggles to find strong enough words to exalt God's greatness and his blessings to believers. He resorts to vivid expressions – like the mountains of God; your judgments are a great deep; the shadow of your wings; drink of the river of your pleasures; the fountain of life. He praises the LORD's mercy and faithfulness (v5); his righteousness, judgments, and providence (v6); his protection (v7); the satisfaction and joy that he gives (v8).

We constantly need the Holy Spirit's help to understand and to express the LORD's greatness and goodness to us. Paul attempts it in Eph. 3:17-21.

The words of verse 9, 'In your light shall we see light' are speaking of spiritual rather than natural light. Without the aid of the LORD, man is totally unable to receive spiritual things (Deut. 29:2-4; John 3:27; 1 Cor. 12:3).[1]

In verses 10-12 David prays for continuance of the mercies that he has already known and experienced (v10). God is able to restrain the forces that are against him (v11). The fall of the wicked is certain and without remedy (v12). By contrast, the believer always recovers his feet when he falls (Ps. 37:24; Prov. 24:16).

---

[1] See Calvin's *Institutes*, Book 2, Chap 2, s.20

Day 74   Psalm 37:1-6

Delighting in the LORD

This Psalm is alphabetical[1]. It is full of promises. Take one with you through today.

It begins with good words of advice regarding the ungodly – 'do not fret' because of them (v1 see v7 too). The English word 'fret' means gnawing, wearing away, tormenting. The root of the Hebrew word means 'to make oneself hot'. Do not get yourself hot and bothered about it!

How we need to see things from God's perspective! Then we will not envy those who shall soon be cut down like the grass. Let us rather trust in the LORD and do good (v3); Delight ourselves in the LORD (v4); Commit our way to him[2] (v5).

If we will take this course of action, we are promised that we will dwell peacefully, and that our needs will be met (v3); that the LORD will give us the desires of our heart! (v4); that he will make things happen for us (v5); he will not allow our integrity and faithfulness to be hidden in darkness, but it shall at last be shown for what it is (v6).

What a promise of undeserved reward there is in these verses! All this comes from an attitude of trust and dependence upon God. Let us cease from our striving and struggling. Rest in him and watch the outcome.

---

[1] Lines start with letters in the order of the Hebrew alphabet
[2] Hebrew, 'cast [or 'roll'] your way'.

Day 75   Psalm 37:7-15

The meek shall inherit the earth

The Psalm continues with encouragement and reassurance. David sees only two classes of people: those who do wicked things and prosper, and those who wait on the LORD, who are meek and live an upright life. Let us also see society around us in the same way. Let us constantly remember the fate of the wicked (v13-15). Let us seek the qualities that mark out a believer in this Psalm.

Some commentators have noted deeper significance in verses 12 and 13. They suddenly shift to the singular, referring to the just one and the wicked, or lawless, one. Christ and Antichrist may be seen in these verses (compare, for example, Ps. 2:4).

We can find all of the beatitudes of Matthew 5 in this Psalm. The Lord Jesus said, 'The meek shall inherit the earth' (Matt. 5:5). This is promised six times in this Psalm.[1] This inheritance and possession will be 'for ever' (v27, 29). It is after the destruction of the wicked (v9-11).

We look for the fulfilment of this in the new earth in which righteousness dwells (2 Pet. 3:13). How reassuring it is that no wicked person and no wickedness will be found in it.

---

[1] v3, 9, 11 ,22, 29, 34.

Day 76   Psalm 37:16-22

David speaking like Solomon

This is a section of comparisons, rather like Solomon gives in the book of Proverbs.

These verses again show the sharp contrast between the godly and the wicked. This is most marked if we consider the Lord Jesus in comparison to the evil one, as in yesterday's portion (v12, 13), but we should always see the world in this light.

There are two classes of people, and only two. The little that a believer has is blessed by God and is better than the prosperity of the wicked (v16a, compare v1, 7). The ungodly relies upon his own strength and it shall be broken, but the LORD upholds the righteous (v16b, 17). For us there will be an everlasting inheritance, but for them eternal punishment (v18-20). The good man and the wicked are both marked out by their actions – one shows true charity and kindness, the other selfishness and greed (v21). The two classes of people are again named in verse 22. They are 'the blessed' and 'the cursed'.

May the LORD give us clear spiritual thinking to always mark the difference. This is not Old Testament teaching. It is Biblical teaching that was also clearly stated by the Lord Jesus himself (Matt. 25:34, 41).

Day 77   Psalm 37:23-28

An old man's wisdom

We have in this portion 1. A promise (v23, 24); 2. A personal testimony (v25, 26); 3. An instruction (v27-29).

(1) The promise concerns a person whom the LORD blesses[1]. Such a man may fall. The promise is that he will recover from his fall. A brief consideration of the men whom God has chosen as leaders will demonstrate this. David, a man after God's own heart, did not live a sinless life, but he arose from his fall. The Lord Jesus did not tell Peter he would not fall, but 'when you are converted (turned again) strengthen your brothers'. The Lord does not prevent all failure, for we need the chastening and humbling, but he upholds and raises us from our failings.

(2) David makes a remarkable statement with the wisdom of old age (v25, 26). A righteous man is not exempt from want and need, but he passes through these things, as Job did. The LORD does not forsake the righteous in their hardships. We need to take the long view of trials and difficulties.

(3) The instruction is what we should do and why. We should negatively go from evil, positively do good, and persevere (v27). The reason given is that this pleases the LORD. He rewards those who do so, and he punishes those who do not (v28).

---

[1] The AV supplies the word 'good' in verse 23. He is rather the person of the previous verse (v22) whom the LORD blesses,.

Day 78   Psalm 37:29-34

Anatomy of a saint

In verses 30, 31 we have the anatomy of a righteous or godly man – his mouth, his tongue, his heart, and his feet are described.

There is a progression here.

1. The speech of a just man is wise because it relies upon God's words and instruction (see Deut. 4:5-6);

2. From his meditation on these things he grows in the knowledge and praise of God (the same word the AV translates 'talks' here, is 'meditates' in Ps. 35:28, and Ps. 1:2);

3. God's law then becomes a part of him – in his very heart; His feet therefore do not slide – he is established.

Paul's description of the Christian soldier in conflict likewise shows how every part of the believer (head, feet, etc) is fully equipped. The peace that the Gospel gives (Eph. 6:15) enables us to stand firmly, even in the midst of battle. Wicked people may plot against us to destroy us (v32), but the LORD is in control.

Let us ponder these things, and deliberately implement them in our Christian lives. Let us 'wait' – patiently wait, look for, hope, expect – these blessings from the LORD (v34; compare v7 and 9).

Day 79   Psalm 37:35-40

The vanishing tree

This Psalm is a theodicy – a vindication of God's providence and justice. We have a summary of its teaching in the first two verses of this portion. The wicked can be disregarded, despite present appearances.

These verses instruct the believer to turn his eyes away from the 'now' situation. 'Now' it may seem that 'the wicked is in great power'. He may be acting like a tyrant, seemingly unstoppable. Thus it was against the early Church: Persecutors flourished as a mighty tree – but they are gone (v35, 36). Thus it shall ever be for wicked men with great power, right down to Antichrist (the Wicked One) who shall be destroyed in a moment.

'The person of integrity' (the perfect man) and 'the upright person', who seem to be so easily set aside by the lying and deceiving actions of the wicked, has a future – he has an end and destiny of peace (v37). The future of the wicked will not be peace – they *shall be* destroyed; they *shall be* cut off. They have no future, but the righteous will finally be saved and delivered.

As the Psalm started, so it finishes. We should not fret about the success of the wicked. We must so live, trusting in the truth that David teaches here.

Day 80   Psalm 38:1-8

Feeble and broken

This is a Psalm written in the midst of great suffering. It is the third of the Penitential Psalms. It contains appeals for God's mercy because of:

1. Bodily affliction (v1-8)

2. Distress of soul (v9-14)

3. Spiritual fear, lest wicked men should triumph (v15-22)

The verses of this portion are a not a prayer for deliverance or blessing. The psalmist simply asks the LORD to moderate and ease his suffering, for he is at the limit of what he can bear. The description of his condition is not a complaint. He appeals to the God of mercy, who will not lay anything upon us above what we are able to bear (1 Cor. 10:13).

He sees his sufferings with the eye of faith, and accepts them as given directly from the hand of God – v2 'Your arrows', 'your hand'. He accepts that the chastening is deserved. It is because of 'my sin' (v3), 'my foolishness' (v5). When we pass through the valley of suffering and trial we too need such a humble brokenness, even when the hand of God is pressing upon us. We will then receive the full benefit of our trial (Ps. 34:18).

Let us use the words of this portion in quiet prayer

Day 81   Psalm 38:9-14

Blind, Deaf, and Dumb

The writer's inward suffering is shown here. He says to God, 'All my desire is before you'. His groans are his prayers (v9). He has no light on his situation (v10). He feels like a leper (v11). There are those who seek to entrap and deceive him (v12). He takes all of this inwardly, and does not accuse others (v13 compare Isa. 53:7). He does not seek to justify himself – 'in whose mouth there are no arguments' is perhaps a better translation in verse 14. The psalmist is completely tongue-tied in his distress. At such a time we must stand before God in disciplined helplessness and look to him, and to him only, for relief and deliverance.

There are three applications. Firstly, this guides us how we should act under the chastising hand of God. Secondly, this teaches us how we should respond to others in distress – not treating them as lepers or outcasts, or even proposing quick remedies as Job's friends did, but rather we should sit alongside in quiet empathy (Ezek. 3:15). Thirdly, this is a window on the soul sufferings of the Lord Jesus Christ (John 19:10; 1 Pet. 2:23).

Let us be submissive under the hand of God so that we may grow in grace and the knowledge of Christ.

Day 82   Psalm 38:15-22

In the furnace

The closing two verses are the essence of the whole Psalm, 'Forsake me not, O LORD: O my God, be not far from me.   Make haste to help me, O Lord my salvation'.

When the Lord Jesus prayed, it was always in submission to his Father's will (Luke 22:42).   How awful it was then when he cried 'My God, My God, Why have you forsaken me?'   It expressed the unimaginable agony of the Saviour's heart, before at last he cried in victory 'It is finished'.

We too must place our hope and trust in God alone (v15).   For us he says, 'I will never leave you or forsake you' (Heb. 13:5).   How often we, God's people, have found themselves in 'Red Sea' situations where we are ready to give up (v17).   Yet our Lord Jesus is with us and will show us his way forward.

Our sinful heart and consequent weakness should constantly suppress our pride, and drive us to repentance and a broken, contrite spirit (v18).   Take the advice of Adolphe Monod[1] 'Read Psalm 38.   Read and ponder every thought'.   'It was in the furnace that he wrote these lines that were to serve for the encouragement of the Church in all time.   O power of the love of Christ!   O renunciation of self will'.

---

[1] Adolph Monod, *Farewell*, p55ff.

Day 83   Psalm 39: 1-6

Knowing our frailty

David's condition is told in this first part of the Psalm. The remedy is applied in the second part, which we shall consider tomorrow. As with the previous Psalm (Ps. 38:13, 14), he speaks of his silence under affliction. He desired to bridle his mouth like a horse, lest he should sin in anger or complaint. He stopped speaking good things, but he found that he had to converse with God in his trial (compare Jer. 20:9). When overwhelmed with grief, we should admit we do not know how we should pray, and await the loosening of our tongue by the Holy Spirit (Rom. 8:26).

After quiet meditation, David is led to think on the shortness and vanity of this present life (v4). He wants to be made aware how frail and short-lived he is, so that he can get things into proper perspective. He declares in words that could have been found in the book of Ecclesiastes, 'every man at his best state is altogether vanity' (v5). He knows his days are short and 'but hand-breadths'.

When we have to endure trial, let us keep a bridle on our tongue. 'Let every man be swift to hear, slow to speak, slow to wrath' (Jas 1:19).

'Take heed to your ways'. Ponder a little on the greatness of God, and the smallness of man.

Day 84   Psalm 39:7-13

Silent under the rod

Thomas Brooks, the puritan, wrote a great and soul-searching exposition of verse 9 under the title *The Mute Christian under the Smarting Rod.*   He encouraged believers 'to be still, quiet, calm, and silent under all changes that have, or may pass upon them in this world'.   It was his view that 'afflictions are a golden key by which the Lord opens the rich treasure of his word to his people's souls'.

We have already seen how David's affliction caused him to see the vanity and shortness of this present life (v6).   Following Brooks, we may say that this godly quietness is not a stoical silence, not a politic silence, not a foolish silence, not a forced silence, nor a despairing silence; it is a holy and gracious silence.   It includes an acknowledgement of God as the author of all the afflictions that come upon us – 'because you did it' (v9).   It acknowledges God's majesty, dignity, and authority in bringing the affliction (Hab. 2:20; Zeph. 1:7).   It shuts out murmuring, fretting, and temper.   It looks to the final outcome of the trial (v7, Job 23:10) - the trial then dims the loveliness of this world that might otherwise entice us (v13).

John Calvin suffered greatly in the last month of his life, and the words of verse 9 were often upon his lips. May the LORD keep us from complaining.   In affliction may we learn to be silent toward man and mighty in prayer toward God.

Day 85   Psalm 40: 1-4

Deliverance worth waiting for

The previous Psalms are full of present problems and trials, but these verses refer to a past deliverance. This portion is a thanksgiving to God for answering prayer, and for faithfully keeping his afflicted servant. The reward is to those who wait patiently ('waiting I waited') for God (v1; Ps. 37:7 see Rom. 12:12; 2 Thess. 3:5).

David waited. The LORD delivered. He heard. He reached out to him. He inclined his ear. He brought him up from the pit. He set his foot on a rock, He made his steps secure. He made him sing. He did everything for him!

This acknowledgement of the sovereignty of God in doing all the work of salvation is not weakness. In verse 4 he says, 'Blessed is that mighty man [Hebrew *gebber*] who makes the LORD his trust'. We are both 'strong in the Lord' and yet, at the same time, we are utterly dependent upon him.

The 'new' song of verse 3 is 'exquisite and extraordinary' (Calvin) just as his deliverance was. It was not composed by the psalmist, but it was 'put in his mouth' by the LORD, who orders all true worship. Likewise, 'the word of Christ' dwells in the believer richly as he sings inspired Psalms, hymns, and songs (see Col. 3:16, 17).

Day 86   Psalm 40:5-10

Lo, I come...

The words of verses 6-8, as quoted in the Book of Hebrews (10:5-10), speak of the first two persons of the Trinity.

In the counsels of eternity, the Only Begotten responded to the Father's purpose. He 'according to the sovereign good pleasure of his own will, purely by grace, has chosen to salvation in Christ a specific number of persons (neither better nor more deserving than the others, but cast down with them in common misery)'.[1]

Christ voluntarily humbled himself and obeyed the Father's will. In fulfilling this purpose, he endured not only without a murmur, he *delighted* in his Father's will - even in the most awful and inconceivable agonies. He alone as God could offer the acceptable sacrifice. A body was prepared for him (Heb. 10:5, Septuagint of Ps. 40:6). Our redemption was accomplished by the free surrender of the Son of God, and his taking up of our cause. So 'none shall perish' of those who are given to him (John 10:28). This glorious truth has been, and will be, declared to all his people (v9, 10).

Dear brother or sister, why are we dumb? Should we not long for a thousand tongues to sing our great Redeemer's praise? Let this mind be in you that was also in Christ Jesus (Phil. 2:5).

---

[1] Canons of the Synod of Dort, Chapter 1, article 7. Quoted from C.W.H. Griffiths, *Chosen – Called – Kept*.

Day 87   Psalm 40:11- 17

Unable to look up?

The closing words of this Psalm are a lament at the suffering cause of truth in this present dispensation. The believer's consciousness of sin and weakness, coupled with the scorn and ridicule of a godless world, should deliver us from hopes and ambitions of worldly greatness.

The psalmist says, 'Make haste to help me' (v13); 'Make no delay, O my God' (v17 – compare Rev. 6:10; Rev. 22:20; Dan. 9:19). Should this not be the constant prayer of our hearts? If we have any concern for God's honour, we must make it so.

There is, in the final verse, an assurance of the LORD's care for us, 'As for me, I am poor and needy, yet the LORD thinks upon me'.

Hawker[1] writes, 'Yes, Jesus! I would be poor, I would be needy; I would feel yet more and more my nothingness, worthlessness, poverty, wretchedness, that Jesus may be increasingly precious, and his salvation increasingly dear. Oh, for grace, as a poor needy debtor, daily to swell my debt account, that my consciousness of need may make Thee and Thy fullness increasingly blessed'.

---

[1] Robert Hawker, *The Poor Man's Morning Portion.*

Day 88   Psalm 41:1-6

The LORD will make my bed

We may take v1-3 as the reward of our God to all who will minister to the weak and sick. The Lord Jesus taught that, in serving such, we are serving him (Matt. 25:35, 36). The word 'poor' in verses 1 and 4 is in the singular (compare 2 Cor. 8: 9; Ps.40:17). This is personal care.

Alternatively, we may read this as the heart and actions of our Saviour himself. This love and care was at the heart of Jesus's earthly ministry (Matt. 11:5; Luke 4:18; 14:13). How comforting it is that the Lord, with His own hand, will minister to our needs. He truly will wipe away every tear from our eye, and make our bed in time of sickness (v3)! And yet outwardly it is not always so as we pass through this vale of tears and pilgrimage.

From v4 the Psalm takes on a different character. As we shall see in tomorrow's portion, the Lord Jesus claims this part of the Psalm as his own. If we read this Psalm as referring to the Lord Jesus, we must take verse 4 as speaking of sin-bearing. Bishop Horsley suggests, 'For I am *as* a sinner before thee'. He took our offence.

The closing hope of His enemies was that his name would perish (v5). How good that we can say of his victory in his suffering 'His name shall endure for ever' (Ps. 72:17). Let us take comfort from these words.

Day 89   Psalm 41:7-13

False familiar friend

This Psalm of David invites us to witness the inner sufferings of the Lord Jesus. We hear his groan as he sighs because even his own familiar friend has lifted himself up against him (v9 and John 13:18-30).

We see the utter abandonment and loneliness of the Saviour in his ministry and last trial. Those who persecuted him desired his complete and final end. He was hung on a tree because 'Cursed is he that hangs on a tree' (Gal. 3:13, Deut. 21:23) - that his destruction might be complete. The hope was (v8) 'now that he lies down, he shall rise no more'. That was the hope of Satan himself, who was a murderer from the beginning (John 8:44).

This Psalm closes the first Book of Psalms. The parallel of the five books of the Psalms and the five books of the Pentateuch has often been noted. Genesis closes with the story of Joseph who was betrayed by his brethren. Ending this first book of Psalms, we likewise ponder on our Greater-than-Joseph who God raised up from all his humiliation.

Let us sing the doxology of this first book of Psalms (v13) with joy and thankfulness.

Book 2

Psalms 42 – 72

Day 90   Psalm 42:1-5

Thirsting for God

This is the soliloquy of a broken and contrite heart. It expresses an intense longing for renewed intimate fellowship with God, as a hunted creature longs for rest and refreshment at cooling streams. Bitter-sweet memories of shared fellowship, of leadership of God's people, and of 'the house of God' pass through his mind. But they are apparently now only memories. He finds himself alone, seemingly abandoned, and facing an uncertain future. It is easy to praise God in a crowd. Although David is now alone, he does not plead to be back with the crowd. He cries out for the Living God (compare John 7:37).

Dr Martyn Lloyd Jones commenced his book, *Spiritual Depression*, with a consideration of this Psalm. He pointedly asks, 'Have you not realised that most of your unhappiness in life is due to the fact that you are listening to yourself instead of talking to yourself?'

The question is more accurately translated, 'Why do you cast yourself down?' We can give 101 reasons for being cast down. In the end it is our response, not the trials themselves, that determine whether we remain that way.

As we worship the LORD through this Psalm, let us remind ourselves that our desires for God are evidence of grace working in us. Let us remind ourselves of former mercies, and then let us reason ourselves back to a quiet confidence - 'Why are you cast down, O my soul?'

Day 91   Psalm 42:6-11

Again, 'Where is your God?'

This Psalm is 'a maschil', which may be translated 'giving instruction' or 'understanding'. It gives a vivid description of the frightening experiences of the man of God. 'Where is your God?' is unanswerable in all that he has gone through, without the eye of faith. The continual taunt is repeated again in v11.

And yet gleams of understanding pierce through the foggy darkness, like rays of sunlight. The writer keeps his balance when all seems lost. He is able to see through 'the frowning providence' and to rise again to the 'I shall yet' of victorious hope. He takes encouragement from past deliverances - the reference to the locations in verse 6 is probably the writer reminding himself of places and times where God had met with him and helped him.

Dan Crawford[1] comments on 'deep calls to deep'. 'The deep of David's longing calling out to the deep of God's longing. The deep of David's emptiness calling out to the deep of God's plenitude'.

We also have in this Psalm a window on the experiences of the Lord Jesus. His adversaries also said, 'He trusted in God. Let Him deliver him now' (Matt. 27:43, compare v10 of this Psalm). God's own hand was in his trial too - 'All *your* waves and *your* billows are gone over me' (v7).

---

[1] Dan Crawford, *Thirsting after God.*

Day 92   Psalm 43

Send Light and Truth!

This Psalm continues where the last Psalm left off. It is joined to it in many manuscripts. It echoes the previous refrain (42:5, 11; 43:5).

The plea of this Psalm is for vindication: not just for the vindication of the one who suffers for righteousness' sake, but vindication of God's name and honour. It speaks of mercies patiently waited for, but not immediately secured and vouchsafed.

The psalmist looks to the LORD to send light and truth. Any awakening or revival, whether national or personal, is in the final analysis a revelation of the Lord, a gift of his mercy.

There may have been no change in his outward circumstances in v4, but his possession of God - 'my God', 'my exceeding joy' - was enough to lift the gloom and stir up his hope at the end of the Psalm.

John Brown[1] concludes his comment on the Psalm, 'Let my heart and flesh cry out for God, the living God, as my God, and mine exceeding joy. And let me still all the tumults of my heart with this, - That he is my God and my All; my God that doth me save'.

---

[1] John Brown of Haddington, *The Psalms of David in Metre with Notes.*

Day 93   Psalm 44: 1-8

Not by might, nor by power

This is a maschil, a Psalm of instruction. Let us be taught by it.

The beginning of this Psalm moves from the intensely personal and present needs of the two preceding Psalms to Israel as a whole – 'we' – 'our fathers' - the body of God's people together.

We are here taught how to pray effectively. The writer reminds the LORD of His former deliverances. This is the method of many men of God in the Scriptures – See for example Jer. 32: 17-23. Likewise, Moses in Numb. 14:13-19 reminds God of who he is, and what he has done, before he makes his request.

The writer moves from 'you did' (v1) to 'we will' (v5). This growing confidence is based only on God, not on weapons, of bow or sword. It is the confidence of faith.

We have here encouragement to prayer, encouragement to trust, and encouragement to praise.

If our perception of present mercies is blinded by tears, let us recite to God what he has done and cheer ourselves that 'his arm is not shortened that it cannot save, nor is His ear heavy that it cannot hear' (Isa. 59:1).

Day 94   Psalm 44: 9-19

The scattered nation

We have in these words a stark contrast to the former days recounted in the first part of the Psalm. Here things seem to be at midnight and hopeless. Bishop Horsley[1] interprets it as: 'The prayer of the new Hebrew Church, in the latter times, suffering under Antichrist's persecutions'. It is otherwise difficult to see where it would fit in Israel's history. Here Israel is 'scattered among the nations' (v11) and 'a byword among the peoples' (v14); and yet able to make a credible claim to faithfulness and freedom from idolatry (v17-18).

Verse 22 is quoted in Rom. 8:36 as applicable to the Christian Church in its various persecutions, but an application is not the same as the interpretation.

In verse 15 and verse 16 this shame is taken to heart personally. Our religion must always be personal, and we must learn to 'suffer with the people of God' in its widest sense, and so water our prayers with tears for the griefs of others.

God requires that we should keep covenant with him in difficult days.

---

[1] Bishop Horsley, *The Book of Psalms...with notes explanatory and critical.*

Day 95   Psalm 44: 20-26

As sheep for the slaughter

In this section the writer and his people do not waver from their devotion to God. And yet, at the same time, there is the strongest perception of God's afflicting hand. As noted in our previous portion, there is a prophetic application of these words to Israel, but they are relevant to all the times when God's Church has known trial.

The writer suggests impossibilities, as if to provoke God to action – that he sleeps through the believer's trial (v23) and that he forgets (v24). In all their trials his people refuse to let go of their faith in God as he is revealed in the Scriptures. Above all, his attribute of mercy (Hebrew *hesed*) is appealed to as their hope in their desperate condition (v26).

'Yea, for your sake we are killed all day long; we are counted as sheep for the slaughter' (v22 quoted in Rom. 8:36) was applied by John Melville to 'the yeir of the bludie massacres in France' - the St Bartholomew's Day massacre of protestants (1685). In their trials, the Huguenots found their supreme consolation in the singing of such Psalms. When burnt at the stake, many had their tongues cut out lest they should stir the crowds with their Psalm singing. May we reclaim the Psalms too, as preparation for the tribulation that Scripture assures us will be our lot in this world (John 16:33).

Day 96   Psalm 45:1-8

Speaking about the King

This Psalm answers the cry of the previous one, just as the Lord's tender comfort follows the 'How long?' of the saints in the Book of Revelation (6:10, 11). We look forward to the Marriage of the Lamb in Revelation 19. In this Psalm we also have the marriage song. It is no ordinary wedding, for Christ is the Bridegroom, and the Bride is his Church. Both Jew and Christian accept it as Messianic.

Let us meditate on the Lord's person. This Psalm is full of Christ. He is *the* King, and King of kings (v1). Although his appearance was marred more than any man (Isa. 52:14), yet he is perfect in his beauty (v2; Song of Solomon 2:1 and 5:10-16). Never did any man speak like this Man (v2; John 7:14). He is the Mighty Conqueror of all his enemies (v3; Rev. 6:2). He is glorious, majestic, true, meek, and righteous (v3, 4). He is expressly called 'God' whose throne is forever (v6, Heb. 1:8, 9).

There is a fragrance, an attractiveness, and a gladness about his Person at this glorious time when he is as a priest upon his throne (consider v6, 7 and the anointing of Exod. 30:22-33). May our hearts 'boil over'[1] as we consider these things. May we exalt the glories of Jesus, our Redeemer.

---

[1] The literal meaning of the word the AV translates as "inditing" in v1

Day 97   Psalm 45:9-17

Introducing the Bride

In our second section of this Psalm we are introduced to the bridal party and to the King's wonderful Bride. Her beauty and adornments are described in language similar that of the Song of Solomon. The identity of the Queen is found in Hos. 2:14-23 – where Israel is restored as The LORD's wife.

In understanding the bride to be restored Israel, there is wide agreement that the King's daughters are the nations subject to Christ.[1] The picture is therefore Millennial, but typical of that final union of Christ with the Church of all the elect (Eph. 5:25-27 and Rev. 19:7-9).

Verses 10 and 11 are particularly precious to me, as I gave them to my daughter as she went to Russia to serve God, and then again as she married, and moved to Israel.

As we sing this 'song of loves' [the Psalm's title], let us reverently submit ourselves to Christ as our beloved spouse. Let us stir up our hopes of his return, and of our joys with him forever. Let look forward to the second coming of our Saviour who will accomplish all of his will, and fulfil everything that has been spoken of by the prophets.

---

[1] So E.W. Hengstenberg, Bishop Horsley, William de Burgh, B.W. Newton, F. Delitzsch, David Baron

Day 98   Psalm 46

He makes wars to cease

This is the first of three Psalms that describe, in order, the events that will take place at the return of the Lord Jesus. We have in this Psalm the Lord putting down all his enemies. Psalm 47 describes his coronation, and Psalm 48 the establishment of his kingdom in 'the city of the great King'.

The previous Psalm (45:3) called upon the LORD to gird on his sword. Here he acts for the deliverance of his people. He is our refuge and strength, a very present help in trouble. Encouraged by this Psalm, Luther wrote his hymn, the *Marseillaise* of the Reformation, 'A mighty fortress is our God'.

This deliverance is marked by great and manifest intervention by the LORD on behalf of his people. Its timing is when he makes wars to cease and when weapons of warfare will be destroyed - when he shall reign, and put down all his enemies (v8,9; compare Mic. 4:1-3; Rev. 11:15-18). May that day come soon!

In his last days, John Warburton[1] remarked that it is impossible to be 'still' in great trial (v10) – the Devil will take care of that!' What is meant is, 'We must be still from helping God. He wants none of our help, neither will he have it!'

---

[1] John Warburton, *Mercies of a Covenant God*,

Day 99   Psalm 47

The Universal King

What a song of praise this is! How well it follows from the previous Psalm, for here we have the LORD seated as the Great King over all the earth, with all nations subject to him.

This is not a description of the successful influence of the Gospel gradually spreading after Christ's ascension, but a mighty and manifest intervention by God, which follows on from the restoration of the people of Israel, who are the chief speakers in this Psalm. It is a coronation scene (compare 2 Kings 11). We must await this consummation, this investiture of Christ, spoken of in Ps. 110:2; Dan. 7:13, 14 and Rev. 11:15. The Kingdoms of this world to be delivered up as the Kingdoms of our God and of his Christ!

Could we be urged to sing, praise, shout, clap, triumph, and exalt the Lord more strongly than in the words of this Psalm? Can we be deaf to its encouragement? Can we be silent now when these words before long shall be upon our lips in celebration of what we see and hear?

A day is coming when the glories and victories of our God will be shouted from the housetops!

Day 100   Psalm 48:1-8

The city of the Great King

A.A. Bonar heads this Psalm 'The Mighty One becomes the glory of Jerusalem'. We have the terms 'Jerusalem', 'Zion' and 'the city of our God' referred to throughout.

Many passages of Scripture make clear that the literal Jerusalem is meant, and it is the presence of 'the Great King' that will be its glory. E. Bendor Samuel writes[1], 'The place that witnessed His humiliation will now witness His exaltation. In place of a shameful cross He will have a glorious throne; in place of the cry, 'Crucify Him' will be heard the glad shout of '*Hosanna to the Son of David*'; the brow that once wore the crown of thorns will now be adorned with many diadems...no longer will He wear the purple robes of mockery, but His royal robes will have written on them 'King of kings and Lord of lords'.

This first half of the Psalm, written prophetically, describes things that the writer has witnessed in God's deliverance of Zion. How wonderful when we will be able to say with the psalmist 'As we have heard, so have we seen' (v8).

Let us rejoice in the Saviour's coming triumph and reign.

---

[1] E. Bendor Samuel, *The Prophetic Character of the Psalms*.

Day 101   Psalm 48:9-14

Sightseeing in Jerusalem

In this portion we are invited to take a tour of the Temple (v9), and of the fortified heights of Mount Zion (v12, 13). We are even promised a divine guide (v14)!

We should deepen our understanding of God's purposes by spending time reflecting and investigating. Ps. 26:6 speaks of compassing (going round) the altar – in this way we can better value the finished work of Christ. We would do well to 'think upon' God's covenant mercy as if standing in the midst of the types and shadows of the Temple. The word used in verse 9 (AV 'thought') is an unusual one. Its root meaning is to compare or liken. It involves a quiet, thoughtful contemplation of all aspects of a subject.

We are told to 'walk about Zion' (v12). This investigating is not simply a mental exercise. 'Walking' is an active process. Having a good look around in this way was designed to stir up the heart in appreciation of all that God had done. This is described in this portion as a careful 'counting', 'marking', and 'considering'.

The expected outcome of this exercise is gladness and praise (v11); a determination to pass this knowledge and heritage to a generation yet to come (v13); confidence in God, who is in control, and who guides us throughout our life (v14). One day we will then worship him as he deserves (v10).

Day 102   Psalm 49:1-5

A call to all

The writer here calls for our earnest attention that we might learn wisdom. He addresses the high and low, the rich and poor from the entire world. As Isaiah, he cries 'Hear, O heaven, and give ear, O earth!' (Isa. 1:2).

He calls for everyone to give attention in verse 1. This is not just a message to Israel, but to all the nations – all who live their brief, mortal lives in this world, whether rich or poor. The word used for 'world' in the opening verse emphasises its temporary and fleeting character.

Alas, carnal men and women cannot understand or respond to the things of God. Only those who are taught of the Spirit can (1 Cor. 2:14). The world is now under the prince of this world, and enslaved to sin.

The psalmist speaks wisdom, discernment, and things that are hard to understand (parables). The LORD likewise spoke on parables, though he knew the people were deaf and blind (Matt. 13:10-17). Let us be diligent, and pray that we might be of the minority that have 'eyes to see and ears to hear' the deep truths of God's word.

He uses whatever means he can to gain their attention (using the harp), but, before he does so, he must 'incline his ear' (v4) to God's voice. He must not speak hastily, but meditate. Here is guidance for any evangelist or preacher. Listen before you speak.

Day 103   Psalm 49:6-15

Things that money cannot buy

We were called to attention in yesterday's passage. This portion unravels the enigma, the mystery. The question considered is 'Why are the wicked often rich and prosperous, whilst the righteous are poor and persecuted?'

The Psalm teaches us that we must see worldly prosperity through spiritual eyes: it cannot buy salvation (v7, 8); it is no safeguard against corruption and decay (v9). Rich men cannot take their riches with them: when they die their riches pass to others (v10); their attempts at permanence and making a name for themselves are futile (v11); they die, just like the beasts of the field (v12). We must beware of accepting the world's estimate of their greatness (v13). Yet the believer is redeemed, received (v15), and will triumph over them (v14).

The Lord Jesus told a parable to express this truth. He spoke of the man who accumulated riches only to hear the words, 'You fool! This night your soul will be required of you' (Luke 12:20). 'What shall it profit a man if he should gain the whole world and lose his own soul' (Mark 8:36)?

Death will be their shepherd and the grave their pasture where all their outward show will be consumed (v14).

Day 104 Psalm 49:16-20

Fading glory

These concluding verses resume the comfort with which the Psalm began. Why should we be afraid when we see the increasing wealth and magnificence of the wicked? The end of all these things is sure. They will at length pass away like all the self-boasting of Ozymandias[1]. It will not be as the prosperous rich man imagines, 'men will praise you when you do well for yourself' (v18b). Care for the fatherless and widows counts more in the balances of God than today's infatuation with self.

Going down unprepared to death is a fearful prospect. The New Testament describes this place as the blackness of darkness for ever (v19; Jude v13). How fearful when moral and mortal blindness ends in the loss of any glimmer of hope, or any 'light at the end of the tunnel'.

This is very much a word for the last days, when the arrogance and pride of men of the world will increase (2 Tim. 3:1-4). They scoff 'Where is the promise of his coming?' (2 Pet. 3:4). They are happy that they enjoy 'their good things', like the callous rich man (Luke 16:19-25). Let the believer 'in patience possess his soul' (Luke 21:19) in such a time.

---

[1] *Ozymandias*, sonnet by P.B. Shelley

Day 105   Psalm 50:1-6

The LORD shining out of Zion

The Mighty God[1] here comes in visible glory out of Mount Zion to judge (v2). The whole earth is summoned, and his saints are gathered to him.

In our days the mocking refrain of the ungodly is 'where is the promise of his coming?' It seems that God remains distant and silent, but these verses speak of a day when his silence will end (v3; Isa. 42:14; 65:6). He 'speaks'. He 'calls'. He 'will not keep silence'. No longer will man ignore the God of gods, for his voice will sound out from the rising of the sun to its going down. A fire, like that of Sinai, will go forth before him. The hurricane of his power will command the attention of all, as did the tempest at Sinai (v3; Exod. 19:18; Heb. 12:18-21).

For the believer there is encouragement in these verses, and we may apply them to ourselves. This is 'Our God' (v3). We are 'his people' (v4). We are the object of his love' (v5). We are safe beneath the blood of the covenant (v5). Such people as us are the focus of this section.

What a heart-warming picture of the coming of the Lord Jesus! Our previous Psalm ended as a dirge proclaiming the end of the prosperous wicked. Here now we have the glorious coming of the Lord, when 'the heavens shall declare his righteousness' (v6).

---

[1] Hebrew: *El Elohim.*

Day 106   Psalm 50 7-15

Offer the sacrifice of thanksgiving

Hengstenberg comments that, after the first six verses of introduction, the next two sections relate to each table of the law[1]. This section relates to the worship of God. Tomorrow's portion relates to responsibility to our fellow man.

The LORD provided the arrangements of the Temple and Tabernacle to teach Israel important spiritual lessons. Instead, they often just observed the external ritual.

This portion upbraids Israel for their formal worship. They offered what was commanded, but without praise from the heart.

Yesterday's portion shows deliverance coming to Israel 'out of Zion' (compare Rom. 11:25, 26), when shall they call upon him in their day of trouble. The veil of formal religion will then be lifted, when the spirit of grace and supplication is poured upon them (v15).

How easy it is to slip into the mere forms of worship! Put your formal religion aside. Read and sing the words of our portion with a heart that longs for worship, not just in truth, but in spirit also.

---

[1] E.W. Hengstenberg, *Commentary on the Psalms*.

Day 107   Psalm 50:16-23

Removing the mask of the hypocrite

There are three categories of people in this Psalm. The first section deals with those who are true believers, those on whom God sets his love, whom he will gather. The second section treats those who rely upon their rituals and works, but who are rebuked that they might repent. This last section is concerned with hypocrites, those who have a pretence of religion, but nevertheless sin against their fellow man.

De Burgh notes the parallels between this description and the New Testament description of the wicked in the last days. These 'take the covenant in their mouth' but hate instruction; in the last days men will have a form of godliness, but deny the power of it, are without natural affection, and so on (compare this section with 2 Tim. 3:1-5; 2 Pet. 3:3,4; and v18 with Rom. 1:32).

In verse 16 and 17 a particular person is addressed. Given the prophetic content of the Psalm (v1-6) this may be identified with Antichrist himself, for verse 16 is singular and emphatic.

There is a solemn warning in verse 22. Consider what a fearful thing it is to pit ourselves against God. May we instead offer true praise from the heart, and humbly order our lives aright before him (v23).

Day 108   Psalm 51:1-6

Owning up to our sins

We come today to David's Psalm of repentance, when he was convicted of his sin with Bathsheba (2 Sam. 11:1 - 12:25).

It reminds us of our need to confess our sin as we meet with God.

David begins with confession in these opening verses. He openly acknowledges his sin before of God. In doing so he feels sin's loathsomeness, and his guilt, as he stands before the Holy One.

The Psalm speaks of his sin. In 2 Samuel 11 it is shown to be a sin of thought (v2), word (v3) and deed (v4). However, in this Psalm, he confesses the root of that sin – 'in sin did my mother conceive me'. At the very point his life began, so did his corruption (v5).

David's broken-heartedness has touched believers in every generation. This Psalm was on the lips of many of the martyrs who died in Scotland and France. It was recited by 16/17-year-old Lady Jane Grey before she was beheaded. Yet today it remains unsung by most true Christians.

Let us use these precious words when we confess our sins to the LORD.

Day 109   Psalm 51:7-15

Wash me

David does not speak in cold selfish regret, nor in dutiful confession after failings have been exposed. Rather, he mingles his tears with those of Peter, who, like David, was a broken and failed leader who denied his Lord.

Having confessed his sin in yesterday's portion, David seeks a remedy. There are eleven short statements in verses 7-12. The first three in verses 7 and 8 are in the future tense, although most English Versions take them as asking God to do something[1]. They may be translated: 'You will purge me with hyssop…You will wash me…You will make me to hear joy and gladness'. These words of confidence rest upon what David knows from his experience of the character of his God. He looks to the restoring and healing hand of the Lord. His requests for cleansing follow in verses 9-12.

Verses 13-15 express his earnest desire to be useful once more. *Then*, he says, will I teach transgressors your ways. *Then* sinners will be converted. *Then* his tongue will sing aloud. *Then* will he will truly praise God.

Let us, like David, commit our failures to the hands of the Potter who is able to remake our marred lives.

---

[1] See Perowne's comments. The Old Greek and the Vulgate translate them as future.

Day 110   Psalm 51:16-19

A broken and contrite heart

In his guilt, David can bring no sacrifice for sin, nor are his tears grounds for forgiveness. Under the law there was no forgiveness for murder. David simply casts himself upon the mercy of God. The LORD 'will not despise a broken and a contrite heart'. This is the figure of speech called litotes. It is a massive understatement. He certainly will esteem, respect, and greatly value such a state and attitude of heart, and he will come soon to heal the broken-hearted. If that is how your heart is when you read this Psalm, then take encouragement.

In verse 18, David is conscious of the impact of his sin on 'Zion' where he was king. We bear responsibility for our actions, whether as a parent, a leader, or a witness to others. Our sin inevitably injures others, however secret we think it is.

We see in David's repentance a type of Israel's final repentance. The closing verse expresses their willing obedience, and the LORD's acceptance, in that day.

Let us make personal application of this sinner's prayer. Thomas Chalmers said, 'This is the most deeply affecting of all the Psalms, and I am sure the one most applicable to me'.

Day 111   Psalm 52

Don't be a Doeg

We have given to us in the title of this Psalm the context in which it was written – 'when Doeg the Edomite came and told Saul, and said unto him, "David is come to the house of Ahimelech"'. We read this story in 1 Samuel 21, 22. David's thoughtless and ill-conceived plans to escape from Saul occasioned the death of the high priest of the LORD (the great grandson of Eli), his whole family, and other innocent people. However, the immediate cause of the massacre was Doeg, a callous and brutal servant of Saul. Let us learn to detest such deceit and cruelty.

However, we do not sing this Psalm to celebrate an ancient wrong, or even to delight in David's vindication. In singing it we witness to the sure final intervention of God to defeat all the schemes of the wicked.

Antichrist shall be rooted out of God's dwelling place (v5), but the godly shall abide like a fruitful olive tree in God's house as a tree beside the waters (v8; Ps. 1:3). Old Testament prophecies are often given in the past tense, which emphasises the certainty of their fulfilment. So we believe it is here. 'Trust in the mercy of God for ever and ever. I will praise you forever, because you have done it' (v8, 9).

The LORD has a set purpose, and has determined what he will do (Acts 2:23; 17:26; Heb. 2:7). Let us sing these words with confidence that he is in control.

Day 112   Psalm 53

Universal depravity and guilt

This Psalm is nearly identical to Psalm 14. The differences are:

1. The titles. Psalm 53 is a maschil – for instruction. Psalm 14 is simply 'of David'.

2. Ps. 53:5 shows God's support of the righteous, compared with 14:5, 6, God's hatred of the wicked.

3. Ps. 53:5 is addressed to Israel ('him that encamps against you ... you have put them to shame'); Ps. 14:5 simply describes the state of the enemies of God and Israel's oppressors ('they were in great fear for God is in the generation of the righteous').

4. Psalm 14 refers to 'the LORD', whereas Psalm 53 refers to 'God'.

Paul quotes parts of verses 1-3 in Rom. 3:10-12 in his great proof of universal guilt. Let us remind ourselves of the utter depravity of the heart of man seen through the eyes of God (Rom. 3:10-12). A man's atheism may be concealed ('in his heart' v1), but it is evidenced by his failure to seek after God (v2), by his failure to do good (v3), and by doing evil (v4).

De Burgh points out the similarities of v5 with 'the Wicked One' of Ps. 10:11, and refers both to a time when Antichristianism shall oppress God's people.

In verse 6 we have the Lord Jesus coming out of Zion (Rom. 11:26) and the restoration of Israel.

Day 113   Psalm 54

By the name and power of God

This is another song of instruction (Maschil) by David, linked to events of his life. The reference is to 1 Sam. 23, during the time that David was an outlaw, when the people of Ziph in the hill country of Judea sought to betray David to Saul. It is a very personal Psalm, frequently using 'I', 'my' and 'me'. The Psalm falls into two halves: v1-3 prayer for deliverance; v4-7 confident assurance, and a vow of thankfulness.

David asks to be saved by the name and power of God (v1). The LORD can use ordinary means to deliver us, but 'when these fail, and every earthly stay is removed, he must then take the work into his own hands'[1].

It is a great mercy to feel and know our complete dependence upon God. How we take for granted our comfort and security. Yet when David had nowhere to lay his head; when all seemed against him, then he had sweet assurance and peace that God had rescued him from all distress (v7). But later, in his prosperity, he sinned (Ps. 51). It was whilst he was a fugitive that he knew most truly that God was his Helper.

Whatever our circumstances, let us acknowledge that our times are in God's hands.

---

[1] John Calvin, *Commentary*

Day 114   Psalm 55:1-8

O for the wings of a dove

David again prays about his affliction in words that are intended for our instruction – it is a maschil. It is generally agreed that the occasion of this Psalm was the rebellion of Absalom and David's flight from Jerusalem (2 Sam. 15-19). He wishes 'to fly away and be at rest' (v6-8).

One of the special privileges of a prayer meeting is that we share in the concerns, burdens, and heart longings of others. The Lord privileged his disciples to be where they would hear him pray, and David likewise lays his heart open to us in this Psalm.

Verses 4 and 5 speak of 'the terrors of death'. Death is a horrible thing. It is a measure of his foolishness and hardness of heart that modern man says he does not fear death, and wishes 'to die in dignity'. Voltaire made the same claims. He rejected the intervention of a priest at his bedside, saying he wished to 'die in peace', but at last went screaming into eternity.

We have comfort that in death, and in all our trials, God will keep us. 'This teaching regarding the perseverance of true believers, and of the saints, and the certainty of it, God, to the glory of his name and the solace of godly souls, has most abundantly revealed in his Word and impresses on the hearts of the faithful.[1] Let us rest in that comfort.

---

[1] Canons of the Synod of Dort, Chapter 5, article 15. Quoted from C.W.H. Griffiths, *Chosen – Called – Kept*.

Day 115   Psalm 55 9-15

Send sudden death

The tone changes. David's prayer continues, but in words directed against his persecutors, and drawing upon accounts of God's past judgments (Babel v9 – Gen. 11; Korah v15 – Numb. 16). These are not idle threats, but words spoken prophetically under the inspiration of the Holy Spirit.

The reference to 'My familiar friend' (v12-14) may well have a reference to Ahithophel who became Absalom's adviser (2 Sam. 15-17). Certainly, we may apply this Psalm to the life of David's greater son and see the Lord's grief at the treachery of Judas.

It is a fearful thing when the LORD acts in judgment and just vengeance upon sinners. However, it is an even more awful thing when he withholds his hand, and wicked men are emboldened, and allowed to wallow deeper in the filth of their sins. We should be jealous for the LORD's cause and plead with him to show that he is the Holy, Living, God 'of purer eyes than to behold evil, and cannot look on wickedness'. We should plead, 'Why do you look on those who deal treacherously, and hold your tongue when the wicked devours a person more righteous than he?' (Hab. 1:13).

All the enemies of God will finally perish.

Day 116   Psalm 55:16-23

A lot to cast

The confidence of the psalmist shines through this final part of the Psalm, although the wickedness of evil men still cuts into him. Verses 20 and 21 speak of the treacherous, deceiving friend who is described on verses 13-14.

This section opens and closes with a double trust in God. David is confident that the righteous will not be shaken, and he is also certain that the wicked will be cut off.

He not only speaks here to himself and to God, but he speaks encouragement to others - 'Cast your burden upon the Lord, and he will sustain you' (v22). How similar are these to the words of Peter - 'Casting all your care upon him, for he cares for you' (1 Pet. 5:7). Spurgeon says of our burden, 'His wisdom casts it on you. It is your wisdom to cast it on him'. We may add the advice of the puritan, David Dickson, 'Whosoever repose with confidence on God in their weighty troubles, shall never sink under them'.

The word translated 'burden' (AV) has the wider meaning of 'lot' or 'condition' Let us lean heavily upon the LORD throughout the life-pathway he has given us. Let us lay our burden upon the LORD.

Day 117   Psalm 56:1-7

Faith and Fear

The historical reference given in the title of this Psalm is the time when David had fled to Gath for fear of Saul (1 Sam. 21:10). We may wonder at David's foolishness, that he should flee to the very home of Goliath for safety. From 1 Samuel 21 we see the humbling of the one anointed to be King of Israel and the 'artful device' (to quote Calvin) that he used to escape with his life. Lest David should be ridiculed for what he did, Calvin notes, 'It is at least apparent from this Psalm what a strenuous contest there was between faith and fear in his heart'. The outpourings of the heart in this Psalm reflect that struggle. Fear and hope are mingled, but hope overcomes fear.

Setting aside the historical context given to us in the title, we can again meditate upon these words as a prayer of the Messiah[1].

The writer speaks of the fight against his enemies that he faces. In it he girds on his armour with three 'I wills'. 'I will trust in you' v3; 'I will praise his word' v4; 'I will not fear' v4. Let us remember that we also must put on the whole armour of God that we may withstand the attacks of Satan (Eph. 6:10-18), let us bind it to us with the same three 'I wills'.

---

[1] So Bishop Horsley, *The Book of Psalms...with Notes Explanatory and Critical*.

Day 118   Psalm 56:8-13

Bottled tears

These concluding verses turn away from enemies and their imminent destruction to tender conversation between David and his God.   His confidence is restored.   Had it been written then, David might have repeated the words of the Heidelberg Catechism![1] 'He also preserves me in such a way that, without the will of my Heavenly Father not a hair can fall from my head, indeed all things must work for my salvation'.

We see a man completely consecrated to God – 'Your vows are upon me' v12.   In its fullest sense this applies to our Saviour who under the Covenant of Grace proclaimed, 'Lo, I come, in the volume of the book it is written of me to do your will, O God'.   In consequence, he can say that his wanderings and his tears (v8), his cries for help (v9), his fears (v11), his soul (v13a) and his feet (v13b) are all surrendered, and in God's safe keeping.

Let us so come in free and glad surrender to our Lord who protects us (v11).   As the hairs of our head are numbered, so are the tears that we shed (v8), until that time when he shall wipe away every tear from our eyes. Let us sing these words without anxiety, casting all our cares upon him.

---

[1] *Heidelberg Catechism*, Question 1

Day 119   Psalm 57:1-5

Under his wings

This Psalm is by its own definition suited to private worship. By its title it is one of only six 'michtams', all of which are by David when he was in grave danger (Psalm 16 and 56-60). We understand the word 'michtam' to mean 'a private prayer or personal meditation'. Parts of this Psalm are very similar to Psalms 60 and 107.

In these opening verses David seeks safety and security (the title says it was written when David 'fled from the presence of Saul, in the cave'). We need to continually remember that we are on a pilgrimage. Daily we should pray for our safety, and the safety of our families and the Church of God from the deceits and attacks of Satan.

How precious is the expression 'in the shadow of his wings' (v1). The picture is of a helpless chick that the parent will defend against all predators.

We could extend the analogy through these verses; the parent bird also performs everything for me (v2), and sends down from the heavens to save me (v3)!

Let us own our dependence upon God for his constant protection in whatever circumstance we find ourselves.

Day 120   Psalm 57:6-11

David's wake-up call

David restates his predicament, but then, as so often in this set of Psalms, he ends with thankful testimony. David emerges from his cave and seeks an ever-wider audience to hear his thanksgiving.

His time of trial has fixed and settled his heart (v7). His joy is such that he feels he can even wake the dawn[1] with his praise and stir to life a sleeping world (v8). We may imagine David seated at the entrance of his cave writing verses 10 and 11 as he views the breaking of the dawn, beholding the heavens, the morning clouds, and the glory of the rising sun.

In all his prayer and thanksgiving his desire for the LORD's glory is foremost. In both sections of this Psalm (v5 and v11) he desires this. He sees God's glory as bound up with the deliverance of his people. He cannot praise God enough. As John Brown[2] quaintly puts it, 'conscious of his own inability to praise God enough, he leaves it on God to exalt and glorify himself'.

In our time with God this day let us bring our concerns to him. Then let us greet those around us with a testimony to God's goodness. Let us prepare our hearts for this delightful task, and ask God to exalt and glorify his name.

---

[1] This is the literal translation of v3.

[2] John Brown of Haddington *The Psalms of David in Metre with Notes.*

Day 121   Psalm 58:1-5

The false judgment of a deceitful heart

This Psalm speaks of the universal sinfulness of man (v3), but particularly the dreadful wickedness of those who have the responsibility to judge, but who give false judgment. It has a past, present and future reference.

It fittingly describes those who sat in judgment upon the Lord Jesus; see Matt. 26:3, 4, Mark 14:55.

It applies to all those with hardened hearts, from the time of Stephen onwards, who shut their ears to the testimony of truth (compare v4 and Acts 7:57) that they might condemn and destroy believers, whether in the name of the 'holy' Inquisition, the Star Chamber, or Sharia law. Foxe's *Book of Martyrs* gives many examples of such people.

It applies to those who lead Antichrist's conspiracy – Ps. 2:1-3 in its final fulfilment (also 2 Thess. 2:11).

The words of the title – Al-tash-heth – meaning 'Destroy not', evidently asks God to spare his people in such difficult times. Compare Deut. 9:26.[1]

---

[1] See J.W. Thirtle, *The Titles of the Psalms, their Nature and Meaning Explained*, He takes the stand-alone Psalm of Habakkuk 3 as a model Psalm. It is preceded by (1) A description – maschil, etc; (2) Its author; (3) The circumstances or object. It is followed by (4) the subscript line "For the Chief Musician". The original Hebrew text lacked paragraphs or punctuation. Adopting the Habakkuk model, "Destroy Not" relates to the preceding Psalm, but it applies to this Psalm as it is also used as a 'title' in 58.

Day 122   Psalm 58:6-11

The vengeance of God

These closing words are very solemn, but we say as Spurgeon does on another Psalm, 'If this be an imprecation, let it stand; for our heart says "Amen" to it. It is but justice that those who hate, harass and hurt the good should be brought to naught'[1].

Our Righteous One shall indeed wash his feet in the blood of the wicked (v10) when he treads out the winepress of the wrath of Almighty God (Rev. 19:15).

Now is the time for mercy (Acts 7:60), but this Psalm shows that judgment will finally come. 'As yet, in this present dispensation, the saints cannot triumph in *judgment*, because it is yet the day of *grace*, and the longsuffering of God waits, deferring in mercy the day of vengeance. But by-and-by they will triumph in it, because by that vengeance Divine justice will be vindicated, and the Divine glory manifested before all'. 'We rejoice now in the *redeeming grace* of Christ; we shall then rejoice in his *avenging power*'[2].

We shall yet know 'that strange, that Divine joy over sin destroyed, justice honoured, the law magnified, vengeance taken for the insult done to Godhead, and the triumph of the Holy One over the unholy'[3].

---

[1] C.H. Spurgeon, *The Treasury of David*. On Psalm 129:4, 5.
[2] William de Burgh, *A Commentary on the Book of Psalms*.
[3] A.A. Bonar, *Christ and His Church in the Book of Psalms*.

Day 123   Psalm 59:1-9
Provoking God's laughter

This Psalm again belongs to the period when David had to escape from Saul. This time it relates to when Saul's servants watched David's house to kill him (1 Sam. 19:11-18). We may wonder that David, escaping for his life, found time for personal prayer and private meditation (the meaning of 'michtam' in the title). We seem to feel that we lack the scope for this in our busy and stressful lives. May we be stirred up by the greater necessity for this at such times of busyness and pressure. Martin Luther allegedly once said that he would be so busy the following day that he would need to spend three hours in prayer before he started!

David looks beyond his personal difficulties. In verse 1 he addresses 'My God' about 'my enemies'. But in verse 5 he takes up the cause of his people, addressing 'the God of Israel' concerning the wickedness of 'all the nations'. Let us also look beyond our own circumstances in our times of prayer.

The reference to the LORD laughing, and deriding the wicked, (v8) is fearful. This Hebrew word 'laugh' is usually used of scornful laughter concerning 'one who threatens to do much, but is able to do nothing'[1]. See Prov. 1:26. Though, for a time, they seem to triumph, Satan, his angels, and wicked men, can, in the end, do nothing against the LORD. 'The LORD is with us. Fear them not' (Numb. 14:9).

---

[1] Gesenius, *Hebrew Lexicon*

Day 124   Psalm 59:10-17

Let them know that God rules

We noted yesterday that David prays for both his personal concerns and, more widely, for his people.

The passage begins with the wonderful thought that, in response, 'the God of mercy will meet (AV 'prevent') me'. Calvin comments, 'God will interpose at the very moment when it is required, however much he may retard or defer his assistance'[1]. Consider the Lord Jesus's perfect timing in his slow journey to raise Lazarus from the dead.

In this passage, David desires the gradual and progressive punishment of the wicked, so that his people might learn more surely that all things are indeed working for good to those who love God. John Brown writes, 'While his honours are trampled underfoot, let me wait on, and trust in God, that at last I may join in the Hallelujahs of his people, when the smoke of his enemies' torment ascendeth up for ever and ever'[2]. There are similarities between verse 8 and Psalm 2. Psalms 56-59 may all be seen in that same context.

We see at the close of this Psalm the evening that leads to night when the 'dogs' threaten; and the morning leading to the day when God's power shall be shown. Let us delight that the morning is coming.

---

[1] John Calvin, *Commentary*.

[2] John Brown of Haddington, *The Psalms of David in Metre with Notes*.

Day 125   Psalm 60:1-5

Raising the LORD's banner

The events referred to in the title of this Psalm are recorded in 2 Samuel 8:3-14. Joab smote Edom in the Valley of Salt. Although written at a more favourable time than the preceding Psalms, the portion we consider today shows considerable apprehension. Hapstone[1] suggests that it was written before that glorious victory.

This section pictures the battle scene. A breach has been made in the ranks (v1, 2 'You have scattered us'. Compare Judg. 21:15, where the same word is used there translated 'a breach'). The earth trembles (v2). Nevertheless, the LORD does raise a banner, or a standard, to cheer their hearts and unite them once again (v4; compare Isa. 11:10). Such a banner ('For Christ's Crown and Covenant') was once raised in the days of the Covenanters in Scotland. O that the LORD would raise a standard once again for poor broken Protestantism!

We face the daily events of our lives without the knowledge God has of the future. Let us rest on him to work all things together for good for us as he has promised (Rom. 8:28). Let us stay close to him. If we begin as those who fear God (v4), we will end as those who are beloved (v5).

---

[1] Dalman Hapstone, *The Ancient Psalms in Appropriate Metres*.

Day 126   Psalm 60:6-12

Vain is the help of man

The verses of this section are repeated in Psalm 108 with a few verbal changes. Those verses are the words of David, spoken of Israel's anticipated future triumphs. In this portion Israel is in possession of their land with all their enemies subdued, as in Isaiah 11.

The imagery of war is continued in these verses; 'the defence of my head' (v7); 'the fortified city' (v9); the LORD going forth with armies (v10); 'doing valiantly' (v12a); the treading down of the adversary (v12b), all paint the same picture.

We, likewise, are in a battle, but do not wrestle against flesh and blood, but against principalities and powers (Eph. 6:12). Let us also be a 'Valiant for the Truth' in our day.

B.W. Newton writes[1], 'these two Psalms of thanksgiving [59 and 60], founded upon typical victories of David, evidently foreshadow that yet future hour, when Israel and Israel's King shall finally triumph over Edom, and all their mighty enemies, and receive the fullness of their inheritance of blessing'. Compare Isaiah 24, where the prophet calls all nations to witness Edom's judgment, evidently yet future.

---

[1] B.W. Newton, *Babylon and Egypt*.

Day 127   Psalm 61

A Royal prayer

The Old Greek version, which was written hundreds of years before any Christian 'hymn' was ever composed, titles this Psalm as 'among the hymns of David'. In 2 Chr. 7:6 it calls these inspired compositions 'the hymns of David'.

The Psalm is a prayer in which David again mingles reflection on past mercies with hope for God's future intervention. The opening verses convey a sense of distance, but a desire to be close and at the LORD's side. He prefaces his prayer with a request that he might be heard (v1). He does not even presume that he will be! He feels he is crying 'from the ends of the earth' (v2a). The rock of refuge that he climbs seems too high for him to reach the place of safety (v2b), so he depends on God's aid. He desires to continually dwell in the Tabernacle where God revealed himself, and under the shadow of the wings of the Almighty (v4).

He then bursts forth with hope and prayer for the establishment of Messiah's kingdom (v6-8). 'The Lord God shall give unto him the throne of his father David; and he shall reign over the house of Jacob forever, and of his kingdom there shall be no end' (Luke 1:32,33). There is similarity with the closing verses of Psalm 72.

Day 128   Psalm 62:1-7

In God alone

In the opening verses David describes the evil purposes of wicked men (v3, 4). For him the LORD is his sole refuge (v2 and 6). He silently waits upon God alone (v1 and 5). What else do we need, but God only? How precious a thing it is to be able to wait on God in silence when confronted with scheming, lying deceivers who are intent on getting their own way.

De Burgh comments that this Psalm is remarkable, because, although again conscious of his enemies, David does not express any fear or dejection, as he does elsewhere. The Psalm seems to be given as an encouragement to himself and to others. It is not a cry for help.

David reminds himself of his relationship to God in many touching ways in the last verses of this portion. He is his Rock; his Salvation; his Defence (Stronghold); his Glory; his strong Fortress (the Rock of my strength); his Refuge.

If we have been converted, and know ourselves to be chosen and elect in him, let us ponder these things and repeat them in our song.

Day 129   Psalm 62:8-12

The God of power and mercy

The theme of dependence upon God and the emptiness of all human endeavour apart from God is repeated in these verses.

'If riches increase, set not your heart upon them'. So reads verse 10. John Brown comments,[1] 'While I sing, go my soul and do likewise. Be weaned from all dependence on creatures; but cleave to, and depend on, this all-sufficient JEHOVAH as answerable to all your needs, all your desires, all your enjoying powers, for time and for eternity. Then, O how fixed in safety! and how filled with the consolations of Christ'. Let us not keep our concerns to ourselves. Let us "pour out our heart before him" (v8)'.

On verses 11 and 12, Augustine says that two things belong to God – power and mercy. 'They are the two wings wherewith we fly upwards to heaven; the two pillars on which we rest'[2]. Perowne writes 'power without love is brutality; love without power is weakness'.

May we sing of our God in the verses of this portion. As Ps. 59:16 urges us 'I will sing of your power; Yes, I will sing aloud of your mercy in the morning'.

---

[1] John Brown of Haddington, *The Psalms of David in metre with notes*

[2] Quoted in John Calvin, *Commentary*

Day 130   Psalm 63:1-5

The best breakfast

The Psalm is a song of David written whilst in the wilderness of Judea (title). It speaks of one who is walking in solitude with his God. The later administrative duties and temptations of Kingship do not trouble David here, as he is able to freely meditate upon God and praise him.

David Baron writes[1], 'A wilderness song! What a strange, unlikely place for a song to proceed from! But it is perhaps the special characteristic of God's people that they can sing in the wilderness. The children of the world also have their wildernesses, but they cannot sing there. When the flowers of outward prosperity fade, and the world's sun begins to set, their music ceases'. But for the Church, 'It is the wilderness, in times of suffering and persecution that she has sung the sweetest'. The world seeks its *joie de vivre*, its enjoyment of this life. The believer can say by contrast, 'Your loving-kindness is better than life' (v3).

This was the daily morning hymn of the early Church. The noun for 'early morning' and the verb 'to seek' are from the same root, hence the AV translation 'early will I seek' (v1). What a privilege it is to be able to sing this Psalm quietly and thoughtfully before the pressures of this day of our lives.

---

[1] David Baron, *Types, Psalms and Prophecies*

Day 131   Psalm 63:6-11

Remembering God in bed

David is not having an easy time in this Psalm. He is awake in the 'night watches'; he needs the 'help' and protection of God's 'wings' over him; he needs to 'follow hard' after God, and to be 'sustained'. Yet his voice is not one of complaint, but of delight that this is his lot. He is thrown hard upon God in his circumstances, and uses that very trial as an opportunity to praise and thank God. His enemies seem to prosper, but they will shortly be cut off. His expectation is not a gloomy defeat. He can say 'But the king *shall* rejoice'. Even in his impossible situation he clings to his kingly calling.

In the expression 'my soul follows hard after you' (v8). The verb means 'to stick', 'to be inseparably joined to', as Adam to his wife (Gen. 2:24) and as Christ and his Church (Eph. 5:25-33).

David remembers the LORD upon his bed, rather than fretting there about the problems he faces. He falls asleep thinking about God. How will it be with you tonight, my friend? Will you take the burdens of the day to bed with you? Matthew Henry asks[1], 'Why do I go to sleep now, but that my body may be fit to serve my soul, and may be able to keep pace with it in the service of God tomorrow?' Let us remember God, in bed this night.

---

[1] Matthew Henry, *A Method for Prayer,* (Chapter: *How to close the day with God*).

Day 132   Psalm 64:1-6

Freedom from fear

The Psalm begins with a cry for help against the vindictive plans of wicked men. It describes their methods, and then confidently predicts their violent end. It thus follows the pattern of a number of Psalms (52, 57, 58, 59, etc).

In the West, we once assumed that everyone is favourable to the Gospel of the love of God. We are waking up to a different world. For our brothers and sisters in the developing world, particularly where the religion of Mohammed holds sway, things are very different. The words given by the Holy Spirit in this Psalm may not be found in hymnbooks, but they are a much-needed consolation to the persecuted Church.

Fearfulness is a cause of spiritual depression. It limits the usefulness of the servant of God and takes away his peace. It may stem from awareness of wicked and satanic attacks which bend their bow at the believer. The Lord Jesus too knew of such plots and scheming against him.

Today's portion is David's prayer for deliverance from fear and dread. If you are anxious and fearful, join with David as you sing and pray to the LORD to hear your voice.

Day 133   Psalm 64:7-10

The Divine Archer

The Psalm now moves from the present to the future; from the arrows of men and the fiery darts of the Satan (v3, 4; compare Eph. 6:16) to the unexpected suddenness of the arrow of God (v7). The Psalm moves from secret slander of the saints to their public vindication.

Surely the message here is that the prayers of this Psalm will be answered, and that it is not wrong to pray for vindication.

Calvin comments that God's usual procedure in dealing with unrepentant, wicked people is to suddenly cut them off. 'It is a consideration which should comfort us, when subjected to long-continued trial, that God, in delaying to punish the ungodly, does so with the express design of afterwards inflicting more appropriate and severe judgments upon them, and when they would say, 'Peace and Safety', overwhelming them with sudden destruction (Jer. 8:11; 1 Thess. 5:3)'[1].

Our comfort is that the 'Day of the Lord' will follow the day of man. God, his Son, and the believer, will then be vindicated. Let us not be afraid to bear reproach in the day of man.

---

[1] John Calvin, *Commentary*.

Day 134 Psalm 65:1-8

The Final Ingathering

This Psalm is closely associated with the Feast of Tabernacles[1], and the Day of Atonement that immediately precedes it.[2] Viewing this Psalm in its prophetic sense, the repentance of Israel and the atonement made for the people ushers in the time of universal blessing (Acts 3:19-21). The wording of verses 1 and 2 links it with that blessing which shall come upon all nations (Isa. 2:2, 3; 66:23 and Zech. 14:16-19).

David Dickson finds in this portion eight reasons to praise God.

1. He hears and answers prayer (v2)
2. He pardons sins (v3)
3. His gracious decree of election (v4)
4. His defence of his Church in all places (v5)
5. His strength in establishing the mountains (v6)
6. His wise and powerful overruling (v7)
7. He sets himself against his people's enemies (v8a)
8. He grants his people joy (v8b)

In this day of small things let us remind ourselves that there will yet be a mighty ingathering. God's arm is not shortened that it cannot save.

---

[1] Or 'the Feast of Ingathering'. Compare v2 and Zech. 14:16 and 8:20-23

[2] *Pardoned* transgressions v3, literally, "covered". It is the same word as "make an atonement" in Lev. 16.

Day 135 Psalm 65: 9-13

Enriched, crowned, and clothed

We are familiar with the words of verse 11, repeated annually at harvest thanksgivings 'You crown the year with goodness'. In accordance with his word, seedtime and harvest, cold and heat, summer and winter, and day and night, have not ceased (Gen. 8:22). Andrew A Bonar writes, 'The yearly return of Spring and Summer is an emblem of Earth's Summer Day, when it shall be renewed'[1].

The language here is beautifully expressive, as if creation is blessed with the regalia of a king. The LORD enriches (v9 compare 1 Sam. 17:25); he crowns (v11); he clothes (v13). How good is our God!

May our thankfulness for oft-repeated mercies lead us on to our future hope. David Baron writes,[2] 'Primarily this Psalm sets forth the blessedness of restored Israel when the LORD shall establish and make Jerusalem a praise in the earth, and when Zion shall be, as never before, the earthly centre for the praise and worship of the one true God'.

Those will be the times of refreshing from the presence of the Lord (Acts 3:19-21); when creation's groan shall end; when earth shall enjoy her Sabbath; and when the earth shall be filled with the knowledge of God as the waters cover the sea.

---

[1] Andrew A Bonar, *Christ and His Church in the Book of Psalms*.
[2] David Baron, *Types, Psalms and Prophecies*.

Day 136   Psalm 66:1-9

All the earth shall worship ... and fear

This joyous appeal to God and man is called in the title 'a song', and if a song, it is certainly a 'spiritual song', as referred to in Col. 3:16 and Eph. 5:19. It is one which Christians are there commanded to sing.

Through the Psalm the writer switches between prayer, praise, and encouraging others (indeed, all the earth) to praise God. The Psalm is a fulfilment of Ps. 65:1 – 'Praise waits for you in Zion'. It is a celebration of God's power and greatness. It is spontaneous from his people, but now compelled from all. For 'at the name of Jesus every knee shall bow' (v3; compare Phil. 2:10).

Joyful as the Psalm is, God's acts are described in verses 3 and 5 as 'awesome' and 'fearful' ('terrible' AV). The same Hebrew word is used in Exod. 15:11 and Deut. 10:17, 21. Modern translations fail to express the Biblical view of the fear of God in strong enough terms. In verse 16 we are called 'those who fear God'. May we be those who 'tremble at his word' (Isa. 66:5) and recoil with dismay when 'Oh my God!' is used as a 'humorous' expletive.

'Who shall not fear you, O Lord, and glorify thy name? for you only are holy: for all nations shall come and worship before you; for your judgments are made manifest'. (Rev. 15:4).

Day 137   Psalm 66:10-15

Through fire and water

In verses 10-12 we have an account of God's actions in proving his people – bringing them through fire and water. This answers to the oppression of the people of Israel in Egypt.

It also answers to the prediction of a future deliverance of Israel – 'When you pass through the waters, I will be with you; and through the rivers, they shall not overflow you: when you walk through the fire you will not be burned; neither shall the flame kindle upon you' – see Isa. 43:2-6.   Compare too verses 5-7 of yesterday's portion with Isa. 11:15 and Zech. 10:11.

'We went through fire and through water; yet you have brought us out to a place of abundance' (v12).   We may safely trust our cause with God as Daniel and his companions did. For many at the Reformation the flame was the means of their death. The waters ended the lives of the two Margarets in the Solway Firth. God brought them through their trials.   So will he certainly bring us through our trials to the many mansions that he has prepared for us.

Let us then, in response to the LORD's promised deliverance (v13-15), 'bring my vows before Him' and serve him to the end. May answered prayers lead to ever greater zeal.

Day 138   Psalm 66:16-20

Bunyan's epigraph

John Bunyan made verse sixteen the motto for his autobiography, *Grace Abounding to the Chief of Sinners*. If we have known the hand of God upon us, in affliction or in blessing, we will not keep his mercies to ourselves. Real experiences of God's mercy and blessing are not meant for enjoyment in secret. They are for the mutual encouragement of all the saints. 'Come and hear, all you that fear God, and I will declare what he hath done for my soul'.

The Gadarene demoniac was denied the role of an anonymous follower so that he might be a fruitful evangelist (Mark 5:18-20). Such has been the pathway of many new converts whose early years have been filled with joyful testimony.

The burning zeal of Howell Harris when he was converted led to him to write often of 'the first summer' as his most precious time[1]. As we grow older, may our mouths be once again opened in praise and testimony by a return to that 'first love' (Rev. 2:4).

What a delightful task to sing this passage and worship God with consecrated hearts!

---

[1] Richard Bennett, *The Early Life of Howell Harris.* Banner of Truth.

Day 139   Psalm 67[1]

The Lord's Prayer of the Old Testament

This precious Psalm four times declares that all peoples (plural) of the earth shall praise the LORD (v3, 5). It is not a call to the peoples. It declares God will cause this to take place. The psalmist longs for that time, when the LORD will 'judge the peoples righteously and govern the nations upon earth'. How much misrule we see! How much injustice! We should long for the time when God's way shall be known upon earth, and his salvation among all nations. What a wonderful day that will be!

The psalmist recognises that the work must begin with the people of God – v1 is before v2.

The primary reference of 2 Chr. 7:14 is to Israel, but we may claim the verse for ourselves. 'If *my people, which are called by my name* shall humble themselves and pray, and seek my face, and turn from their wicked ways...' May our hearts and desires be moved. God sets his people to pray when it is his time to act (Dan. 8:2).

The early Church called this Psalm 'the Lord's Prayer of the Old Testament'[2]. We should daily ask for the kingdom, the power, and the glory to come.

---

[1] This Psalm's title in Rahlf's edition of the Old Greek version is, "among the hymns: a song; a psalm". Compare Eph. 5:19 and Col. 3:16. The inspired Psalms provide what the New Testament requires for our worship in song.

[2] John Ker, *The Psalms in History and Biography*.

Day 140 Psalm 68:1-6

Smoke and wax

This Psalm describes the commencement of the Day of the Lord, when God finally intervenes.[1]

The opening words were shouted when the Ark went forward in the wilderness (Numb. 10:35). It has been suggested that the Psalm was written for the bringing up of the Ark to Jerusalem by David (2 Samuel 6; 1 Chronicles 15).

We must wait for God to indicate when we should go forward. How disastrous it was that the sons of Eli took the Ark into battle, presuming that they could force God's hand, and make him fight for them (1 Sam. 4; but compare Numb. 14:44)!

The psalmist longs for God's open intervention in the plight of his people. When he intervenes, his enemies will perish. As Luther says, 'smoke disappears before the wind, and wax before the fire' (v2).

Let us, with the psalmist, place all our hope in God's sovereign intervention in the affairs of men. Let us not proudly boast that we are on the winning side, but humbly depend upon the Captain of the Lord's host[2] (Josh. 5:14) to lead us forward in this day.

---

[1] See B.W. Newton, *Expository Teaching on the Millennium, and Israel's Future* (On Psalm 68).

[2] Bishop Horsley comments on the remarkable proof of the Lord Jesus' Divinity in this Psalm. As he returns it will be "By his name JAH" (the LORD) that he is known (v4; Isa. 62:10-12).

Day 141   Psalm 68: 7-14

If God goes before us, who can be against us?

The psalmist recounts what God did in former days in expectation of what he is about to do. The opening verses are an echo of the Song of Deborah (Judg. 5:4, 5). This passage relates Israel's miraculous deliverance from Egypt; their 'ordinary' sustainment in the land with rain, etc; the trial of God's people through conflicts; and their deliverance from their trials. Commentaries will clarify the various events alluded to in this passage, which relate especially to the times of Joshua and the Judges.

We must ever recall God's past deliverances. From these events Dickson[1] finds 11 reasons why we should praise God. We must remember that those who have gone before us faced great trial and difficulty too. The LORD sustained them in remarkable ways. So too he can for us. The words are also a prophecy of what Christ will do when he returns. Then, no more defiled and rebellious, Israel shall be 'like the wings of a dove covered with silver and its feathers with glistening gold' (v13).

'May the reader's heart adore the God before whom the unconscious earth and sky act as if they recognised their Maker and were moved with a tremor of reverence'.[2]

---

[1] David Dickson, *A Brief Explication of the Psalms.*
[2] C.H. Spurgeon, *Treasury of David.*

Day 142   Psalm 68:15-23

Christ exalted: His enemies crushed

The prophetic character of these verses is shown by their use by Paul in Eph. 4:8-16. Paul applies them to the Ascension, but they also apply to the time when Christ will put every enemy down[1].

For the purpose of his application, Paul stops short of the words in v18 that point to this final event, when Christ is described as giving gifts to rebellious Israel also, that the LORD God might dwell among them. Both the Ascension and Return of Christ are marked by gladness, glory, deliverance, triumph, and the outpouring of gifts.

When the Lord Jesus left his disciples, he told them to wait 40 days until the Holy Spirit descended upon them. Through Christ's glorious Ascension, gifts of blessing and ministry were poured upon his Church. It was then equipped for service. Gentiles have been grafted into 'the goodly olive tree' so that they may bear fruit (Rom. 11:14-36). However, there is a fuller, yet future, fulfilment of his triumph for which we yet wait. 'If the casting away of them is the reconciling of the world, what shall the receiving of them be'?

Praise the Lord Jesus. Rejoice at his past and coming triumph, and the largesse of his mighty victory.

---

[1] Dr John Gill, *Commentary*. On v24 "So much carnage will be made of Antichrist and his followers, that the fowls of the heavens will be called upon to eat the flesh of kings, captains, and mighty ones" (Rev. 19:17,18)

Day 143 Psalm 68:24-35

Celebrating glorious victory

There is much of Christ's future dominion in this Psalm.

The triumphal procession of God's people is described in verses 24-28. The Gentiles (kings) are also there (v29). The nations who delight in war are scattered. It is the reign of the Prince of Peace (v30, 31). The nations sing Psalms to the LORD (v32). Compare this with Isaiah 19:19-25; 45:14-17.

There have been past tokens, as the conversion of the Ethiopian eunuch, but, O for the promised time when the words of Isa. 19:22 shall be fulfilled. What a glorious song of praise is given in verses 32-35! It is a command to willing people to praise, awed by the holiness and power of God.

At that time his excellent majesty will be peculiarly over Israel (v34). As B.W. Newton observes[1], they have for so long been the nation who hates their Messiah (Isa. 49:7). In that day, the LORD will be known as 'the God of Israel' and strength and power will be given to them (v35).

O for that time when all nations shall serve him, and the cry shall go up 'the Kingdoms of this world are become the Kingdoms of our and of his Christ' Rev. 11:14)! Let us celebrate his anticipated, manifest, victory as we sing.

---

[1] B.W. Newton, *Expository Teaching on the Millennium, and Israel's Future* (On Psalm 68),

Day 144 Psalm 69:1-5

The prayer of the Suffering Servant

The New Testament refers to this Psalm in connection with the life and death of the Lord Jesus (e.g. v4 in John 15:25 and v9 in John 2:17). All the expressions that we find here must therefore be interpreted in this light.

The inmost agony of the Lord's heart is shown in these verses, and we need to tread reverently as we pass through. These are sufferings endured on account of imputed sin. Here was the Substitute, in all his purity, bearing and suffering under the wrath of man, the wrath of Satan and, most terribly, the wrath of God, for our sakes.

So closely is he identified with us that he confesses our folly and guilt as his own (v5) - 'who was most free of what men laid to his charge, although, in another reckoning, all the iniquities of the elect were charged upon him by imputation'[1].

The prayer of this Psalm is a model for our praying[2]. It gives reasons why the LORD should answer.

1. For the danger he was in (v1, 2).
2. For he had waited long and patiently (v3).
3. For his enemies were many and strong (v4).
4. For he was innocent of their accusations, and free of hidden sins (v5).

Lord, teach us to pray.

---

[1] David Dickson, *A Brief Explication of the Psalms*.
[2] *Ibid*.

Day 145   Psalm 69:6-12

Holy zeal

We see the Man of Sorrows again in these verses. The zeal for God's house had eaten him up. He was deeply affected by the dishonour done to God. Verse 10 literally reads 'I wept away my soul in fasting'. He pleads for deliverance. The cause of God was upon his shoulders. God's honour was at stake in all his sufferings. His grief that 'He came unto his own and his own received him not' (John 1:11) is clear in these verses.

Bunyan reminds us that Christ had to go through the Vanity Fair of this world and that we must pass through it too. How well do we stand when we are treated as Pilgrim was? - 'made the objects of any man's sport, or malice, or revenge, the Great One of the Fair laughing still at all that befell them'[1].

Dear reader, how is it with your soul? Do you burn inwardly that Christ might be glorified? Do you bear his reproach? Can we repeat the words of Paul? 'We are fools for Christ's sake … we are weak … we are despised…we hunger and thirst … are naked … are buffeted …have no certain dwelling place … labour, working with our own hands … reviled … persecuted … defamed. We are made as the filth of the world, and are the offscouring of all things' (1 Cor. 4:10-13).

---

[1] John Bunyan, *The Pilgrim's Progress.*

Day 146   Psalm 69:13-21

Scorned and broken-hearted

David, the writer of this Psalm, turns to God in prayer as the only one who is full of great mercy; and who saves us according to his sovereign will (v13). His words are pleading, anxious, desperate. He is in the mire, in deep waters, in danger of being washed away by the flood, of falling into a deep pit (v14, 15). He longs for an answer, for a glimpse of God's face, for a feeling of the LORD's nearness to him (v16-18). He pleads with the LORD to draw near and comfort – for he finds no comfort from man. No one gives him sympathy (v20).

Again and again, we have inspired words that we can use in our petitions to God. If we sing them regularly, these words will be familiar to us and help us in our prayers. Could we not start all our prayers with verse 13? Can we make a stronger reason for God to answer than we find in verse 16?

The believer who has been called to suffer for his Master can surely understand these words and feelings, but, as we have already noted, we also have here an insight into the heart of the Saviour as he undertook his mission for us. For him the bitter gall and the vinegar were literal, as well as describing the bitter sorrow he suffered (v21). He was alone and forsaken, even by the Father.

Let us pray and sing these wonderful words.

Day 147　Psalm 69:22-28

A time for every purpose under heaven

The tone of the Psalm changes in this section. It now focusses on the wicked and those who persecute the godly. It calls God's wrath and punishment down upon them.

We need to remember who is saying these things, whether David ('the man after God's own heart' Acts 13:22), or the Lord Jesus himself. There is a time for mercy and the longsuffering of God, but there is also a time when the wrath of the Lamb will be seen, and will cut men down with fear and despair. It is of such a dark time that this passage speaks.

We must never forget that, down the centuries, Israel has been a nation under judgment. Wrath has come upon them 'unto the uttermost'. Their privileges have aggravated their guilt. Their rejection of the Messiah has brought judgment upon them and their children (Matt. 27:25). And yet, we too need to heed the warning of judgment on Christendom, which has apostatised from the truths that were entrusted to it, and is ripe for judgment also (Rom. 11:13-24). It is a fearful thing to fall into the hands of the Living God (Heb. 10:31).

This is a solemn passage to read and sing. May it give impetus to our evangelism in the day of grace.

Day 148   Psalm 69:29-36

Pleasing God with song

The tone of the Psalm again changes in these verses, to the joy and hope that springs from his 'poor and sorrowful' servant (v29). 'For the LORD hears the poor, and does not despise his prisoners' (v33). We learn the goodness and severity of God in this Psalm. It is applied in the New Testament to our blessed Lord Jesus, and to the sufferings that have befallen that nation which brought him to the cross. Nevertheless, we are told that 'God will save Zion…and they that love his name shall dwell therein' (v35, 36).

Verses 30 and 31 will reward our meditation. We are told:

1. The LORD desires our obedience in how we worship (sacrifice of ox and bull were appointed by God).
2. It is possible for God's people to please him!
3. Praise and thanksgiving are a means of pleasing him.
4. The LORD desires not just praise in our hearts, or in our speech, but in our song.

However low and hopeless our condition may seem to be, the Lord is able to, and will at length, bring us out from it. As we read elsewhere 'Many are the afflictions of the righteous, but the LORD delivers him out of them all'. Let us praise him for all that he has done, and what he will do.

Day 149   Psalm 70

An urgent cry for help

This Psalm is almost identical to Ps. 40:13-17. It is entitled, 'A Psalm of David; to bring to remembrance'. Perhaps it is repeated because David wanted to think on these words again! It has been provided a second time by the Holy Spirit with some significant differences. It is a cry for help from David. Its urgency is more marked than in Psalm 40.

Sometimes we make an urgent call to God, as a child cries for a parent in the dark (v1 and 5). Such was the request of Mary and Martha on behalf of Lazarus. It seems at such times that our short span of life here is passing quickly. We should remind ourselves that, though the Lord then seemed to 'tarry', it was for the glory of God. So it is with all God's delays.

However, as we do not want God to delay when we need him, we should not delay in going to God. 'Man is apt to think that he will have ample leisure to repent. Man needs to be continually put in remembrance that … he has no time to spare'[1].

We may not have human enemies as David did (v2, 3), although the days are darkening for Christians. But there is one who goes about as a roaring lion against us (1 Pet. 5:18), whose cruel, lying, and murderous hatred desires the destruction of our souls. Let us seek the LORD's protection and lay all our problems at his feet.

---

[1] Charles Girdlestone, *Commentary on the Bible*.

Day 150   Psalm 71:1-8

Youthful trust

The opening prayer (v1-3) is very similar to the first three verses of Psalm 31. It is the voice of one harassed and persecuted. The words 'escape', 'rescue', 'strong habitation', 'rock', 'fortress', 'strong refuge' all speak of physical jeopardy. In the midst of such physical dangers the writer is able to rest on his God. He says, 'Deliver me in your righteousness' in verse 2. For the believer, God has given commandment (v3) that we should be protected and preserved to the end (Ps. 91:11). In the Psalms the righteousness of God is frequently linked to the faithfulness with which he acts (see Psalms 4:1; 119:138; 143:1).

The writer's dependence is a habitual and a proven trust. We trust those whose love has stood the test of time. Just so, he can look back to his youth (v5) and even to his earliest years – from 'his mother's womb' (v6) and see the way the LORD has helped him. That strengthens him when he is confronted with present difficulties. Happy if that is also our experience.

Whatever our present perplexities, let us also depend upon our God. Let our praise be continual (v6), all day long (v8), uninterrupted by our trials and difficulties. Then our mouth will be 'filled' with his praise (v8). So shall we be a wonder – a sign, a miracle, a special display of God's power – to those around us (v7).

Day 151   Psalm 71:9-18

Not forsaken in old age

In these verses the writer starts with the cares, weakness and feelings of uselessness that often accompany old age.

His response to this is:

1. Steadfast hope (v14)
2. Desire to praise God more and more (v14)
3. Longing to share God's salvation with others (15)
4. Reliance on God's strength (v16).

We live in a disposable society. When something is outdated or worn out; when shoes let water; when a suit gets shabby, we dispose of them and get new ones. A worker is retired when he loses his usefulness to his employer.

It is not so with the LORD. The elect of God may still bring forth fruit in old age (Ps. 92:14). David's desire was to live long enough to declare and show the strength of God to the next generation (v18). We may say with the wise man, 'the hoary head is a crown of glory if he be found in the way of righteousness' (Prov. 16:31). The LORD has promised, 'Even to your old age, I am He; and even to grey hairs I will carry you' (Isa. 46:4).

May faith, hope, and love be our portion in old age. As we grow older may we praise him more, speak more of him, and demonstrate that his strength is made perfect in weakness.

Day 152   Psalm 71:19-24

Up from the depths of the earth

In these verses the writer's troubles disappear as his thoughts are taken up with the greatness of God. The first use of the title 'the Holy One of Israel' in the Scriptures is found in these verses. The psalmist is overwhelmed by the righteousness of God, his omnipotence, his providence, and his resurrection power (v19, 20).

Such a view of God awakens his desire to praise and to sing. His very lips and redeemed soul rejoice at the joy of praise, and his tongue cannot cease to speak of the righteousness of God.

May we sing these verses when we look back on the 'great and severe troubles' that the LORD has brought us through. As we stand at the threshold of eternity and face our approaching death, may we share David's confidence (v20). In our flesh we will see God (Job 19:26). He will bring us up from the depths of the earth. Then, singing the immortal song, our lips shall greatly rejoice, our redeemed soul shall sing praises, and our tongue shall talk of the LORD's righteousness all the day long, in that land where there is no night.

May we know a quickening and reviving touch from the Lord as we take these words on our lips and apply them to ourselves.

Day 153   Psalm 72:1-7

The song of Solomon

Commentators are divided as to whether this Psalm is by or for Solomon, but the link with David's son is accepted by all. The application of the Psalm to our King Messiah is equally clear. It is expressed powerfully in James Montgomery's Psalm imitation, 'Hail to the Lord's Anointed'. In a parallel passage to verses 1 and 2 (Ps. 96:13) he is called 'the LORD'.

After the prayer of verse 1, these verses are a prophecy. The AV rightly follows Calvin who translates the Psalm in the future tense, rather than some modern versions that see it as just a pious wish.

As David is the type of our victorious and conquering King at his second coming (Psalm 2), so Solomon in this Psalm is a type of Him who shall then rule and reign in righteousness and peace.

Solomon started wisely. The Queen of Sheba marvelled at his wisdom (1 Kgs. 10), but, in his latter days, he fell far short of the type described in this Psalm (1 Kgs. 11:4; 12:14). Not so with our King; right judgment and righteousness shall mark his rule.

What wonderful words are in this opening portion! How we need his merciful justice in our troubled world. As we sing the words of our portion, our hearts will inwardly cry, 'Even so, come Lord Jesus'.

Day 154   Psalm 72:8-11

All kings shall fall down before him

A careful examination of the extent of the rule of the King in verses 8-11 shows him as one who rules 'from sea to sea', 'unto the ends of the earth', 'all kings shall fall down before him' and 'all nations shall serve him'. We do not charge the writer as guilty of exaggeration in speaking of an earthly monarch, but recognise that he speaks in the spirit of prophecy of him who shall reign as King of kings and Lord of lords (Phil. 2:10,11; Rev. 21:24). He came first in lowliness, but he shall reign in power (Zech. 9:9, 10).

This is not a mere Jewish king. He will rule over all. 'All nations shall serve him' (v11). All will pay homage to this King. Alas, when 'Christianity ascended the throne of the Caesars' in the time of Constantine, it was assumed that the universal Christian rule was established, and the doctrine of the Millennium was lost. Romanism too, in its pretence of earthly rule, continues the fiction. Overseas visits of Pope John Paul were blasphemously accompanied by the singing of the chorus, 'He's got the whole world in his hands'.

Shall we not bow at Christ's throne now? Shall we not pour out our needs and wants to him now? As Cowper wrote, 'Thou art coming to a King, large petitions with thee bring, for his might and power are such, none can ever ask too much'. Let us raise our voices in joyful anticipation of what shall be.

Day 155   Psalm 72:12-14

My blood is precious

In these verses our Lord's rule is described. It speaks of a glorious future day when earth shall have its Sabbath.

In prophecy, Christ's reign comes after unparalleled tribulation (Matt. 24:21-31). At that time Babylon is presented as 'drunk with the blood of the saints' and 'drunk with the blood of the martyrs of Jesus' (Rev. 17:6). Then a great and wonderful change takes place. The saints shall no longer cry out 'How long?' (Rev. 6:10).

All those who oppress God's people will learn then to their cost that 'precious shall their blood be in his sight' (v14). This Sovereign Lord has a father's care for those who cry to him for help.

We know of a Christian father who was greatly affected at seeing the blood-stained clothes of his self-harming son. In the same way, we are taught in this Psalm that the LORD views any hurt or injury to his elect, his children, with great tenderness.

How would you describe yourself? Are you 'needy'? Are you 'feeble', 'oppressed', subject to violence from others? If so, cry to the Saviour. He is the one who can deliver. He has great compassion.

Day 156   Psalm 72:15-20

The whole earth filled with glory

These verses speak of the prosperity and blessedness that shall accompany Messiah's reign. This earth, blighted and poisoned by man's efforts at advancement, is in stark contrast to the abundant flourishing of all things under this wonderful King. The cornfields will stretch from the valleys to the mountains.

This glorious King - shown in many ways through this Psalm, is extolled and blessed in verses 17-19. So too 'men shall be blessed in him'. The expression used is the same as in Gen. 22:18 and 26:4.

There are 'benedictions' at the end of this Psalm and other Books of the Psalms (41, 89 and 106). Therefore, some suggest that v20 is an uninspired and inaccurate addition[1]. Almost all metrical Psalters ignore it.

We believe that this 'benediction' declares that, when the things prophesied in this Psalm shall have come to pass, the prayers of David will have been answered (see 1 Chronicles 17 and Psalm 89, esp. v3,4,34-37)[2]. Let us joyfully sing these verses until they reach their high watermark of praise.

---

[1] It is suggested that this ended an early collection of Psalms. There are 18 more Psalms by David in Books 3,4, and 5.

[2] So the Jewish commentators Aben Ezra, Kimchi and Bishop Horsley, A.A. Bonar, B.W. Newton. See too Calvin. "Ended" is the same word in the Hebrew as in Ezra 1:1 and Dan. 12:7, there translated by the AV as "fulfilled" and "finished"

Book 3

Psalms 73 – 89

Day 157   Psalm 73:1-12

Almost gone and well-nigh slipped

There are times after a near accident, after recovering from a serious illness, or when we suddenly become aware of a danger that threatened us, that we need a few moments of quietness, when trembling and thankfulness combine. I can recall on a winter's day being encouraged by Sam, my six-year-old son, to cross a frozen lake with him to reach an otherwise inaccessible island. We could see that skaters had been on the ice, but no-one had made that crossing. How thankful I have been in retrospect that I did not yield to the desires of my precious young son and run a dreadful risk. That is how Asaph responds in this Psalm, as he considers the danger that he had placed himself in by envying the wicked.

This Psalm is a confession of Asaph. He regrets yielding to his own natural judgment on things, rather than viewing things through God's eyes.

The Devil is a liar from the beginning. At whatever cost, against seeming impossibilities, we must cling to God's truth. Let the wicked scoff 'How does God know?' May we rather tremble, confess our lack of understanding, and live a life of utter dependence upon God. Let us turn aside from doubting his wisdom and his care.

Let us acknowledge our past folly, and thank God for his overruling providence.

Day 158   Psalm 73:13-22

Understanding in the Sanctuary

These verses describe the slippery slope that Asaph was on, and then his realisation and confession of his error. For a time, he saw the condition of himself and others through worldly eyes. He lost sight of the mercy and grace that the LORD was giving to him. He could only see the present prosperity of the wicked. He could not see beyond 'many are the afflictions of the righteous' (Ps. 34:19).

He then reasons himself out of this negative frame of mind (v15). Augustine paraphrases, 'Am I to say something different from that which Abraham said – which Isaac said – which Jacob said – which all the prophets said? For they all said that God does care for human beings. Am I to say he does not care?'[1]

However, it was not until he went to 'the sanctuary of God' that he regained a true perspective. So it is with us. Listen to what the New Testament says, 'Having therefore, brethren, boldness to enter into the holy place by the blood of Jesus…let us draw near with a true heart in full assurance of faith, having our hearts sprinkled from an evil conscience and our bodies washed with pure water. Let us hold fast to the profession of our faith without wavering' (Heb. 10:19-25).

See in verse 22 what a discovery this will make, and what repentance it will bring!

---

[1] Quoted by de Burgh

Day 159   Psalm 73:23-28

The God who holds my hand

Here we see all the fresh consolation and strengthened hope that has come to Asaph from drawing aside 'into the sanctuary'.

1. He saw that, through it all, God had been with him (compare the *Footsteps* parable), and that he had been kept through the powerful sustainment of the LORD – 'you have held me by my right hand' v23.

2. This gives assurance of his final perseverance through God's grace – 'You will guide me with your counsel, and afterward receive me to glory' (v24).

3. He rests upon God, as the source of all true contentment – verses 25 and 26.

4. He reflects now upon the fate of the wicked. Just as they are far from God and heading for destruction, he desires to get yet nearer to God – verses 27 and 28.

David Dickson comments on these verses, 'The Lord's child profiteth by the hardest exercises, and his temptations, being resisted by faith, leave him in a better case than they have found him: his knowledge of God's ways, his faith, his love to God and hatred of wicked courses are augmented'. May it so be with us as we sing and reflect upon Asaph's words, which were the dying meditation of Charles Wesley.

Day 160   Psalm 74:1-4

Cast off forever?

The words of this pensive Psalm are well suited to times of apostasy when the Church of God is oppressed. The words in the old Scottish Psalter were sung by the Covenanter host before the battle of Rullion Green in 1666, one of the first Covenanter actions against their oppression (the Pentland Rising). It grew from the actions of those who disarmed soldiers who were beating an old man for not attending the Episcopal services. They must have been yet more mournful as their action was crushed, and ministers and good people were slain in battle or executed. God's relief came twenty years later, but it did come.

Through these opening verses of the Psalm, the writer struggles with the seeming contradiction between the spiritual reality and the facts that he sees before him. God's people are 'the sheep of his pasture'. They are 'purchased', 'redeemed'. The LORD's fixed place was Zion. And yet, God's people seem to have been 'cast off forever'; 'perpetual ruins'; the 'holy place' made a place of wickedness, with God's enemies roaring like lions among his people.

Yet, throughout, the psalmist maintains his hope. Let us, in our trials, see them all as from the hand of our loving Father. Let us turn to him for relief, for the LORD says 'my salvation shall not tarry (delay)', Isa. 46:13. It will come in its time.

Day 161   Psalm 74:5-11

Does God really know?

We can imagine these words on the lips of Jews during at the Destruction of Herod's Temple[1] or, more recently, during the Holocaust. B.W. Newton considers it as one of the songs of Israel under the oppression of Antichrist[2]. The writer knows that Israel is precious, but there is little confession and little recognition of the sin that has brought the calamities in this Psalm.

In verse 10 the suppliant cries 'How long?', and it seems to him almost as though these desolations will never end. However, he looks to the LORD for his arm to be once more brought forth to help, and to destroy the enemy, as he did with Egypt. Our God shall surely act to bring deliverance to his people.

As we wait for God to deliver, let us be as Nehemiah. There was no king, no prophet, and no miraculous signs in his day (v9). And yet he attempted and succeeded in a work for God.

Let us look for God's intervention, and not be slack to take up the sword and the trowel (Neh. 4:8). Let us see what can be done in our day.

---

[1] The title of the Syriac version refers to it as prophecy of this event. There is perhaps comparison of felling of trees to build the Temple with the destruction of its ornamental work and the burning of the Sanctuary (v5-7)

[2] B.W. Newton, *Prophetic Psalms in their relation to Israel*, p15,16.

Day 162   Psalm 74:12-17

Pondering past mercies

In these verses, Asaph declares, and takes comfort from, the greatness and power of God shown in the past.   He reminds God of his works of old, particularly, it seems, in relation to Israel's deliverance from Egypt by God's outstretched arm (compare v11ff with Deut. 26:8).

The verses make reference to that deliverance in a figurative way, with the dragon symbolising Egypt (v13, 14; compare Ezek. 29:3 and Isa. 51:9, 10).   We also have reference to the cleaving of the rock (v15 compare Exod. 17:6) and the drying up of mighty rivers (v15; compare Josh. 3:13).

From God's particular intervention in the past, the psalmist reflects upon his power manifest in the heavens, on earth, and in the seasons (v16, 17).

When cast down, it is good to meditate upon past mercies, either to us personally, or to God's people generally.   If we recall the LORD's power shown in the past and remember that this is still the God who sustains all things by the word of his power, we shall be able to go forward confidently, knowing that 'his arm is not shortened that it cannot save'.

Let us remind ourselves of God's power and greatness.

Day 163   Psalm 74: 18-23

God pleading his own cause

The psalmist returns to petitioning the LORD for his help. He leaves to God's wisdom the action that God will take.

First of all he seeks to stir up God's pity for his broken and bruised people who are greatly threatened, as a helpless dove. Secondly, he pleads for the LORD to vindicate his honour against those who despise and reproach him - he asks God to 'plead his own cause' (v22). These twin prayers are surely requests that God will always hear.

If we should ask the context of this prayer, we must say that this is a time of great emergency and of great wickedness, as Scripture warns us it will be at the last time. It is therefore not surprising that some expositors hear these words upon the lips of persecuted Israel before their redemption and deliverance as a people. Having said that, these are surely precious words that the Church can apply to any situation of great need, seeking that God would 'have respect unto the covenant'.

This is a maschil, a Psalm of instruction; let us learn from it how we should petition God. Let us raise our voice to our God in the words of the Psalm.

Day 164   Psalm 75:1-6

Just judgment is coming

Motyer[1] comments that Psalm 74 and Psalm 75 belong together.   Psalm 74 speaks of a dreadful calamity. Psalm 75 looks back at the way the Lord has resolved the problem.

The Psalm begins with the word 'we' in verse 1. Asaph rejoices *with God's people* that the LORD is near, and that his character and power (his 'name' and his 'works') will be declared.   What joy when we have this assurance!

In verses 2-6 the pronoun changes to 'I', as God or the Messiah responds. We see here Asaph praising in faith, and the Lord responding.

The promise is given that the Lord will come to judge righteously, and deal with the pride and haughtiness of the ungodly.

In v2 it is best to read with the AV margin.   The Hebrew word translated as 'the congregation' is there translated 'the set time'. The phrase then means 'when the set time is come'. The word is so translated in the AV in Ps. 102:13.

Despite all the heartaches and disappointments, God does have 'a set time', when he will remedy earth's wrongs. Let us encourage ourselves in this.

---

[1] Alec Motyer, *Psalms by the Day.*

Day 165   Psalm 75:7-10

God casts down and raises up

With this portion, we return to the LORD coming in judgment, which is declared in verse 2. This judging is not merely deciding and sentencing: the complete administration of justice and right rule is included. The same word is used here as of the 'Judges' who led the people after Joshua. The LORD promises that, in his dealings with Israel, he will 'restore your judges as at the first' (Isa. 1:26 - where the word is used). So the Prince of Peace will come and will put down 'all the wicked of the earth'. They shall 'drink of the wine of the wrath of God' (v8; Rev. 14:10).

The word 'horn' is used in verses 4, 5 and 10. Verse 10 says, 'All the horns of the wicked [ones] will I cut off, but the horns of the righteous [one] shall be exalted'[1]. In commenting on Zechariah 1:18ff, David Baron writes, '"Horns" are used in Scripture as emblematic of power and pride of conscious strength (Amos 6:13; Psalms 75:4, 5; 92:10), and are sometimes explained by the sacred writers themselves as representing *the ruling powers of the world* (Dan. 8:3ff; Rev. 17:3-12)'[2]. The Book of Psalms continually expresses a longing for the ending of the rule of the wicked, and for the Messiah to exercise his righteous rule. It does so here with this graphic symbol.

---

[1] Compare Zech. 1:18-21
[2] David Baron, *The Visions and Prophecies of Zechariah*, p45.

Day 166   Psalm 76:1-6

In Judah's land God is well-known

The title of this Psalm in the Septuagint Greek version calls it a 'Hymn', a 'Psalm', and a 'Song' – the threefold description of the songs which the Church is instructed to sing in Col.3:16 and Eph. 5:19.

In these opening verses the LORD is described as:

1. Known and great in Israel (v1).
2. Dwelling in Jerusalem (Salem, Zion) (v2).
3. Triumphant in battle[1]. The focus of that battle ('there' v3) is Jerusalem.

These verses, and the title in the Septuagint Greek – 'to the Assyrian', have led most commentators to link it with the destruction of Sennacherib's armies (2 Kings 18, 19, and Isaiah 36, 37).

However, William de Burgh and B.W. Newton see this as but a foreshadowing of the great and future intervention of the LORD in the affairs of men, when Antichrist is destroyed (Zech. 12:2-5; Isa. 10), and when Jerusalem is blessed by God's presence (Isa. 2:1-3;12:6; Ezek. 48:35). Then, indeed, the earth will be still, and all the meek-afflicted of the earth will be saved (v8, 9).

We worship a great and mighty God. Let us celebrate his past and future victories.

---

[1] The two words translated "tabernacle" and "dwelling place" in v2 are also used of a "covert" and "lair" of a lion, and the idea may be of the LORD going forth as a lion from Jerusalem (see Amos 1:2 and Isa. 31:4)

Day 167   Psalm 76:7-12

The earth feared and was still

In these verses, the great act of judgment has been carried out. The consequences, and the lesson to be drawn from it, are given in this portion.

The noise of chariot horsemen and warriors has been silenced (v6). The earth was afraid and still (v8), for God has come in judgment to save the meek and afflicted. The wrath of man, so frightening to the afflicted and helpless child of God, will be turned to God's glory; he puts limits on the fury and rage of men, and makes even the wrath of man to praise him (v10).

The fear of the LORD is spoken of four times in these verses as the motivating force for obedience and service. The references to the fear of God are in verses 7, 8, 11, 12. In verse 12, the expression 'He is terrible' may rather be translated as a name of God. He is 'The Fear' - 'the sum of all that is awe inspiring'[1]. is used again as a name of God in Isa. 8:12, 13.

Dear reader, Isaiah says, 'Let him be your Fear. Let him be your Dread'. May we live as in his awesome and holy presence. May it govern our thinking, our actions, and our service. May this holy God draw near to us as we meditate upon these things.

---

[1] So Keil and Delitzsch, *Commentary on the Psalms.*

Day 168   Psalm 77:1-6

Trouble, trouble, trouble, nothing but trouble

Have we had such experiences as the psalmist, who says in this Psalm, 'I am so troubled that I cannot speak' (v4)?

Asaph describes his deep emotion as he feels deserted by God. He remembers God; reflects on past blessings; and is troubled. Night does not bring its rest, and he lapses from the loud crying of verse 1 into silence.

Robert Brown, a man greatly used by God in the nineteenth century, recounts an experience he had, when for a year and a half he was afflicted by Satan in such a way as he almost despaired[1]. In commenting upon this, he quotes the remark of John Newton who said that he believed that Satan was ever issuing command to his 'angels' regarding godly ministers, as the King of Syria did. The king told his forces – 'Fight with no one small or great, but only with the king of Israel' (1 Kgs. 22:31).

Let us pray for the upholding of godly ministers in our day. Let us not be Job's comforters to such brothers under attack, and in affliction. They are our standard bearers.

---

[1] He gives a full account of this in the Preface to *Scripture Truths, together with Divine Unfoldings*

Day 169   Psalm 77:7-15

Anxious questions

Asaph is still in great turmoil in these verses. He asks six questions, all of them with the same sentiments, beginning with 'Will the LORD cast off forever?' (reject for evermore). His experience seems to be in direct contrast to all that he knows of God, and faith wrestles for an explanation. It has often been so for the Church of God when the enemies of truth seem to have triumphed. Is this not the experience of the Reformation Churches of Western Europe at this time?

His way through the darkness is given in three words. (1) He *remembered* (v11): this has not so much to do with memory, as with calling to mind so that it affects present feeling, thought, or action. (2) He *meditated* (v12a): the root meaning is murmuring or muttering in a low voice - thinking aloud on what God's. (3) He *talked with himself, or pondered* (12b), especially on God's deeds[1]. These are three things we can all do alone.

His meditation (v13-16) recalls Israel's deliverance from Egypt. Verse 13 may be read (literally) 'your way is in holiness', rather than 'in the sanctuary' (compare Exod. 15:11).

Let us apply the psalmist's remedies to our troubles.

---

[1] The same word is translated by the Authorised Version as "complain" (v3), as "commune" (with his own heart) (v6) and "talk of" (v12b). He was certainly not complaining against God in the modern sense of the word.

Day 170   Psalm 77:16-20
Led like a flock through thunder and lightning

The last verses of this Psalm celebrate the mighty power of God, particularly shown during the Exodus, when the LORD led his people by the hand of Moses and Aaron.

However, as Hengstenberg notes, the description exceeds the reality and we have no other suggestion in Scripture that the parting of the Red Sea was accompanied by storm and tempest[1].

William de Burgh therefore refers to unfulfilled prophecies of a second exodus from their bondage (Isa. 11:11-16; Zech. 10:10-12), and suggests that the heartfelt cries of verses 7-10, and Israel's 1900 years of experience of desertion by God, will at length end with God intervening on their behalf.

There is a wonderful contrast between verses 16-19 and verse 20. His tender shepherd care for his people is shown after his great and awesome power. What comfort we have if we can say of this great, all-powerful God, 'The LORD is my Shepherd'.

Let us rejoice in God's great power as we sing these words. Let us praise him for past and future interventions on behalf of his people.

---

[1] E.W. Hengstenberg, *Commentary on the Psalms,*

Day 171   Psalm 78:1-8

Asaph's dark sayings

The opening verses of this Psalm have been a puzzle to many, as Asaph says that he will open his mouth in a parable and in dark sayings, and yet what follows appears to be a clear narrative of the LORD's deliverances of Israel.

We think that the explanation is this. The hardening of the heart of Israel ('my people, v. 1) is at least one of the 'dark sayings' of this Psalm. We read here that their unbelief followed God's intervention, time and again.

As we consider the New Testament, we find that it continued to be so. In his ministry the Lord Jesus spoke in parables - so that the heart of the people might be hardened (Matt. 13:10-17). This is the mystery of this Psalm. Paul said in Rom. 11:25 'I would not, brethren, that you should be ignorant of this mystery ... that blindness in part has happened to Israel, until the fullness of the Gentiles be come in'.

God's sovereignty in revealing himself is ever a mystery. How we should long that he would open our eyes to his truth and make known to us things kept secret since the foundation of the world. And if he has done so, let us instruct our children in these things, as the LORD commanded Israel of old (v3-5).

Day 172   Psalm 78:9-16

Running away and giving up

God's mighty works are related in these verses, but first the failure and blindness of 'Ephraim' is described. Ephraim was, at first, the ruling tribe of Israel.

Four failures are recorded.

1. They turned back in the day of battle.
2. They did not keep the covenant.
3. They refused to live according to the law.
4. They forgot the remarkable things that God had done for them and had shown them.

We may sum up their failure as lack of perseverance: they entered the battle, but turned back: they committed to the covenant but did not keep it: they went outside the commands of the law for their lives: they failed to keep in mind the power and mercy of God on their behalf.

In this Psalm, Zoan is twice identified as the place where the LORD did his miracles in Egypt (v12 and v43). This is the only knowledge we have of this, although Zoan is referred to elsewhere in Scripture[1].

Let us persevere in the path of obedience that we have taken and that God has fully set before us.

---

[1] See Numb. 13:22; Isa. 19:11; Ezek. 30:14

Day 173   Psalm 78:17-29

Wilderness provocations

We have here the continuing and persistent sin of the people against their God.

In their rebellion they put the LORD to the test (v18): they showed their impudence and challenged the LORD who had brought them out of the bondage of Egypt: Israel demanded meat from God in the wilderness. The amazing thing was God's response.

Instead of cursing them, and cutting them off, he rained food upon them in abundance. He worked a mighty miracle. He gave them manna - the bread of angels! (v25; John 6:31). He delivered a feast of poultry to them in the desert. In his providence, he gave them more than they expected in their wildest dreams. He does not deal with us according to our sins.

He is a God who is 'able to do exceeding abundantly above all that we ask or think'. He knows our needs. Let us quietly and humbly lay them before him.

How foolish if we 'do not believe God, nor trust in his salvation' (v22). Do we have any grounds to shout angrily at heaven for what we want, and to provoke the LORD with our unbelief and ingratitude?

Day 174   Psalm 78:30-39

Many times God turned his anger away

We see repeatedly in these verses the hardness of men's hearts. They turned back to God when he chastened them, but insincerely. More wonderfully in these verses, we see the compassion of the LORD. Whom he loves he chastens, in order that they might repent.

He knew their hypocrisy, which was only 'flattery' to God from their mouths. Their heart was not in their words. He knew that what they were saying was really a lie.

Man looks upon the outward appearance, but God looks upon the heart. He could see 'their heart was not right with him'. He knew they were 'not steadfast in his covenant' (v37) whatever their words or deeds pretended.

And yet...and yet, 'He, being full of compassion forgave their iniquity and destroyed them not. Yea, many a time turned he his anger away, and did not stir up all his wrath, for he remembered that they were but flesh' (v38, 39).

And is it not so in God's dealings with us? How false and fickle we are to him who has set his love upon us, even from before the foundation of the world! O that these words might stir us up to serve God with a pure and faithful heart!

Day 175   Psalm 78:40-51

Failing to remember

The waywardness of God's people is again described in these verses.

In verse 39 we saw that God 'remembered that they were but flesh', but in verse 42 we read 'They remembered not his hand, nor the day when he delivered them from the enemy'. The Hebrew word for 'remember' does not just mean 'not forgetting'. The full meaning is to 'remember, recall, call to mind, usually as affecting present feeling, thought, or action'[1]. This is a discipline that God requires of us – to constantly bring to our minds who he is, what he has done, and what he requires of us. This is why his dealings with Egypt are again recorded in verses 43-51.

It is a litany of things that 'he' did. Things do not happen by chance or by luck. This is not a God who sits back and lets the world run its own course. He is continually intervening – more than this – everything is directly ordered by his hand.

Let us 'remember', so that we may not 'provoke him', 'grieve him', 'turn back', 'tempt God', 'limit [or 'vex'] the Holy One of Israel'. Let us reflect on the 'outstretched arm' of the LORD in these verses, and his deliverance to us.

---

[1] Brown, Driver and Briggs Hebrew Lexicon.

Day 176   Psalm 78:52-57

Sheep in the wilderness

When Israel was in Egypt, and Egypt experienced the plagues, the Israelites were spared them. All the children of Israel had light in their dwellings (Exod. 10:23). God does not always deal with his people in this way. Sometimes they too suffer with the ungodly.

In Exodus, and in the history recounted in these verses, God's reason for dealing with Israel differently was 'that they might know'. Like a flock of sheep that learns to trust the shepherd, he 'guided them' and 'led safely'. But yet again, we are told, they 'tempted God', 'provoked', 'kept not his testimonies', and 'turned back', 'acted unfaithfully'.

The LORD's kindness is that he nevertheless brought them to their destination. Verse 54 speaks as though the destination was the sanctuary, the very place where God himself dwells. What an amazing blessing it was to be brought out of the alien land of Egypt. But what a yet greater blessing it was to be brought into the holy land, to Emmanuel's land.

And how has it been with our souls? Have we no examples of God's mercy in sparing us from things that have happened to others? Do we have no sense of his goodness and blessing to us? How faithful are we in following and obeying such a gracious God? He is leading us, and will lead, until we enter the many mansions that the Saviour has promised to us.

Day 177   Psalm 78: 58-64

Chastisement in Canaan

The provoking of God to anger that is referred to in these verses seems to be the period of the Judges (v58 and Judg. 2:12). The LORD's punishments seem to particularly relate to the events of 1 Sam. 4.

Their provocation in the land of Canaan began with their 'high places' or 'hill altars', and their 'graven images'. Spurgeon called this 'will worship'. He saw parallels to this departure from the worship of the true God in his day. He comments 'Doubtless God, so far from being honoured by worship which he has not commanded, is greatly angered at it'.

God withdrew from the tabernacle at Shiloh (v60) and, although the 'worship' no doubt continued, it was an empty shell, and further provoked God.

We need to humble ourselves also. No doubt when Ephesus's candlestick was removed from the heavenly tabernacle (Rev. 2:5) a congregation continued in the city, but without the Lord Jesus's supervision and blessing. How is it with our gatherings? Does he delight in them, or do they provoke him?

May we worship God carefully, reverently and in obedience to his Word, so that his presence and blessing may abide with us.

Day 178   Psalm 78: 65-72

The Shepherd King

The history follows on from yesterday's portion. The ark had been lost (1 Sam. 4), and, with the reign of Saul quickly passed over, the rejection of 'Ephraim' leads to the establishment of Mount Zion, the 'sanctuary', and the throne of David.

However, verse 4 of this Psalm says that the purpose of the Psalm is to show 'to the generation to come the praises of the LORD', and we may therefore justifiably ask what this passage teaches us.

One key lesson is that God shepherds his people. This recurs in Asaph's Psalms – Psalms 74:1; 79:13 and 80:1. In this Psalm, verses 52, 53 speak of the LORD shepherding his people and then, in these closing verses, this shepherding is delegated to the Shepherd-King David. Verse 71 'to feed Jacob' may be translated 'to shepherd Jacob' and the word 'guided' (AV) of verse 72 is the same word as in the '*leading* in the paths of righteousness' of Ps. 23:3. Oh for the time when Israel shall turn and shall confess his shepherd care!

We also find this theme in the Book of Revelation, where the Lamb will be the believer's shepherd, and will lead him into living fountains of waters (Rev. 7:17). Let us own the loving, watchful, care of our Saviour throughout our earthly journey.

Day 179   Psalm 79:1-4

Blood shed like water

This Psalm speaks of destruction of the Temple and Jerusalem, and of a prolonged expression of God's anger. Many commentators take this Psalm as simply a lament for Nebuchadnezzar's destruction of Jerusalem. But Asaph was pre-exilic (1 Chr. 16:4, 5). What is described is surely more than the 70 years of Babylonian Captivity. We cannot imagine a more appropriate context than that period which Scripture calls 'the last end of the indignation' (Dan. 8:19). Indeed, the fate of those whose 'blood they have shed like water' (v2, 3) with 'none to bury them' is closely parallel to that of the two witnesses in the Book of Revelation (Rev. 11:7-10).

The lament of the opening verses longs for the LORD's intervention. It is grounded on God's honour and glory – 'your inheritance', 'your holy temple', 'your servants', 'your saints'. This is a prayer God will always hear, even though there may be a good reason for us to wait (compare Lazarus 'he whom you love', John 11:3).

Our prayers are too much about 'I', 'me', 'my'. Rather, we should rest wholly upon his mercy and his loving-kindness (or as the Scottish Metrical Psalter quaintly expresses it in Ps. 40:10 'his kindness which most loving is'). How good if we seek him in this way. 'He must increase and I must decrease'.

Day 180   Psalm 79:5-9

Mercy not merit

Here is a cry of God's people tried and tested to their limit. It is a contrite cry that recognises past sins, and the anger of God which those sins have brought upon them. It is a prayer based not on merit, but on mercy. As such, it is fitting upon the lips of any believer. 'O remember not against us former iniquities; let your tender mercies speedily prevent[1] us; for we are brought very low' (v8) were the last words of John Owen.

Much has been carelessly spoken of 'imprecatory Psalms' which call down wrath and vengeance. Some reject them as unworthy for use in Christian worship. This label might be put on the prayer of verse 6, 'Pour out your wrath upon the nations that have not known you'.

However, a comparison with the New Testament will show that such is indeed the purpose of God (2 Thess. 1:7, 8) and these are therefore appropriate words upon the lips of Christians. All men are guilty of rejecting natural light, and are without excuse. The time of judgment must come. The LORD's righteousness will be vindicated. The suffering of God's elect will then cease.

'The kingdoms that do not call upon his name' must one day all yield, and bow at the name of Jesus.

---

[1] Come to meet

Day 181   Psalm 79:10-13

Let God be known among the nations

Israel is described here as a people without any evident help or defence. They cannot rely upon their own strength.

To the world, they are beyond help. Those who oppress them can see no supernatural power that can save them. The world boldly says, 'Where is their God?' They are but sighing prisoners, and those appointed to die.

There is a danger that we will just accept the world's verdict.

And yet, if the LORD's people will but cast themselves on him and see that it is really God who is being reproached, and it is only he who can deliver, then what a change there can be!

In a world situation and a Church situation where the forces of darkness seem to be able to act with impunity, will we despair and give up? Will we try to solve the situation in our own strength? Or will we pour out our supplication to the Most High God, acknowledging that we are his people and the sheep of his pasture? Will we use that alone as the ground for our hope? Will Israel not at last cry this prayer too?

Let us pray this prayer, and end it with the joyfulness of the closing verse. We will give thanks for ever, and we will let our hallelujahs ring to all generations.

Day 182   Psalm 80:1-3

The Shepherd of Israel

David Baron describes this Psalm as 'a very important Scripture which briefly, but very graphically, depicts Israel's present state among the nations, and looks prophetically to God's dealings with them in the future'[1].

Asaph again takes up his shepherd theme at the beginning of this Psalm[2]. The Psalm describes a relationship in which LORD seeks, heals, strengthens, feeds, rests, and satisfies his flock. David Baron links it with Ezekiel 34, where it is promised to Israel that God will 'set up one shepherd over them' and they will 'dwell safely' (compare too Ezek. 37:24-27). The psalmist longs for the time when the LORD, who sits enthroned between the cherubim, will shine forth his glory and lead his people.

The tribes of Ephraim, Benjamin, and Manasseh (v2) walked behind the ark in Israel's wilderness journey. They would therefore have been encouraged by always having sight of the place where the LORD dwelt, and where the pillar of fire led. There is a mixture of rich metaphors and pictures here!

May all who read these pages know Israel's Shepherd as 'my Shepherd'.

---

[1] David Baron, *The Shepherd of Israel and His Scattered Flock.*
[2] See notes on Ps. 78:65-72.

Day 183   Psalm 80:4-7

Tears for food, and tears for drink

Verses 5 and 6 very graphically describe the lot of the Jewish people.

Cut off from God by their rejection of their Messiah, they have known tears in great measure down the centuries. There is irony in the full title 'LORD, God of hosts' in v4, for Israel will not even take his name (JEHOVAH or Yahweh) upon their lips today, and his 'hosts' seem to have been withdrawn.

God has always preserved 'a remnant according to promise' (Rom. 11:5): yet how long will it be before they as a people utter the prayer of verse 7 and verse 19? How long before the LORD pours upon them the Spirit of grace and supplications, and they will look upon him whom they have pierced, and will mourn for him? (Zech. 12:10). The only consolation is that that time will come, and, in their blessing, all nations shall be blessed (Rom. 11:15ff). It will not be dependent upon them turning, but upon God turning them.

Christians should pray for the peace of Jerusalem. May our hearts be touched to say, 'For Zion's sake I will not hold my peace, and for Jerusalem's sake I will not rest, until the righteousness thereof goes forth as brightness, and its salvation as a lamp that burns'. (Isa. 62:1).

Day 184   Psalm 80:8-14

Visit this vine!

These verses record the mercy of the LORD in taking Israel out of Egypt.

They tell of his singular care and provision for that people, planting them as a vine, and 'causing them to take deep root'. They tell of the prosperity that followed his singular care, but then tell how that prosperity became spoiled, laid waste, devoured, and broken down.

Israel could not, and nor can we, trade on past mercies. We need to walk with our God today. Our children looked around a town in Wales with amazement during a recent holiday. It had chapel buildings on nearly on every street corner. But the glory had departed. Two had closed that very week and the remainder were kept going by a handful of older people.

Israel expresses puzzlement at what had happened (v12, 13), and asks God why he has done this. A plea goes up in verse 14, as in verses 3 and 7 – return – look down – visit – take care of this vine.

May a prayer for revival be on our lips too. O for the tide to turn again in Wales, that 'land of revivals', and amongst the scattered companies of God's children throughout this hostile world.

Day 185   Psalm 80: 15-19

Turn us again

We have here a prayer of dependence, a prayer for God to act for his own honour, to bless the work of his hands. Such prayers may seem to go unanswered for a time, but they touch the heart of God, and are surely answered in his time.

There is a reference in verse 17 to the Advent of the Son of Man, who will turn away ungodliness from Jacob (Rom. 11:26). It is helpful to study Romans 11 in connection with this Psalm, although there the symbol is an olive tree, rather than a vine. There is much warning in it for Gentile Christians. If Israel was cut off because of unbelief and the Gentiles grafted in, we should know that God's punishment will also fall on our sins.

God is sovereign, v18, 19. We need his regeneration, his new creation, his raising from the dead, his making alive, which he works 'in us without us'. We need his 'supernatural, most powerful, most delightful, wonderful, mysterious and inexpressible' work[1] if we are to call upon his name.

The refrain goes up again at the end of the Psalm, pleading for God to turn his people and to shine his face upon them. Whether as a prayer for Israel or as a supplication for the fallen state of Gentile Christendom, let us pray that prayer.

---

[1] Canons of the Synod of Dort, Chapter 3/4, Article 12. Quoted from C.W.H. Griffiths, *Chosen – Called – Kept*.

Day 186   Psalm 81:1-5

Remember and rejoice

We have here a Psalm to be sung at one of Israel's solemn festivals. From verses 5, 6 and 10, it would seem to be for the Passover.

The psalmist urges joyfulness at the remembrance of what God had done for Israel. This was no doubt the distant past when it was written, and yet a cause for rejoicing for God's people still. How often do we think of God's past dealings with his people and rejoice? November the 5th used to be such a day for solemn thankfulness in England. Reformation Sunday is still kept by some, but we have failed to keep alive to the rising generations the memories of God's mighty deliverances in the past.

As believers, we have all had our personal Passover deliverance from the bondage of sin. How much do we remember it and rejoice?

Verses 2 and 3 urge the use of instruments, 'for this was a statute for Israel' (v4). Calvin comments, 'But now, when the clear light of the Gospel has dissipated the shadows of the law, and taught us that God is to be served in a simpler form, it would be to act a foolish and mistaken part to imitate that which the prophet enjoined only upon those of his own time'.

Let us this day, with all our heart, sing and declare the greatness of our God for all he has done for us.

Day 187   Psalm 81:6-10

Open your mouth wide

We have God speaking here, reminding the people of his tender care. What affectionate words come from his mouth, 'Hear, O my people'. Can we doubt the loving, personal care of our God for us? He calls Israel 'my people'. Are not all who trust him likewise the children of God? He says, 'Open your mouth wide and I will fill it' (v. 10). Then why should we strive and struggle? Why should we lust after our own desires and walk in our own counsels when we have such a loving and caring God to supply our needs?

Israel was brought through the wilderness. It was a desert place. It was not easy with searing temperatures, hunger and thirst, and seemingly meaningless wanderings, but God had a purpose. He was proving them. He desired his people to be dependent upon him. Why do we not accept God's daily instruction and leave the outcome of our pilgrimage with him?

Just like Moses, we may not enjoy the rest in Canaan in this life. But, if we look to God for all our needs, we may say with Job, 'He knows the way that I take, when he has purged me, I shall come forth as gold' (Job 23:10). Until that time comes let us continue to 'call in the time of trouble' (v7).

Day 188 Psalm 81:11-16

If they would only listen

This is an amazing statement of God's unrequited love for Israel. We have here a parallel with the Lord Jesus's weeping farewell to his people in Matt. 23:37, 'O Jerusalem, Jerusalem, you who kill the prophets and stone them which are sent unto you, how often would I have gathered your children together, even as a hen gathers her chickens under her wings, and you would not'.

Here we have the great mystery of God's sovereignty and omnipotence and his love. 'God may permit his gracious desires to be frustrated, but not his counsel or determined will' (B.W. Newton).

The appeal of God's love is general, but is largely rejected, and man bears full responsibility for that rejection. 'Then, alas, there is no plague more deadly than for men to be left to the guidance of their own counsels' (Calvin on v12).

The Lord continually came to Israel with mercies greater than they could comprehend – their land bearing 'the finest of the wheat' and honey flowing even from the barren rocks.

May it never be said of us 'My people would not hearken to my voice'. Let us make sure that we listen for his voice in all the affairs of our lives for his promise of blessing extends to us also.

Day 189   Psalm 82:1-4

Crooked judgment

We have here a Psalm that focuses upon Government. 'Judges' in verses 2 and 3 were rulers, not the judiciary. The Psalm may certainly be applied to the unjust government of the nations as a whole. Bishop Horsley interprets it of those unjust judges who condemned the Saviour, and we may meditate on it in that context. The Lord Jesus was indeed the helpless, fatherless, afflicted, and poor one (singular in v3, 4).

In the context of democracy, the rule of the people, anyone may aspire to rule a country. We have forgotten the importance God's Word places upon right government and authority answerable to our Maker. Governors are called *elohim* – gods - in verses 1 and 6 (compare John 10:34-36).

Scripture calls governors 'higher powers', 'ordained by God' and even 'ministers of God' in Romans 13. We are instructed to pray for them (1 Tim. 2:1, 2).

Would that we had a Government like the Parliament that affirmed the Solemn League and Covenant (1643). 'Because these kingdoms are guilty of many sins and provocations against God, and his Son Jesus Christ, as is too manifest by our present distresses and dangers, the fruits thereof; we profess and declare, before God and the world, our unfeigned desire to be humbled for our sins and for the sins of these kingdoms'.

Day 190   Psalm 82:5-8

Rulers who don't know where they are going

These verses deal with the failings of governors and rulers. The condemnation appears to be universal. They lack the knowledge of God. They lack understanding of his righteous standard. That authority which was delegated to the nations in the visions of Daniel chapters 3, 7 and 8 has been grossly abused. We can rightly say, 'They walk in darkness; all the foundations of the earth are out of course' (v5). How salutary was the lesson to King Nebuchadnezzar, who strutted in his palace and boasted of 'great Babylon that I have built' only to brought down to eating grass in the field as a brute beast (Dan. 4). We are taught again and again in Scripture to respect and honour those in authority, not as placed there by men (democracy), or exalted by good fortune or personal charisma, but rather as appointed by God (see Rom. 13). And yet 'they shall die like men' (v7) – as mere children of Adam who return to the dust.

The psalmist knows that 'the Most High rules in the kingdom of men and gives it to whomsoever He will, and sets up over it the basest of men' (Dan. 4:17). He therefore pleads for the coming day of God's judgment and rule, 'Arise, O God, give justice to the earth: for you shall inherit all nations'. 'Even so, Come Lord Jesus'.

Day 191   Psalm 83:1-8

A silent God in a tumultuous world

The silence of God in the face of oppression and persecution is a fearful thing. How long did Israel cry in their bondage in Egypt, seemingly to the silence of God?

Yet such circumstances stir up the spirit of expectancy and hope in the believer's heart. They lead to earnest cries for God to turn the tide, or to minister grace to the afflicted.

Such is the situation of Asaph in our Psalm today. He sees the noise and clamour of God's enemies. They hate God. Despite their varied beliefs and backgrounds, they are agreed on this – that God's people must be destroyed. They seem to be an invincible force.

We do not know what specific event that occasioned the Psalm, although one of the few references to the Hagarites (v6) in 1 Chr. 5:20 may give a clue, when Israel 'cried out to God in the battle, and he was entreated of them'. We do know from this, and ten thousand times ten thousand unrecorded cases, that God did not keep silence. He ever cares for, and protects, his 'hidden ones' (v3 - see Psalms 27:5 and 31:20).

The plans of evil men will soon fail, for the wicked are like the chaff which the wind drives away (Ps. 1:4).

Day 192   Psalm 83:9-12

Telling of Gideon and Barak

The writer is responding to the malice of God's enemies who desire the complete destruction of God's people. So we must look to God as our Helper and Defender. As Martin Luther wrote,

For still our ancient foe,
Doth seek to work his woe
His craft and power are great,
And armed with cruel hate
On earth is not his equal'.

The two events to which Asaph appeals in our Psalm (v9-12) are those of Barak over the Canaanites (Judg. 4 and 5) and Gideon over the Midianites (Judg. 6 and 7). Both of these deliverances occurred in the valley of Megiddo (Armageddon), otherwise known as the valley of Jehoshaphat. These two instances of deliverance are very significant. They are not forgotten even in the New Testament (Heb. 11:32).

In this Psalm the peoples around Israel attack, with the help of Assyria (v8). Such a threat is repeatedly associated in Scripture with the assault of Antichrist upon Israel (see Ps. 2; Isa. 10:24-27; 11:11-16; Joel 3:12-14; Zech. 14:1-3; Rev. 16:13-16).

The time shall shortly be when our Jesus shall come forth conquering and to conquer. Let us be patient and look to God for help until that time comes.

Day 193   Psalm 83:13-18

That they may know JEHOVAH reigns

The psalmist, on behalf of his beleaguered people, pleads for God to send whirlwind, fire, tempest, and storm against his (and their) enemies. We think of the destruction of the fleet of the greatest navy on earth when God 'blew with his wind and he scattered them' (v15), and the Spanish Armada was lost.

The USA, the world's most powerful nation, was overwhelmed by one of its worst natural disasters, as a hurricane hit New Orleans (2005). Well might men be confused, terrified and dismayed (v15-17) when God shows his hand. O that God may not hold his peace! O that he would work in righteousness and in mercy in the earth! Mercy is yet needed, if men, faced with great calamity, are to 'seek God's name' (v16), and know that the Most High is over all the earth (v18).

The Authorised Version only uses the word 'JEHOVAH' here (v18) and in three other places (Exod. 6:2; Isa. 12:3; 26:4). In this it follows Coverdale's Bible (1539), which translates here, 'They shall know that thou (whose name is IEHOUA) art only the most hyest ouer all the earth'. Strictly speaking, JEHOVAH (Yahweh) is the only personal name given to God in the Scriptures. He alone is the true God.

Day 194   Psalm 84:1-7

Making the valley of Baca a well

Today we leave the series of Psalms by Asaph. The writer of this Psalm strikes a different, a devotional, note.

This first half of the Psalm contains no requests. It is simply the outpouring of a man delighting in his God. These are not the sentimental words of someone whose desire is for the familiar outward forms. Nor is it the lonely longing of one who misses the company of other worshippers. There is, in fact, hardly a mention of other worshippers here.

His yearning, his desire, his whole notion of blessing, is to be in the presence of his God. It is a place for the weak and the insignificant – the swallow and the sparrow. It is a place for those who feel the sadness and barrenness of the valley of Baca as they journey to Zion. All the ancient versions translate 'the valley of Baca' as 'the valley of weeping'. Trusting in our God, we may make such a 'valley', and even 'the valley of the shadow of death', a place of comfort.

O that we too may be able to say from our experience of meeting with the LORD, 'My heart and my flesh cries out for the living God'. Let us meditate on these precious words.

Day 195   Psalm 84:8-12

I'd rather be a doorkeeper

The writer's prayer in these verses begins with the desire that the LORD would see and hear him. What can we say of the delightful heart outpourings of this portion? Can we add to them by commenting on them?

It is as though he gazes up with hands raised and face looking to the heavens and cries, 'Look upon the face of your anointed'. Such was the circumstance of the Lord Jesus (Luke 3:21, 22): and the voice came from heaven, 'This is my beloved Son in whom I am well pleased'.

'A day in your courts is better than a thousand. I had rather be a doorkeeper in the house of my God than to dwell in the tents of wickedness' (v10). There is an intense joy here that changes our perspective on our lives and ambitions. There is a contentment that the writer had come to know.

The house of God – the place where his people come together, is glorious. It is wonderful for the backslider who comes to himself, recalls 'what peaceful hours I once enjoyed', and finds his way back again to the assembly of the saints.

Let us rejoice over the words of this portion and sing them meaningfully. 'No good thing will he withhold from those who walk uprightly'.

Day 196   Psalm 85:1-7

Revive us again

It is impossible to place the full realisation of the blessings of the first three verses of this Psalm at any point in Israel's past history. When could it be said of Israel 'You have covered all their sin; you have taken away [literally, 'utterly removed'] all your wrath'? Israel can rejoice in partial and momentary situations when God's favour was upon them. Christians can do likewise. But this refers to complete fulfilment. This can only refer to the time when the LORD 'shall turn away ungodliness from Jacob' (Rom. 11:26).

Let us delight in the sovereign power of God to deliver. Mercy and favour are his prerogative. These verses show God as the great prime mover in salvation and deliverance. It is all 'you', and not what 'we' have done or might do. The cry of the psalmist's heart is 'turn us', 'revive us'. Without that sweet, irresistible, constraining and saving grace we have no hope.

'He opens the closed heart; softens the hardened heart; circumcises that which was uncircumcised; infuses new qualities into the will; makes the will from being dead, alive; from being bad, good; from being unwilling, willing; from being stubborn, compliant'[1]

---

[1] Canons of the Synod of Dort, Chapter 3, 4. Article 11.   Quoted from C.W.H. Griffiths, *Chosen – Called – Kept.*

Day 197   Psalm 85:8-13

Listen when the LORD speaks peace

After all the thanksgiving, and pleas for help, in the first half of the Psalm, the writer sets himself to listen (v8). Does our daily time with God give time for listening, as well as speaking and reading?

The Psalm gives a pattern for coming to God in worship that it would be useful to follow. When we come before God:

1. We must not be so full of speaking that we have no time to listen ('I will hear what God the LORD will say' v8a).

2. We must be obedient to him ('not turn back to folly' v8b).

3. We must not forget that he is close at hand to help ('Surely his salvation is near to those who fear him' v9).

4. We must rest in the sure and certain basis for our deliverance ('righteousness and peace have kissed each other' v10).

The Psalm is one of great comfort. The opening verses speak of the Lord's full deliverance of his people. Their captivity will end. The Psalm concludes with a vision of a full harvest of blessing (v11-13) when mercy and truth have met, and righteousness and peace have kissed. This is the same blessing that we have already seen described in Psalm 67.

Day 198   Psalm 86:1-5

The servant's petition

The title of this Psalm is 'A Prayer of David'. It is his conversation with God. After each of his requests in the opening verses, he gives the basis of his hope that the LORD will answer.

Here he does not base his hope on God's character, as so often in Scripture, but upon his needs, and because he is the LORD's servant (v2). He claims it as one who is loved and favoured by God. It is better to translate verse 2 with the AV margin. He is 'one whom you favour' (v2). What an amazing thing it is to be able to say, in full assurance of faith 'the Son of God loved me, and gave himself for me' (Gal. 2:20).

Bishop Horsley gives a guide to how we are to distinguish Messianic Psalms. His rule is that Psalms of David which are personal and do not have application to any particular circumstance are to be taken as Messianic. If we read the words of this Psalm as words of the Lord Jesus, they have their truest and fullest meaning, as a prayer uttered in his humiliation. As such, we have a unique view of the inner spiritual life of the Saviour during his time on earth.

Whether thinking of the Lord Jesus, or bringing our own needs to the LORD, let us sing these lovely words thoughtfully.

Day 199   Psalm 86:6-13.

Calling in the day of trouble

These words refer to the Lord Jesus. The book of Hebrews provides a commentary on what is said here.

1. We have the prayer and supplications of the Lord 'in the day of trouble' (v7). So the book of Hebrews says, 'Who in the days of his flesh, when he had offered up prayers and supplications with strong crying and tears unto him who was able to save him from death, and was heard in that he feared' (Heb. 5:7. See Isa. 53:11).

2. 'All nations that you made shall come and worship before you, O Lord, and shall glorify your name' (v9). The coming of all nations to the house of the LORD is recorded in several important Scriptures (Isa. 2:2; 56:6-8; 66:23; Zech. 14:16-19; Gen. 49:10, Compare Ps. 87).

3. Hebrews says of our Lord Jesus, 'Though he were a son, yet learned he obedience by the things which he suffered' (Heb. 5:8). The psalmist asks the LORD to 'teach' him and to 'unite my heart to fear your name'.

5. Lastly, the psalmist writes in verse 13, 'You have delivered my soul from the depths of Sheol. So in Hebrews, 'that through death he might destroy him that had the power of death, that is, the devil' (Heb. 2:14).

Well might the Lord Jesus say of the Scriptures, 'these testify of me' (John 5:39).

Day 200   Psalm 86:14-17

Show me a token for good

We have in these verses David's predicament (v14), his praise (v15) and his plea (v16, 17). As we have noted earlier, these words may be very aptly heard from the mouth of the Lord Jesus in his humiliation.

In their malice against the afflicted one described here, the proud and violent are shown to be against God also. Note three sins that bring judgment – pride, violence and 'not setting God before them'. Dr Gill amplifies this phrase, 'they did not set his omniscience, omnipresence, omnipotence, justice, goodness, or glory before them'.

There is a beautiful and encouraging description of the LORD in verse 15. It is good to uplift and praise God when we are under attack!

In verse 17 David says, 'Show me a token for good'. The word 'token' has become devalued. The Hebrew means 'a sign' or 'a proof'. Think of God's patience to Gideon. He gave all the reassurance that he needed – and that he requested. Compare the 23rd Psalm, where David says that the LORD has 'spread a table before me in the presence of my enemies'. De Burgh comments that the resurrection was the sign given for the true David.

In whatever circumstance we find ourselves today, may we have a token, a clear and unmistakeable sign upon us of the LORD's favour.

Day 201   Psalm 87

Glorious things spoken of the City of God

Having set Mount Zion as the object of God's past choosing, present love and future blessing in verses 1-3, it follows that the references to 'there' and 'in her' in the following verses refer to Zion - the city of God.

We believe this Psalm speaks of Israel's final restoration, when the nation shall at last 'look on him whom they have pierced' (Zech. 10:12-14) and 'a nation shall be born at once' (Isa.66:8). Then all Israel will have the birthright to the city of God. The Hebrew phrase used in verse 5 means 'each and every one'.[1]

The Psalm speaks of the nations as able to claim their (new) birth as of the city of God. However, for them it is not universal – it is 'this one' and 'this one' (v.4 and 6). It appears to us too that a distinction is made between proud Egypt (Rahab, Ps 89:10, and Isa 51:9) and Babylon (which is to be permanently destroyed Isa.13:19-22) and the other nations which the Psalmist points out ('Behold Philistia', etc). We believe the correct translation of v4 is 'and I will bring to remembrance … to those who know me' (v.4), i.e. with a view to punishment (compare Rev. 16:19).

Glorious things are spoken of this city, but what joy there shall be for us in the heavenly Jerusalem with all the chosen of God (Heb. 13:14; Rev. 21:10-27).

---

[1] As in Esther 1:8 'every man', and Lev. 17:10, 13 'whatsoever man …'

Day 202   Psalm 88:1-8

A sad Psalm

Over this Psalm, a previous owner of my Bible has pencilled 'the saddest Psalm'. I do not know whether he was quoting another writer, or has just been struck by its solemnity.

The writer is conscious that his affliction comes directly from the hand of God (v.6-8) and yet it is God to whom he turns for strength and mercy.

However, in its sadness, there are still embers glowing in the darkness. Indeed, the whole Psalm breathes a spirit of communion between a man and his God. He does not despair, accuse God, or question his wisdom. His hope is grounded in him who is eternal and all-powerful.

De Burgh comments, "That the speaker in this Psalm is the suffering Messiah is abundantly evident. In the words of Bishop Horne, 'The nature and degree of the sufferings related in it; the strength of the expressions used to describe them; the consent of ancient expositors; the appointment of the Psalm by the Church to be read on Good Friday: all these circumstances concur in directing an application of the whole to our blessed Lord'"

Let us then tread carefully and reverently, thinking of the sorrows and sufferings that our beloved Saviour bore for his people.

Day 203   Psalm 88:9-12

Where is Death's sting?

He who speaks these words (and we can imagine the Lord Jesus uttering them) has been in deep darkness of soul in the opening verses. 'The LORD, God of my salvation' (v1) is his only hope. All other acquaintance is gone. In these verses he calls upon God alone.

His eyes fail [literally, 'are dissolved'] through his weeping, as day and night he cries out to God with hands outstretched imploringly (v9). In verses 10-12 he contemplates death – death with all its darkness – a death where God's mercies are absent. Christ must pass alone through the valley of the shadow of death so that we might fear no evil, knowing then that nothing can separate us from the love of God.

In verses 10-12 he longs for a display of God's mercy and power, before death closes in. Such must have been the thoughts of the Redeemer as he passed through Jericho for the last time, healing the blind men; as he was greeted by acclamation on 'Palm Sunday'; as he wept over Jerusalem (Matt. 23:27, Lk. 19: 44). Such longings must have filled his heart as he prayed in Gethsemane. Death, destruction, and darkness were closing in.

Much of his human endeavour (the thirty hidden years for example) would soon be forgotten, as will ours. How our spirit rebels against the loss of such things in death. And yet 'for the joy that was set before him, he endured the cross, despising the shame'. So should we.

Day 204   Psalm 88:13-18

Friendless and forsaken

In the fearful last lines of the Psalm the writer heaps up expressions of utter abandonment.   Here is the Redeemer's cry, 'My God, My God, why have you forsaken me?' His soul is cast off like an unwanted garment. The face of his Father is hidden from him. He is afflicted and ready to die – from his youth he has been more like one dying than living.   He suffers terrors – *your* terrors – even the fiery wrath of God against sin. Raging seas of terrors are about him, and all who know and love him are gone – he is alone. So the Psalm ends.

But his confidence and resolve was stronger than all these waves of darkness.   In verse 13 he declares, 'I have cried to you for help, in the morning my prayer comes to meet you'. No cry to our merciful God goes unanswered. At the earliest possible moment, it will have answer in the morning of his goodness.

We have focussed on the vicarious sufferings of Christ for us in this Psalm, but it also holds comfort for the afflicted believer. We are confident that all his saints can whisper its words

But unto Thee, JEHOVAH, I have cried:
My prayer shall rise to Thee with morning-tide[1].

---

[1] *The Book of Psalms for Singing,* RPCNA, 1973, Ps. 88:13.

Day 205   Psalm 89:1-5

Making his faithfulness known

This joyful song commences with a happy commitment to endless praise. The speaker alternates between the LORD and the psalmist. The psalmist speaks in verses 1 and 2. The LORD declares his everlasting mercies to David in verses 3 and 4. In verse 5, the psalmist extols God's future glories.

In every verse of this portion God's 'faithfulness' is celebrated. This is the theme of the Psalm. The Hebrew word is linked to 'steadfastness' and 'truth'. 'Amen' comes from the same Hebrew root. So, God's mercies are forever, his faithfulness will be made known to all generations. His faithfulness is as secure as the heavens. So the LORD declares his covenant with David and to his seed - that his throne shall be built up to all generations. We may say with William Gadsby 'Immortal honours rest on Jesus' head'. He shall reign and fulfil every iota of his covenant with David.

We agree with the comments of de Burgh. 'How is the spiritual kingdom, which Christ administers as Head of the Church, 'the throne *of His father David*'? or His reign over a Gentile election during Israel's rejection a 'reign over *the house of Jacob*'?' We believe that the true wonders of his faithfulness to unworthy sinners and unbelieving Israel have yet to be seen in their fullness.

Day 206   Psalm 89:6-14

Our incomparable LORD

What clear skies extend over the psalmist as he writes the words of today's portion! There is nothing of his personal circumstances. All his thoughts are upon the LORD. Words of praise just flow from his mouth. We need to be reminded that our pilgrimage does have such times, as well as those when thick darkness seems to surround us.

All the wonders of nature belong to the LORD, for he has made them – 'and the fullness thereof' (v11). Can we walk around natural history museums without wonder and awe that these things are so. And yet ungodly man has made them temples to Darwin! The believer sees things differently. It is a distinguishing mercy of the elect that he responds 'God is greatly to be feared in the assembly of his saints, and to be had in reverence [literally, 'be feared'] above all them that are about him' (v7).

As we ponder on this portion, let us pause for a moment on verse 9. 'You rule the raging of the sea: when the waves thereof arise, you still them'. We wonder whether these words came to the minds of the disciples on the Sea of Galilee as the Saviour spoke to the fury of the storm, and then there was a great calm. 'And they feared exceedingly, and said to one another, 'What manner of man is this, that even the wind and the sea obey him' (Mark 4:41). May we know reverence and peace in the presence of the Lord today.

Day 207　Psalm 89:15-18

Waiting for the shout to go up

Most of yesterday's portion concerned the glories of God in creation and providence. The bridge with today's reading is verse 14, which begins to speak of the LORD's throne of mercy and truth, of that time when he will be exalted and praised. With this in mind the psalmist delights in the joys of fellowship and worship.

However, the words here are not just a testimony to personal experience. They are the collective voice of a nation saved and redeemed by him. The beginning of this section declares the happiness of the people (not 'a people', but 'the people') who know 'the glad sound' (v15). The word ('glad sound') is used of 'when the shout of a king is among them' (compare v18; Numb. 23:21), or at the New Year when the shofar was blown (Lev. 23:24). The section ends with 'the Holy One of Israel is our King'. It will indeed be a happy time when the cry goes up 'the Kingdoms of this world are become the kingdoms of our Lord, and of his Christ, and he shall reign for ever and ever' (Rev. 11:15ff; see too Psalm 47, especially v1 and v5, where the word is again used). What a difference from the time when Israel said, 'We will not have this man to reign over us' (Luke 19:14) and they cried out 'Crucify him!'

Let us rejoice as we enter into the fellowship of God in song, and, if we refrain from shouting, let us at least make a joyful noise!

Day 208   Psalm 89:19-29

The youngest son made the firstborn

This section is full of promises to David. Surely, God's choice of David is remarkable. He was the youngest and least of all his brothers. The Old Testament is ruthlessly candid about his flaws and weaknesses - his adultery with Bathsheba; the murder of her husband; his doting weakness towards Absalom, and so on. This is a man like us, and like so many rulers and governors of men.

And yet, God, in his sovereign election, chose David. And yet, God drew out his affections, so the LORD could say that he was 'a man after my own heart which shall fulfil all my will' (1 Sam. 13:14; Acts 7:46; 13:22). Is this marvel of grace not the experience of every true believer? May we not all speak, as John Bunyan, of 'grace abounding to the chief of sinners'?

Here in these verses, we have incomparable blessing promised to one insignificant monarch, ruling over a small country in a distant place for a short period. And yet, God had his eye upon him; he shall be 'the highest of the kings of the earth'; 'his throne shall be established as the days of heaven'.

Our God chooses 'the things that are not to bring to nought things that are' (1 Cor. 1:28). The youngest son is made the firstborn (v27).

This is yet to be finally fulfilled in 'David's Greater Son'.

Day 209   Psalm 89:30-37

My Covenant I will not break

We have 'the sure mercies of David' in these verses. In the story of the Northern Kingdom, each of the lines of kings ended, because of their failing and iniquity. So it was with Jeroboam, Baasha, and Ahab (1 Kgs. 21: 22). It would not be so for David, even though he sinned, and though wicked Ahaz and Manasseh should sit upon his throne.

Just as such promises of permanent covenant were made to David as a person, likewise, great and precious promises were given to the people of Israel, to their land, and to the city of Jerusalem. We cannot understand how any believer should doubt that God will also fulfil these promises to the very letter.

Note in these verses the experience of chastening. It is a mark of God's love. It is a sign of his faithfulness to his covenant. It is for the good of his children (v32 and 33).

The Lord Jesus said, 'the one who comes to me I will by no means cast out'. We have a God who cannot lie, and who likewise says reassuring words to David, 'My covenant will I not break, nor alter the thing that is gone out of my lips' (v34). 'My covenant shall stand fast with him. His seed also will I make to endure forever' (v28, 29).

Let us thank the LORD for his faithfulness by singing the words of this Psalm.

Day 210   Psalm 89:38-45

The night

One commentator[1] simply called this section 'the night'. It stands in sharp contrast to yesterday's portion. It speaks of a time when all God's covenant promises seem to have failed, when God himself has cut off, abhorred, and been angry with 'David'.

Nothing in David's life would complete the meaning of these awful words. Ezekiel gives the key, 'Thus says the Lord GOD; Remove the diadem, and take off the crown … I will overturn, overturn, overturn it: and it shall be no *more*, until he come whose right it is; and I will give it *him*' (Ezek. 21:26, 27). The day has not yet fully come for David's Greater Son, 'whose right it is', to manifestly reign. 'The night' continues.

The 'triumphal entry' (Luke 19:38; Mark 11:10) was a false dawn. Soon he word was spoken, 'You shall not see me henceforth, till you shall say, 'Blessed is he that comes in the name of the LORD'' (Matt. 23:39).

The Archangel's prophecy has yet to be fulfilled. 'He shall be great, and shall be called the Son of the Highest: and the Lord God shall give unto him the throne of his father David: And he shall reign over the house of Jacob for ever; and of his kingdom there shall be no end' (Luke 1:32, 33).

We sorrow for the night, but we know that 'joy comes in the morning'.

---

[1] B.W. Newton, *Dark Sayings upon the Harp* (from notes of his lectures).

Day 211   Psalm 89:46-52
Where are the sure mercies of David?

The discouragement of the previous section is followed by growing light towards the end of the Psalm, until it ends with the doxology of verse 52.

'How long?' is an expression of faith which has not given way to despair. Reasoning with God is often a mark of true prayer. The psalmist does this as he 'reminds' the LORD of his purpose in creating man, and of the shortness of life. In verses 49-51 the psalmist 'reminds' God of his former loving-kindness, of his truthfulness, of the reproach of his enemies, and of how that reproach personally affects the writer. We need to wrestle with God in prayer in this way.

In verse 51 (his delayed footsteps) it is as though the LORD's enemies were saying in New Testament language 'Where is the promise of his coming' (2 Pet. 3:4). Most leading Jewish commentators and the Talmud interpret this verse of the coming of Messiah, 'which, because delayed, or was not so soon expected, was scoffed at, and reproached by wicked men'[1].

This third book of Psalms then ends with words of praise, as do the first two books of Psalms (see the end of Psalm 41 and 72). So may we end today in praise.

---

[1] Quoted in Dr John Gill, *Commentary on the Whole Bible*.

Book 4

Psalms 90 – 106

Day 212   Psalm 90:1-6

Mortality and eternity

This great and majestic Psalm is about the shortness of human life and the eternity of God. In the opening verses, words are piled up in describing God and man.

The LORD is 'to all generations'; 'before the mountains were brought forth'; before 'you had made the earth'; 'from everlasting to everlasting'. A thousand years to him is as yesterday.

Man, however, passes through many 'generations'; we are but 'sons of Adam' – fallen humanity; we are turned to destruction (or 'dust'); a flood of water sweeps us and all we have away[1], as fleeting as sleep, as insignificant and temporary as grass.

And yet, man may find his strength and refuge in God. The Psalm is written by Moses the 'man of God'[2]. God can be 'our dwelling place'. In contrast to all the transient affairs of men, our mighty God is constant 'through all generations'.

These words have been a comfort before many an open grave, and I trust they will be a comfort to your loved ones at yours. They will only be so if we have been known as 'men of God'. We shall then exchange our fleeting habitation here for an eternity in the many mansions prepared for us, when he shall truly be 'our dwelling place' for evermore.

---

[1] Consider the 2005 Tsunami, and the New Orleans floods.

[2] Literally, 'man (Hebrew *ish* – an individual of worth) of the God'.

Day 213   Psalm 90:7-11
Our years are soon gone

The mention of death and mortality leads to consideration of the cause of death in these verses. The life of man, which at one time extended to nearly 1000 years, is now reduced to a span. The cause of this is rooted in God's anger at man's sin (Gen. 6:3). It is for this cause that he is destined to 'return' to the dust (Gen. 3:19).

As a comment on verse 10, I can remember my wife's father in his eighties saying in a moment of weariness, 'I have lived too long'. He desired to enter into the promised rest.

Modern man considers it inappropriate to give serious thought to such things. The time for reflection is relegated to the closing days of one's life. The urgency of death's approach is often is dulled by 'palliative care' and antidepressants. O how we need to remain aware that we tread upon fragile boards throughout our lives, and be prepared for our time to come.

Such thoughts are not morose and negative, although they are opposed to the spirit of the age, which says, 'Let us eat, drink, and be merry for *tomorrow* we die'. May we spend our lives in a godly fear, aware and ready, for we will soon meet God.

Day 214   Psalm 90:12-17

The beauty of the LORD our God

This Psalm is 'the prayer of Moses the man of God', and here in the second half of the Psalm we have his requests.

I recall a Gospel tract from the 'Victory Tract Club' that my father carried with him. It had the title 'Three score years and then'. Its object was to bring people to consider the shortness of life and, in the words of our Psalm, 'to number our days'. Moses does not tell other people to number their days, nor does he make a resolution to do so himself. He asks the LORD to teach him to do it. We must see in infirmity, sickness, and loss, the lessons of our Heavenly Schoolmaster for our good.

Verses 15-17 request gladness in exchange for affliction. Verse 17 asks 'Let the beauty of the LORD our God be upon us'. From this we learn that: (1) Beauty is a characteristic of the LORD; (2) Through our association with him (he is 'our God') that beauty may characterise us too; (3) Bearing the beauty of the LORD is a thing to be desired and enjoyed; (4) It is not something we can attain by our efforts, but something which he can bestow (5) A gathering of God's people may exhibit this grace ('us').

Do you take the beauty of the LORD on your travels in this wicked world? Do your friends, associates, and work colleagues see it too?

Day 215   Psalm 91:1-7

Under his wings

Psalm 90 began by calling God 'our dwelling place'. The first four verses of this Psalm take up the same theme (see too v9). *Dwelling* 'in the secret place'; *Lodging* 'under the shadow of the Almighty'; 'The refuge' is a place of safety when sin and Satan harries and hounds us; 'The fortress' defends us when we face overwhelming odds in our conflict.

The covering of his wings and feathers warm and protect the helpless believer from malice and harm (compare Deut. 32:10-12; Matt. 23:37). The 'shield and armour' are a defence in the heat of the battle (see Eph. 6:10-18).

De Burgh helpfully draws the parallel between this Psalm and Israel's protection from the plagues of Egypt. There it could be said, 'Neither shall any plague come near your dwelling' (compare v5-7 with Exod. 8:22; 9:4, 6; 10:23; 11:7; 12:13).

Scripture teaches us that God will send his plagues specifically on the ungodly at the last time (Rev. 16:2). This Psalm will then have direct relevance. In the meantime, we may say with John Ryland,

> Plagues and deaths around me fly;
>
> Till he bids, I cannot die;
>
> Not a single shaft can hit,
>
> Until the God of love sees fit.

Day 216   Psalm 91:8 -16

The believer's guardian angels

Verses 8-13 promise complete protection from plague and destruction. Many commentators apply it to all believers. We are protected from spiritual harm, but not from all physical harm. Satan tested the Son of God with verses 11 and 12 at his temptation. The Lord's response guides us on how we should use these and similar promises.

The word used to describe love in verse 14 is unique in the Psalms. It echoes the intense desire and love that God has for his people (Deut. 7:7). What pleases God is longing after him, and heart-understanding and delight in all that he is (his 'name'). Horatius Bonar writes, 'Let us learn to love him. For what he is in himself; for what he has done, and for what he has promised to do for us. Let us love him for his love, and for his loveableness. We love him because he first loved us. He has set his love on us. Let us set our love on him'[1].

God's gracious reward for that love and knowledge is deliverance, exaltation, response, comfort, and reward. Bishop Horne writes, 'All these promises have already been made good in our gracious Head and Representative'.

What more do we need than 'I will be with him in trouble' (v15)? Let us delight in God.

---

[1] Horatius Bonar, *Light and Truth* (on this Psalm).

Day 217   Psalm 92:1-4

A Sabbath song

The title of this Psalm is 'a song or Psalm for the Sabbath Day'. It is most probable that this was a regular song for the Temple worship, rather than (as Jewish commentators imagine) a Psalm written by Adam soon after the first Sabbath! Its connection with the Sabbath is threefold: Firstly` (v1-4), it celebrates 'the work of God's hands' (Exod. 20:11); Secondly (v5-9), it celebrates God's work in deliverance, and his destruction of the wicked (Deut. 5:15); Thirdly (v10-15), it looks forward to that final Sabbath of rest promised to the children of God (Heb. 4:6).

We have in this first section the psalmist's desire to worship God (v1). For him it is 'a good thing'. It is not a chore or a burden. Can we say this of our daily 'quiet time' with God? Are these our feelings as we leave for the prayer meeting on a dark and cold winter's evening?

We see too the psalmist's diligence in worshipping God (v2 and 3). It is his delight morning and evening, and he makes due preparation for it to be the best he can offer.

Finally, we have the source of his desire to worship God. It is not worked up, nor is it a natural desire. It is God-given – '*You* have made me glad'. May the LORD stir up our hearts to praise him too. May we sing for joy at all the works his hands have wrought (v4).

Day 218   Psalm 92:5-9

Flourishing now: Doomed for ever

We saw yesterday that it is the LORD who gives the desire to worship. Only the man whose mind has been opened can understand the deep thoughts of God (compare v5, 6 and 1 Corinthians 2).

The object of the natural man is to prosper in whatever he wants to do. He will use whatever means he can to achieve that end. But they will soon be destroyed forever (v7). Those who seek such things – all the workers of iniquity – are God's enemies, and will perish. They will be 'scattered', the form of the word here means separated, divided from each other, as bones being out of joint (Ps. 22:14). So shall the tares be separated from the wheat (Matt. 13:30, 41-43): so will the wicked be cut off: so their fate will be different from that of God's people. For them the sea of death will be destruction, but the believer will pass over as on dry land (Heb. 11:29).

In this 'Psalm or song for the Sabbath Day', we see the person, whose heart the LORD has opened, stirred to worship him for his mighty works. We see the redeemed soul made wise. Only such a person can truly call the Sabbath, the reminder of these things, 'a Delight!' (Isa. 58:13).

Day 219   Psalm 92:10-15

Planted now: Flourishing for ever

Here prosperity, blessing, and long life to the godly are described. They have never been consistently given to God's people in this dispensation. They are associated with a different time, which is yet future, when, as it was at the beginning of the world, the years of a man shall be as the years of a tree (compare v12-14 and Isa. 65:19-25).

Dickson encourages us to apply the truth given in these verses. 'The best condition of the godly, is not in what they are for the present, but in what they shall be hereafter ... whatsoever weakness or grief the godly lie under for a while, they shall have in due time restful refreshment, comfort and encouragement from God's Spirit and powerful providence, and that renewed unto them from time to time, as need requireth'.

Often, as we considered yesterday, the prosperity of the wicked seems a disturbing problem, but God's future actions will 'show that the LORD is upright' and 'there is no unrighteousness in him' (v15).

We look forward to the rest that remains for the people of God, when we shall personally and collectively enjoy these blessings (note the changes from 'my' to 'they' in these verses). Let us sing these words in anticipation.

Day 220   Psalm 93

The LORD reigns!

This Psalm begins with the shout at the accession of a King to his throne (see 2 Sam. 15:10). As Hengstenberg comments, 'it does not apply to the constant government of God'[1]. The picture is of an event, the enthronement of a monarch, clothed with the robes of his office, whose kingdom is secure.

Even the roaring of the awe-inspiring waves (v3 and 4) is dismissed because 'the LORD is mightier'. This links with the Day of the LORD in Luke 21:25 with 'the sea and the waves roaring'. But, in this Psalm, this disturbance is past. The cry has already gone up 'Rule in the midst of your adversaries!' (Psalm 110). The Messiah has taken his great power to rule and to reign (Rev. 11:17, 18).

What pleasant words are these to hold in our mind this day, when we are everywhere confronted with all the 'roaring of the waves' of this world's turmoil and rebellion against God. But comforted with the words of this Psalm, we will have a quiet inward peace. We will have a confidence that says, 'The LORD on high is mightier than many waters', and we will prepare ourselves to join the loud voices in heaven, saying, 'The kingdoms of this world are become *the kingdoms* of our Lord, and of his Christ; and he shall reign for ever and ever' (Rev. 11:15).

---

[1] E.W. Hengstenberg, *Commentary on the Psalms*

Day 221 Psalm 94:1-7

Vengeance belongs to God

Our journey through the Psalms is rather like travelling cross country on an inter-city train. The scenery changes as we gaze through the windows. In this Psalm, we have a remarkable change. We had been in bright sunlight and now suddenly we find ourselves passing through a dark tunnel. This is not the personal darkness that we have seen elsewhere, but a darkness that has engulfed God's people.

It is a cry for justice. It sees the widow and the fatherless oppressed. It sees God's people nearly broken in pieces. It hears the proud, dismissive words of evildoers, 'the LORD shall not see, neither shall the God of Jacob regard it'. So it is for many scattered Christian communities across the world at this time. Thus it will be as the end time approaches, when 'the Devil comes down having great wrath, because he knows that he has but a short time' (Rev. 12:12).

Let us continue to plead, with the saints of all ages, the 'How long?' prayer. The Hebrew puts it slightly differently. It is not so much 'how long' will we suffer; but rather 'when' will the promised change arrive. Let us set out all the LORD's justice, mercy, and power in our petitions, and plead that we may soon see the glories of his final intervention.

Day 222   Psalm 94:8-15

If the LORD chastens, we are blessed

Those who see the opening cry of this Psalm for vengeance as 'unchristian' fail to grasp that the Psalm relates to the period when at last our Saviour treads the winepress of the fierceness and wrath of Almighty God (Rev. 19:15).

The words of verses 9 and 10 are vivid. They rebuke our unbelief too. We must hold as certain that God sees and hears, and will, in the fullness of time, demonstrate his righteousness. He not only sees and hears the outward rebellion of the nations, but he knows the thoughts of all men (v11). What an awesome God we have, who brings all such things into his reckoning for perfect justice!

Verses 12-15 speak of chastisement for God's people. The experience, though painful, is a cause of happiness! God sets his people aside by chastisement. We believe this speaks particularly of the time of Antichrist. It is yet future, as the believer is kept 'until' (v13) the destruction of the wicked – not of the wicked generally, but (in the singular) of the Lawless One.

If we are under chastening and do not prosper now. Let us still count ourselves 'happy' and 'blessed'.

Day 223   Psalm 94:16-23

Unless the LORD had been my help...

The psalmist, in his feelings of abandonment, cries out, 'Who will rise up for me against the evildoers?' We must learn the lesson well that 'vain is the help of man' (Ps. 60:11). Consequently, verses 17 and 18 demonstrate God's help and consolation in trial – 'unless the LORD had been my help...'.

The expression 'the throne of iniquity...which frames mischief by a law' (v20) is a striking one. Scripture makes plain that there will be such a throne which shall be hostile to God's people (Revelation 13; Dan. 7:24, 25). It is only when we grasp the quintessential evil of that last time before the Lord returns that we can understand the cries for vengeance in this Psalm and others. It is only then that we can fully enter into the plea 'How long?' and can gain peace from the assurance that God will at length 'cut off' the wicked.

Now we plead for God's mercy upon the wicked, we turn the other cheek, we suffer wrong for his sake, but a time will come when it is right and just that God should judge, and the believer will rejoice that that time has come. At length there will only be one throne.

Let us leave all our circumstances, and the LORD's dealings with men, in his sovereign hands. 'There is no unrighteousness in him' (Ps. 92:15).

Day 224   Psalm 95:1-5

Make a joyful noise with Psalms

This Psalm was used by the early Church at the beginning of its services[1]. The 33 who survived the 2010 Chilean mining disaster emerged with verse 4 of this Psalm emblazoned on their tee-shirts 'To him the glory and honour'.

.Bishop Horsley views Psalms 95-100 as one prophetic poem quoted by Paul in the Epistle to the Hebrews. He writes, 'Each Psalm has its proper subject, which is some particular branch of the general argument, the establishment of Messiah's Kingdom'[2]. He gives the theme of this Psalm as 'JEHOVAH's Godhead and his power over all nature'.

It is fitting that David (Heb. 4:7) begins with the words 'O come let us sing unto the LORD'. In Western society, although we hear a great deal of music, we sing very little. We do not sing out of doors. We rarely sing praise to God in our homes. In Churches the music group takes over, often with heavy percussion. The congregation's singing is shepherded (often drowned out) by the volume. In their efforts to stop the Covid 19 virus, Governments banned Church singing. Yet God commands singing.

The words 'let us' and 'our' are used repeatedly. It is a personal invitation to united worship.

---

[1] De Burgh quotes Ambrose, 4th century.
[2] Bishop Samuel Horsley *The Book of Psalms...with Notes Explanatory and Critical*.

Day 225   Psalm 95:6-11

Today – not yesterday or tomorrow

This passage begins with a strong call to worship, to bow down, and to kneel (literally, 'prostrate oneself') before God. We come before (the face of) our Maker!

The Psalmist then shows the habitual disobedience of his people, even when under the LORD's shepherd care (v7). They hardened their heart. They tested God. They grieved him. They erred in their heart. They were wilfully ignorant of his ways. There is specific reference to *Meribah* and *Massah* in verse 8 (Exod. 17:1-7, 'provocation' and 'trial' AV).

Yet the emphasis of these verses is not grief for a sinful, sorrowful past, it is a call to respond to God's mercy 'Today' - The LORD's word breaks in suddenly. A.A. Bonar[1] translates, 'Today, O that you would hear his voice'. Likewise, in the Book of Hebrews the writer emphasises the need to 'hold fast', 'exhort one another daily', 'labour to enter our rest' … 'Today' (Heb. 3 and 4). Whatever happened in the past, the call is to respond now - at this critical moment. We are to seize this moment, or it will be gone forever.

For blind Bartimaeus, and for the dying thief, the day of mercy came once. Perhaps it came once for Felix (Acts 24:25). Let us heed the warning, and seek the LORD with all our hearts today (Jer. 29:13).

---

[1] A.A. Bonar, *Christ and His Church in the Book of Psalms*. So too Perowne.

Day 226   Psalm 96:1-6

Let the whole earth sing!

The Psalm starts with a proclamation and a command. It is a summons to all the earth to sing God's praise, and for his glory and wonders to be declared among all the nations. Alas, although the call might go out, it has been unanswered by all but a few since the triumph of Calvary.

The closing verse (v13) indicates that it will be responded to in a future day, when the LORD comes to judge (or govern) the earth and rule with righteousness. This Psalm is for the time when all nations shall see his glory (Isa. 66:18, 19), not in token, but in fullness.

The call to sing a new song is not an invitation to write new hymns or choruses. The 'new song' here spoken of is this very prophetic Psalm, and (as it refers to a time then far future) it precludes, rather than encourages, the use of uninspired compositions in worship.

How we long for the time when the earth will be filled with his glory (Ps. 72:19); when the call of this Psalm shall receive a ready response. Let us now be the vanguard, the first-fruits of that great harvest of praise, when his great salvation will be shown forth from 'day to day' (v2) for endless years.

Day 227   Psalm 96:7-13

The LORD is coming

How glorious these verses are! When will we say among the nations, 'The LORD reigns?' When will men give to him the glory that is due to his name? When will he be seen and worshipped all the beauty of his holiness?

Creation is in groaning and travail now, but then it shall be different: even the fields and the trees shall rejoice that His time has come. Amidst all the injustice, violence, sin, and boasting of man, we yearn for the justice of, and the reign of, our Redeemer.

He comes as Judge – as the Samson or Gideon who will deliver. Bonar writes, 'It is not a time of mere adjudication of causes or pronouncing sentences – it is a day of jubilee. It is the happiest day our world has ever seen. Who would not long for it? Who is there that does not pray for it? It is the day of the Judge's glory, as well as of our world's freedom – the day when the judgment of this world (John 12:31 and 16:11) which his cross began and made sure, is completed by the total removal and suppression of Satan's reign, and the removal of the curse. All this is anticipated here'.

The repetition of 'for he comes' in the last verse vividly suggests that the psalmist is an eyewitness of an event taking place. We would add again, 'Even so, Come Lord Jesus!'

Day 228   Psalm 97:1-6

But who can abide the day of his coming?

The cry, 'The LORD reigns' goes out again in this Psalm. Although God is Lord of all things as the Creator (Acts 17:24), although the Lord Jesus could say 'All power is given unto me in heaven and in earth' (Matt. 28:18), yet the manifestation of these things in this earth have yet to be. The word has yet to go out to the Son, 'Rule in the midst of your adversaries' (Ps. 110:1, 2). The earth shall yet 'see and tremble' (v4).

Some have inferred from the quotation of this Psalm (v7) in Hebrews 1:6 that it refers to his first coming, but the correct translation of the New Testament author is 'and when he brings in <u>again</u> the First Begotten into the world'. When the word 'again' is joined to a verb in Hebrews it always has the sense of 'a second time' (4:7; 5:12; 6:1, 6). It refers to his second coming.[1]

He comes in glory, and his coming will be a source of gladness to the ends of the earth (v1), but nevertheless it will be a day of judgment. The clouds and darkness (v2; Exod. 20:21); the fire going before him; the burning up of his enemies; the lightning, are all an awful prospect to the ungodly.

The LORD shall reign. Let us own his rule and kingship over our lives as his people here and now.

---

[1] See Alford's Greek New Testament, de Burgh, Vincent's *Word Studies*, Dr Gill, etc.

Day 229   Psalm 97:7-12

Let those who love the LORD hate evil

At the Reformation images and relics were rightly destroyed by the people. They did not spare the 'accursed idolatry'[1] of the mass either. The LORD's rebuke to 'all they that serve graven images' is given in these verses. The golden calves of Jeroboam, although dedicated to the worship of JEHOVAH, are repeatedly condemned in Scripture as the sin 'wherewith he made Israel to sin'. The LORD will one day be known as the one who is exalted above all false gods. O that our so-called Christian leaders of today would proclaim the one true God, rather than dabbling in multi-faithism. 'You who love the LORD, hate evil!' (v10).

Our God is a jealous God who forbids an image of anything in his created works being used in worship or reverence. We believe that portraying the Lord Jesus in human form falls under this ban, 'the making of any representation of God, of all or any of the three persons'[2].

We can take the psalmist's encouragement from these verses and be glad and rejoice that God's judgments, justice, and holiness will one day be seen and manifest. Let us begin that song of gladness now.

---

[1] *Heidelberg Catechism*, Lords Day 30, Answer 80.

[2] See *Westminster Larger Catechism* Q109, and *Seeing Jesus* by Peter Barnes (Banner of Truth).

Day 230   Psalm 98:1-3

The ends of the earth shall see

This Psalm does not urge us or instruct us to write new songs to God's praise for use today. It does not say 'sing to God new songs of worship'. The newness of which it speaks is not a newness of man's invention. It is a response to a new situation - the great change wrought by God when Christ comes in glory. The Psalm is for the time when 'all the ends of the earth have seen the salvation of our God' (v3).

De Burgh expounds that coming and consummation from this passage. Firstly, it is a work of power, not of grace. It is a victory by his right hand and his holy arm (v1). The LORD 'openly shows' his righteousness in the sight of the nations (v2). It follows apostasy, which the New Testament uniformly teaches will precede the Lord's return. Secondly, the salvation of Israel is associated with this deliverance, 'He has remembered his mercy and his truth toward the house of Israel' (v3). Thirdly, the conversion of all nations follows his 'victory' and mercy upon Israel; 'All the ends of the earth have seen the salvation of our God' (v4). So the earth shall be filled with the knowledge of God as the waters cover the sea.

Can we hold back from singing this 'old' Psalm? It is impossible now to make up new words to express the joy that the Church will know when the Lord takes his great power and begins to reign (Rev. 11:16, 17).

Day 231   Psalm 98:4-9

A joyful noise

The melody of the harp (v5) is associated with joy (Gen. 31:27, Job 30:31; Isa. 24:8), the pouring out of the Holy Spirit (1 Sam. 10:5, 6), and with joyful song (Psalms 33:2; 71:22; 147:7). As it was the instrument of David, so here it is called for at the coming of the Son of David. It is associated with the destruction of Antichrist (Isa. 30:32) and, of course, the worship of the glorified Church, when the 'new song' is again mentioned (Rev. 5:7-10). A.A. Bonar notes that, when a new king began his reign in Israel, it was marked, as here, by the shout of triumph, the clapping of hands and the blowing of the trumpet (v6).

The last verses of Psalm 96 and Psalm 98 are almost identical. 'Before the LORD, for he comes to judge the earth. With righteousness shall he judge the world and the peoples with equity' (Psalm 96 speaks of the LORD judging in truth). The call for a new song which even inanimate things join in – the sea, the trees, and the hills – are likewise parallel. They speak of the same time in earth's history. It is the time of universal deliverance when 'his wonders are seen among all the nations' (Ps. 96:3) and when all the earth shall 'make a joyful noise unto the LORD' (Ps. 98:4).

The earth waits in groaning and travail for such a day (Rom. 8:22). Let us sing these blessed words with joy.

Day 232   Psalm 99:1-5

The LORD is great in Zion

The Kingship of Christ is again the theme of this Psalm. Here we have not just the expectation, or even the realisation, of his coming as in Psalm 97 and 98, but here his throne established in Mount Zion. His reign from Mount Zion is the theme of many of the Psalms, and 'Mount Zion' is not simply an allegory, or pseudonym, for 'the Church'. Psalms such as this and Psalm 2 are free from confusion if we understand them literally, and therefore as describing future events. By doing so, we follow the pattern of prophecy and literal fulfilment which characterised the Lord's first coming.

The psalmist piles up words to describe the nature of Christ's reign: strength; justice loved and executed; equity; righteousness; holiness. As words fail him, he draws upon powerful images of the LORD's greatness. 'He sits between' or is 'enthroned above' the cherubim (those awesome creatures described in Gen. 3:24; Ezek. 1:4-14; 10:1-22 and Rev. 4:6-8; 5:8-14) manifesting God's irresistible, almighty power. He is 'high above' observing and viewing everyone. Nothing is hidden from him. Men should tremble at 'his great and terrible *name*' (all that God has revealed himself to be).

Let us rejoice at the sure word of prophecy, as a light shining in a dark place (2 Pet. 1:19). Let us bring these wonderful words to God in song, for we shall one day sing such words in glory.

Day 233   Psalm 99:6-9

The worship at his holy hill

This Psalm is a part of the series that runs from Psalm 95-100. It is concerned with the establishment of Messiah's kingdom. In this portion, his people are conscious that they worship in the company of Moses, Aaron, and Samuel. God will show his power in that day, as he did in their day. He will answer the prayers of his people, as he answered their prayers (see Jer. 15:1).

The psalmist is describing the character of Messiah's reign, when the Lord will restore to Israel 'judges as at the first' (Isa. 1:26).

In the closing verse, the psalmist says that such will be the worship of God 'at his <u>holy</u> hill' in that day. Compare too Ps. 132:7 with v5. Jerusalem will again be the centre of worship.

The Lord Jesus prophesied that Jerusalem would, for a time, cease to be the required place of worship (John 4:21). The Church continued to worship at the Temple until it was destroyed in 70 AD: since then, the veneration by Christendom of 'holy places' has been misguided foolishness.

Nevertheless, Scripture speaks of a restored Temple (Ezekiel 40-46), and of the Gentiles being required to go up from year to year to Jerusalem (Zech. 14:16-21). However, that (as here) is when Christ shall bring in the new order of things.

Day 234   Psalm 100

We did not make ourselves

This glorious 100th Psalm brings to an end the series that began with Psalm 95. It calls upon all creatures to praise the LORD.

The false science of evolution says, 'We have made ourselves through the survival of the fittest'. Here redeemed mankind says, 'It is he who has made us, and not we ourselves' (v3).

All nations (Mark 11:17) will not just acknowledge creation, but also God's redemption and shepherd care; 'We are his people and the sheep of his pasture'. Their praise will be constant. The gates of God's house (v4) 'shall be open continually (Isa. 60:11); they shall not be shut day or night' (Isa. 56:6, 7).

B.W. Newton writes[1] 'nor does God authorise anyone to say to the nations now, "Make a joyful noise unto the LORD <u>all ye lands</u>". How can nations, fast bound in misery and iron – nations whom gross darkness covers – nations tyrannised over by Satan and Satan's servants, how can such make a joyful noise before Jehovah, and come into His presence with a song? Can he that is bound in iron dance? Can he who groans in agony sing? God asks not for joy where no joy is. He asks not for worship from those whom Truth has not brought into the knowledge of his love'.

But one day it will be different.

---

[1] B.W. Newton, *Prophetic Psalms in their relation to Israel*.

Day 235   Psalm 101:1-4

The Prince's Psalm

This Psalm of David commences with the words, 'I will sing of mercy and of judgment'. Those who only sing from a hymn book often sing of mercy, but rarely of judgment. Literally, translating the second half of the verse explains how it is to be done, 'Unto you, O Jehovah, will I sing-Psalms'[1].

This has been called 'the Prince's Psalm'. In it David sets out the manner in which he intended to govern. King David had to act with integrity in affairs of state. God's Word makes clear that Government should only be exercised by people of high moral integrity, and there must be consistency in their personal lives. We have abandoned such principles as a nation.

David's question, 'O when will you come to me?' seems to date the words during the long period of waiting, whilst he was a fugitive from Saul. All true Christians know such times of waiting, often in apparent hopelessness. In such times we can claim the New Testament promises. The Lord Jesus said that he and the Father will come to the man who loves him and keeps his word (John 14:23). Let us keep faithful in the place and in the way that he has set us, for he knows best and will fulfil his promises to us as he did to David.

---

[1] Calvin's translation: 'Sing-psalms' Hebrew 'zamar', the root of the word 'mizmor', a psalm.

Day 236   Psalm 101:5-8

Justice and Judgment at last

We find in verses 5 to 7 the principles by which David was determined to reign: rewarding the just and excluding the deceitful. If indeed this is 'the prince's Psalm, concerned with judgment and justice', it will come as no surprise if we find the Lord Jesus in these verses acting as the king.

In the last verse there is the clearest indication that this does indeed refer to Christ's future reign. No king has ever (for Israel, or any other nation) destroyed all the wicked of the land. Where reference is made explicitly to cutting off all evil doers from the city of the LORD the meaning is plain. We should take the literal meaning. It will be fulfilled in Christ's millennial reign over his people. Revelation 21 refers to a city into which is brought the glory of kings, and nations will walk in the light of it. It is written there, 'And there shall in no wise enter into it any thing that defiles, neither whatsoever works abomination, or makes a lie: but they who are written in the Lamb's book of life'.

Most commentators take this to be a description of heaven, but, unless we reduce the words to mere poetry, the description more naturally refers to a time when this Psalm will also find literal fulfilment[1].

---

[1] B.W. Newton sees this Psalm as a whole as having a reference both to the commencement of the millennium and to the New Heavens and the New Earth (in *Dark sayings upon the Harp*, from notes of his addresses).

Day 237 Psalm 102:1-5

Reduced to skin and bones

The title of this Psalm is 'A prayer of the afflicted, when he is overwhelmed, and pours out his complaint before the LORD'. It is one of what Luther called 'Paul's Psalms' and shows great brokenness and dependence upon God. It is a penitential Psalm.

These opening five verses speak of the outward circumstances of the psalmist – his prayer, his cry, his days, his bones, his heart, his groaning. The earnest pleading of verses 1 and 2 is a longing for the LORD's closeness. He wants the LORD to see, and hear, and answer.

We shall see the reference of this Psalm to 'The Man of Sorrows' as we consider it, but it has often been upon the lips of his suffering servants too. As Dr Gill says, 'all the people of God are more or less a *poor* and *afflicted* people; outwardly afflicted in body, in estate, and in their good name and character; inwardly with the corruptions of their own hearts, the temptations of Satan, and Divine desertions'.

This Psalm was sung at the bedside of David Brainerd as he lay dying, burnt out from his missionary labours at the age of 30.

A broken and a contrite heart God will not despise. Let us sing these words in this spirit.

Day 238   Psalm 102:6-11

Alone and in tears

We continue with this Psalm of the one who is overwhelmed with affliction.

In the verses before us, his grief goes beyond external burdens to an aching heart. It is a heart bowed down by solitariness and loneliness. Three times the phrase 'I am like' is repeated, and each time the writer thinks of solitary birds in the wilderness or alone at night on the rooftop. If this is the reader's experience, let him think of the Saviour's experience too.

The Lord Jesus was tried by Satan for forty days alone in the wilderness. It was often his habit to spend nights in prayer alone. He got up a great while before dawn to pray. He said to a would-be disciple, 'The foxes have holes, and the birds of the air have nests; but the Son of man has not where to lay his head' (Matt. 8:20). He is seen alone in Gethsemane, where 'Backwards and forwards thrice he ran, as if to seek some help from man'[1]. Betrayed by his familiar friend, he was abused and spat upon. On the cross he made that dreadful cry, 'My God, My God, why have you forsaken me?' This indeed was the last blow, as the psalmist says in verse 10, 'Because of your indignation and your wrath: for you have lifted me up and cast me down'.

Let us sing these words thoughtfully and reverently.

---

[1] Joseph Hart.

Day 239   Psalm 102:12-17

The time to favour Zion has come

We have meditated upon the grief of the Son of Man in the earlier portions of this Psalm and we can say 'Was there any sorrow like his sorrow?' (Lam. 1:12).

We can now go further and see the outcome of that sorrow. 'He shall see of the travail of his soul, and shall be satisfied' (Isa. 53:11). There was a time when the disciples marvelled at the great stones of the Temple, but were told that they would be cast down, and Jerusalem's 'house' left desolate (Matt. 23:37 – 24:2). Here the Psalm looks forward prophetically to when 'the time to favour her, yea, the set time is come' (v13). Then even the very stones and dust of Zion will be a source of reverence and compassion (v14). The Lord will build up Zion, and will appear in his glory (v16). That time, although long prayed for and seemingly forgotten, shall at length come (v17).

The timing of these events is made clear in these verses. It is when, 'the heathen (the nations) shall fear the name of the LORD, and all the kings of the earth your glory' (v15). De Burgh notes that we have here, as so frequently set together in prophecy, the restoration of Israel, the subsequent conversion of the nations, and the coming of the Lord in glory.

Let us look beyond present difficulty or destitution to that glorious time.

Day 240   Psalm 102:18-22

Written for a generation yet to come

Israel in their bondage in Egypt appeared unaware that the time of their deliverance was drawing near – the 400 years that were appointed (Gen. 15:13; Exod. 12:40, 41). They cried out under their bondage, but there is no record in the opening chapters of the book of Exodus that they cried out to the LORD. Yet in spite of this, the LORD saw and heard (Exod. 2:23-25) and, in his time, led them out, humbling the greatest king and empire upon earth in the process.

So it will be when the Lord Jesus returns. When the things that are written here are fulfilled, he will look down, he will hear the groaning of the prisoner, and he will set free those who are appointed to death v19, 20). He will declare the name of the LORD in Zion, and his praise in Jerusalem, when all peoples and kingdoms shall serve the LORD (v21, 22; Zech. 2:11). This wicked 'generation' continues to this day, but it will pass away when all these things are fulfilled.

How we should be watching the signs of the times! How we should be learning of the parable of the fig tree, for by it we may know when he is even at the doors, waiting to come (Matt. 24:32-34).

Let us sing these words in hope and expectancy, confident that they will reach the ear of God.

Day 241   Psalm 102:23-28

Christ is still the same. His years will never end

This portion is interpreted for us by Hebrews 1:10-12. We learn from Hebrews 1 that the speaker changes after verse 24. The Lord Jesus in his affliction cries out in verses 23 and 24, 'O take me not away in the midst of my days'. The reply comes back to him from the Father (v25-27). 'Unto the Son he says' (Heb. 1:8), "Your years are throughout all generations. Of old you have laid the foundation of the earth: and the heavens are the work of your hands. They shall perish, but you will endure, yea, all of them shall wax old like a garment; as a vesture you will change them, and they shall be changed. But you are the same, and your years shall have no end"'.[1]

The passage identifies the Lord Jesus as the Creator of all things (v25 and Heb. 1:10; John 1:1-3, 10). Our Saviour is therefore identified with the LORD. He is Alpha and Omega, the one whose years have no end (v27). We say with the apostle, 'Great is the mystery of godliness'! (1 Tim. 3:16).

It is on his unchangeableness as God that the security and perseverance of his people, and the covenant promise to their children, rests (v27, 28).

Let us sing these words in awe and wonder as we ponder upon the incarnate Son of God, and his covenant mercies to us.

---

[1] See Adolph Saphir, *Expository Lectures on the Epistle to the Hebrews*.

Day 242   Psalm 103:1-5

Do not forget his benefits

Bishop Horne calls this an 'evangelical and most comfortable Psalm'. Spurgeon writes, 'There is too much in the Psalm for a thousand pens to write, it is one of the most all-comprehending Scriptures, which is a Bible in itself, and it might alone suffice for the hymn-book of the Church'.[1]

In these opening verses, David is speaking to his own soul. He is reminding himself of God's goodness and mercy. He recounts what the LORD has done for him, and urges his soul to give a response of praise.

In a busy world, how rarely do we take time to ponder God's dealings with us, and all that he has done for us. How easily does a dull and prayerless spirit dominate our lives! This opens the way for us to disobey the LORD and to give way to temptations, because we forget how much we owe him, and all the tokens of his care.

Take a little time to ponder over these five verses and make them personal to you; then sing them with heartfelt conviction. Sing them in battle against spiritual coldness, so that you may be stirred up and refreshed in your walk with God. This Psalm was sung by James Renwick, the last martyr of the persecuted Covenanters, at the place of his execution. May our dying breath also recount the mercies of the LORD to our souls.

---

[1] C.H. Spurgeon, *The Treasury of David*.

Day 243   Psalm 103:6-13

Abounding in love: Plenteous in mercy

Mercy, mercy, mercy is the subject of these verses. God's loving-kindness shines through every line. He defends the cause of the oppressed. He made known his ways to a rebellious people. He sets limits upon his righteous anger. He does not deal with us according to our sins. His mercy is as high as the heavens above. He has removed our transgressions as far as the east is from the west from us. And why is he merciful? Is it that we deserved it? No. Is it that God needed to find some to reward? No, he us utterly sufficient in himself. It is because he has a fatherly compassion on us as his children (v13).

The psalmist declares these things; and are our hearts unmoved? Sinner, will you not venture on such a God who is the overflowing fountain of all good? Backslider, will you not return with tears to such a father who will run to meet you as to a prodigal from a far country. Believer oppressed and perplexed by misfortunes that you cannot understand – he will not chide forever. Christian soldier struggling in the battle for truth under the accusations and fiery darts of the Evil One – none of his accusations can stand, for God has removed your transgressions from you.

Let us sing with glad hearts this celebration of God's mercy.

Day 244   Psalm 103:14-18

Forgotten flowers, but measureless mercy

This passage reminds us of the frailty and mortality of man. 'As for man, his days are like grass; as a flower of the field, so he flourishes. For the wind passes over it, and it is gone, and its place remembers it no more'. (v15, 16).   Although we often forget, in our preoccupation with pleasure and ambitions, God remembers we are dust (v14).

'But' – what a glorious 'but' – 'the mercies of the LORD are from everlasting to everlasting upon them that fear him' (v17 and 18). The words of C.T. Studd come to mind, 'he is no fool who gives up what he cannot keep, to gain what he cannot lose'. Fearing and obeying God may cost us dearly in a world that is intent to eat, drink and be merry, but we shall afterwards enjoy God's mercy from everlasting to everlasting.

The covenant promise here is yet more precious on the lips of Mary – 'his mercy is on them that fear him from generation to generation' (Luke 1:50). He will cause our children and children's children to inherit our blessings. Is this not incentive enough to fulfil the condition that is given? – to 'fear him', to 'keep his covenant', and to 'remember his commandments to do them'.

May the wanderings and backslidings of our children drive us to greater faithfulness and fear: not that we can earn his blessing upon them, but because he has promised it (v17, 18 and Luke 1:50).

Day 245   Psalm 103:19-22

The praises of the heavenly host

The words of the previous portion may well have led our minds to think solemnly onward to death, and to giving account to God. For the psalmist, God's reign, rule, and judgment is rather a cause for rejoicing. He does not dwell on his own condition. His thoughts are taken up with the LORD. The LORD has set up his throne, and will truly rule and judge.

It is almost as though the psalmist marvels that creation can be silent at such wonderful truths. He urges the mighty angels to bless the LORD – surely, they will! Perhaps he calls upon those archangels most capable of praising our God – those who excel in strength, that do his word, hearing his very voice. He then turns to the ministering spirits and 'hosts' of the LORD 'that do his pleasure' – 'an innumerable company of angels'. He calls to 'all God's works', 'in all places of his dominion'. He lastly, as he began the Psalm, stirs up his own heart to bless the LORD.

We rejoice that one day the appeal of the psalmist will be answered. When Christ's work on earth began, archangels announced, and a 'multitude of the heavenly host' took up the song. They were only heard by a few shepherds. It will be different when all God's creatures greet his glorious coming with praise. Let believers join in the singing of this Psalm in preparation. These words were used at the close of the communion service by both Martin Luther and John Knox.

Day 246   Psalm 104:1-5

In the beginning ...

Bishop Horsley calls this 'a Psalm for the Sabbath Day'. It is a meditation on God's power and goodness. It celebrates his creation and providence, and it is therefore a good Psalm for the day that God gave us to remember his works (Exod. 20:11; Deut. 5:15).

As the previous Psalm, the writer begins by stirring up his own heart to praise the Lord. In verse 1 he commands his soul to praise God. As David says at the start of Psalm 34 'I will bless the LORD at all times: his praise shall continually be in my mouth'. Whatever the circumstance, he is determined that it should be so.

The inspired writer directs his praise personally to the LORD – 'O LORD *my* God...' (v1; compare v33, 34). He follows on with a description of God's splendour – as an encouragement to his own heart, praising God, and appealing to others to worship him too.

We have in these five verses light, the heavens, the earth, the waters, the sky, the angels, and the 'foundations of the earth' -all subserving his glory. There are echoes throughout of the account of creation in Genesis 1.

These words have been given by the Holy Spirit for us to use in praise. Let us sing them as inspired worship now.

Day 247   Psalm 104:6-9

Lord of the mighty waters

The earth is described here as a watery planet before the LORD caused the dry land to appear (the third day of creation - compare Gen. 1:9). It only took a word from God to move the mighty oceans. A momentary tremor can cause a tsunami. How great is the God who caused continents to emerge, and the waters to recede, at his word!

After the mighty outpouring of waters at the Flood, God once again set the limits of the oceans, and has promised never again to flood the earth as he did then.

This is the God who causes dry land to appear in the midst of the Red Sea that his people may cross over; who parts the river Jordan for Joshua; and who divides that same river for Elijah and Elisha.

We think of him who seemed to be drawn to the Sea of Galilee, whose company was fishermen, and who rebuked the waves, and they became still. And then, another time, when he walked on the waters, they upheld him.

Our God is a God who restrains things that would be harmful to us. He is a God who sets limits upon evil forces too, for the Scripture says, 'When the enemy shall come in like a flood, the Spirit of the LORD shall lift up a standard against him' (Isa. 59:19).

Let us worship God for his power, and for his care to us.

Day 248   Psalm 104:10-15

Wine, oil, and bread

The Lord Jesus said in John 14 'I go to prepare a place for you'. Creation is presented in this Psalm in a similar way. The earth was prepared for man. In his newly-made earth the LORD sent springs into the valleys – to give drink to every beast of the field – even for the untameable wild asses, to quench their thirst (v11; see Job 39:5-8). He makes provision for the birds of the air. He waters the hills so that the earth may be fruitful. He causes grass to grow for cattle and vegetation to serve man's needs. What a spirit of thankfulness should flow from this! Food is not produced by the supermarket. God lovingly provides it as a gift.

Different words are used for 'man' in the Hebrew, in verses 14 and 15. The emphasis in verse 15 is on man's weakness.

Three items are given as evidence of the LORD's special care for frail man in verse 15 – wine, oil, and bread. He provides not just bread – the staff of life, but wine, that can cheer the heart in sorrow, and oil that brightens the countenance. Wine, oil, and bread are all also spoken of in a spiritual sense in Scripture (see Acts 2:13; Eph. 5:20; Ps. 45:7 and John 6:33-35).

In the quaint words of Thomas Goodwin, the puritan, God provides for our 'strength, ornament, and delight'.

Day 249   Psalm 104:16-19

JEHOVAH Jireh – the LORD who provides

The psalmist continues his description of God's provision for the natural world in these verses. All creation is owned and sustained by him. Verse 16 refers to 'the trees <u>of the LORD</u>', and, although we should not become too taken up with 'the green agenda', we should constantly remind ourselves that the natural creation around us belongs to God. There is a sense in which this world has been given to man to cultivate and keep, as the Garden of Eden was given to Adam. God's eye is upon the sparrow (Luke 12:6, 7); not a single fir cone falls to the ground and takes root, but God plants it (v16).

His work in creation and providence is not random, but purposeful – the trees are to provide a home for the birds, the mountains for the wild goats, the cliffs for the conies (or rock badgers). Even the moon and the sun were created purposefully to set times and seasons for man (verse 19; compare Gen. 1:14).

Above all the turmoil and disorder that man seems to create in this world through his sin and selfishness, let us recognise in these verses that God is over all, and causes 'even the wrath of man to praise him'. And we look forward. What shall the New Heavens and the New Earth be like that he prepares as the Garden of Eden for redeemed men and women?

Let us sing these pleasant words, and praise our God.

Day 250   Psalm 104:20-24

Night and Day

These verses describe in beautiful language the coming of night and day (Gen. 1:16-18). The psalmist speaks of the beasts of the forest 'creeping forth' or 'prowling' in the night, of their retreat to their dens at the dawn, and of the daily cycle of man's labour. How distant from this daily pattern set by God are our urban lives, with 24/7 work and pleasure. God desired our time to be broken up; time for work; time to be with family; and, especially, weekly time for worship, and rest on the Sabbath.

If even wild beasts roar – 'seeking their food from God' - we too should acknowledge our dependence upon our Father and pray 'Give us this day our daily bread'.

The writer is meditating upon the fourth day of creation, but then thinks on man's place in it (v 23). He cannot hold back praise to the LORD for what he has done (v 24). He gives God praise that everything is from him and through him in this world. As we noted yesterday of 'the trees of the LORD', everything belongs to him – 'the earth is full of your riches', or 'your possessions'. To quote an earlier Psalm, 'the earth is the LORD's and the fullness thereof' (Ps. 24:1).

Let us praise God, who gives us richly all things to enjoy (1 Tim. 6:17).

Day 251   Psalm 104:25-30

The wonders of his providence

Here we pass on to the fifth day of creation's work - the seas. It is as though the writer is transported to the sea shore. He exclaims 'This, the sea...There go the ships...' Who has not gazed in wonderment at 'this great and wide sea'? The writer speaks of creeping things innumerable, and we are still finding new sea creatures more than two and a half thousand years after these words were written!

The author then returns to his theme, 'these all wait upon you that you may give them meat in due season'. We would do well to learn our dependence on God for things great and small. The Syro-Phoenician woman spoke well when she pleaded for help on the grounds that 'yet the dogs eat of the crumbs which fall from their masters' table' (Matt. 15:27).

In these verses we have dependency upon God for supply ('in due season'); for sufficiency ('you give them what they gather'); for satisfaction ('you open your hand, they are filled with good'); for solace ('you hide your face, they are troubled'); even for survival ('you take away their breath, they die') and finally in sustaining all creation ('you send forth your spirit, they are created, and you renew the face of the earth'). We can usefully ponder all of these things with a thankful heart.

Day 252   Psalm 104:31-35

Waiting for the New Heavens and the New Earth

The psalmist has pondered on God's merciful and plenteous provision to all his creatures, reflecting on the six days of creation. At the end of the sixth day God also considered his creation. He 'saw every thing that he had made, and, behold, it was very good'. So here the psalmist writes, 'the LORD will rejoice in all his works' (v31).

These closing verses look forward prophetically to the renewal of all creation. Creation now waits in groaning and in travail (Rom. 8:22). When the times of restitution come (Acts 3:21) he will look on the earth, and it will tremble. He will touch the hills, and they will smoke. He will cause sinners to be consumed out of the earth, and the wicked will be no more.

Then at last shall the long 'Hallelujah!' sound, when the New Heavens and the New Earth, in which righteousness dwells, shall appear (2 Pet. 3:13)[1]. Our longing is for the LORD's return; for earth's Sabbath; and for eternal glory.

Let us join in the words of the psalmist here. 'I will sing unto the LORD as long as I live: I will sing praise (literally: 'sing-psalms') to my God while I have my being. My meditation of him shall be sweet. I will be glad in the LORD' (v33).

---

[1] Rev. 19:1-5. The Psalm ends in Hebrew with "Hallelujah" – "Praise the LORD"

Day 253   Psalm 105:1-7

Raise his praise

This portion is the introduction to the Psalm, which recounts the history of Israel. The Psalm starts with short, sharp invitations - Give-thanks; call; make-known; sing; sing-psalms; talk; glory; rejoice; seek; enquire; remember. The writer is stirring up God's people from their passive and unresponsive state, to wake from their spiritual sleep.

Let us stir ourselves up in today. Take each of the psalmist's exhortations and 'meditate' and pray over them, for they focus on the works of God.

Who should be the focus of our thinking and praying and praising? It is 'the LORD' himself, to whom we have access through the blood of Christ (v1). It is 'his name' – all that God has shown himself to be in all his perfections. We should glory in the LORD because he has made known his holiness ('his *holy* name' v3). We should do more than praise him for what he is. We must make him known for what he has done ('his deeds' v1). The Psalm goes on to speak of 'his wondrous works' – 'his strength' – 'his face' – 'his marvellous works' – 'his wonders' – 'his judgments'.

This is '*our* God' (v7). As Israel of old, we too are '*his* chosen' (v6) – elect from before the foundation of the world. All his marvellous works; all his wonders; all the judgments of his mouth; all are for the good of his elect.

Day 254   Psalm 105:8-15

Covenant mercies

Our relationship with God is defined by covenant. He enters into covenant relations with his people. He makes promises to them that he never breaks – not even though a thousand generations should pass. He is always the same. He is always a faithful God. He calls us 'his servants', 'his chosen'. We are bonded to him, and only to him, for he is 'the LORD our God'.

David Baron wrote, 'This Psalm deals throughout with God's unfailing faithfulness to Israel from the call of Abraham to the Exodus'[1]. In this portion we have God's merciful care over a very small and insignificant number of people (v12); over a remnant with no rights; with no settled home (v13). He did not just care for them, he made sure promises (v10, 11). He did not just observe their fortunes, but intervened on their behalf – 'Touch not my anointed and do my prophets no harm' (v15).

The people of God must always remember their insignificance and dependence upon God. In the West, and in some other parts of the world, we used to expect the world to order things favourably for the Church. Not so now. Let us read *Foxe's Book of Martyrs* again. Let us read the stories of the Covenanters, and of missionary self-sacrifice. Let us bring ourselves back to appreciation for every mercy we enjoy, for the Lord loves and cares for us.

---

[1] David Baron, *Israel in the Plan of God* (on Psalm 105).

Day 255   Psalm 105:16-23

The word of the LORD tested Joseph

14 chapters of Genesis are summarised in these 7 verses. They narrate the life of Joseph. The closing words of the previous section –'he suffered no man to do them wrong' and 'touch not my anointed and do my prophets no harm' seem to be contradicted by Joseph's early life. But, in his life, and in ours, we must see the bigger picture. We do not yet know the end, and must trust God by faith. Far from allowing his people to be cast off, 'he sent a man before them' (v17). Joseph's life was planned with this in mind. Joseph himself later acknowledged God's goodness in all the trials that he endured (Gen. 45:7, 8; 50:20).

Will it be said of us, as it was said of Joseph (v19), 'Until the time that his word came to pass, the word of the LORD tested him'? Are we still waiting for a promise that God gave us long ago? Do things seem to be running contrary to God's promises in Scripture? Let us continue to be strong in the LORD. Let us still wait for 'the time that his word came', for often (as it was with Joseph), the darkest hour comes before the break of day.

David Baron writes, 'Like Joseph, we receive at the very beginning of our Christian career the revelation and pledge of our future greatness, but between the promise and its final realisation there is often a long and dark valley of humiliation to pass'[1].

---

[1] David Baron, *Israel in the Plan of God* (on Psalm 105).

Day 256 Psalm 105:24-36

What God did through Moses

These verses describe Israel in Egypt. Beyond all the detail of the LORD's dealings with them, and his plagues on Egypt, we see the over-arching control of the Sovereign Lord. The psalmist sees God as ordering and controlling everything.

The book of Exodus refers to what appears to be a natural population increase in Egypt and a reasoned response from Pharaoh, but here we see behind the scenes. 'He increased his people greatly and made them stronger than their enemies'. 'He turned their heart to hate his people'. God is in control throughout, and is able to make even the wrath of man to praise him[1]. In all their groaning and affliction, few can have realised that God had a great plan and purpose.

Does all seem confusion and contrary to God in the world around us? Do our prayers seem to be unanswered? 'The God of peace shall bruise Satan under your feet shortly' (Rom. 16:20). Let us believe it.

We have a God who is in total control. Everything obeys him knowingly or unknowingly. The word 'He' occurs again and again as the source of all that happened in Egypt. He did it all, from commanding the locusts to the smiting of the firstborn.

---

[1] See Ps. 76:10

Day 257 Psalm 105:37-45

They asked and God gave

Yesterday's portion was concerned with Israel's deliverance. Today's portion is to do with all the blessings that God showered upon them. They got silver and gold (v37). He satisfied them with the bread of heaven (v40). Water gushed out in the dry places of the desert (v41). He led his people with joy, and his chosen with singing (v43). They inherited the property and labour of others (v44).

Our deliverance from sin and the Devil goes beyond mere rescue. We are 'blessed with all spiritual blessings in Christ' (Eph. 1:3). The theme of this Psalm is God's wonders. Nothing is said of their sin or failings (this is recorded in all its unflattering detail in the following Psalm). Notice how God passes over all their weaknesses, and even delights in the opportunity that their unbelief gave to manifest his power. Can we not ponder over our past days and, without excusing our failings, marvel at the grace of the LORD in bringing good out of bad, and overruling to his own glory?

Verse 45 gives the object of all the LORD's dealings with Israel - that they might observe his statutes and keep his laws. These laws, and this obedience, marked and separated them out from all the nations. Saved by grace alone, we too are 'his workmanship, created in Christ Jesus unto good works, which God has before ordained that we should walk in them' (Eph. 2:10).

This God is our God. Let us praise him.

Day 258   Psalm 106:1-5
Keep judgment: Do righteousness

Psalms 105 and 106 are a pair. Psalm 105 sets out God's faithfulness, and this Psalm sets out Israel's faithlessness. However, it begins with a similar call to praise as the last Psalm. In the Hebrew, it commences with 'Hallelujah'.

We are to praise him for he is 'good', 'merciful', constant, and consistent ('his mercy endures for ever'), and because he is a God of action, who performs his will with mighty power ('his mighty acts').   He is benevolent, compassionate, and engaged with man.

God's nature and deeds demand a response from man, and we have this in verses 2 and 3. We should 'show forth all his praise', 'keep judgment', and 'do righteousness'.   In this, we will be strangers in this present world. As we shall see in the verses that follow, Israel failed again and again to give such a response. Yet a day is coming when it will be otherwise, both from Israel and from the whole world, for justice and righteousness are the characteristic of the times of Messiah (Psalms 9:8; 33:5; Isa. 56:1; Hos. 2:19).

Verses 4 and 5 conclude the portion with a request for personal faithfulness, blessing, and gladness in a day of apostasy. We may be strangers and pilgrims, but yet, by faith, we can enter in to all his promised blessings, and will one day share the glory of his inheritance.

Day 259   Psalm 106:6-12

We sinned: He saved

In Jonah 2:9 the erring prophet was brought to the realisation that 'salvation is of the LORD', and this is surely the message of these verses. In this description of what God did for his people in bringing them out of Egypt there is no human cleverness, or act of chance. Salvation is God's work, not ours. Here the psalmist simply confesses his sin, and the sin of his fathers (v6, 7 and throughout the Psalm). He then says 'Nevertheless ... God' (v8, 44). What a contrast to the preceding verses where he looks forward to rejoicing, glory, and gladness.

We must ever learn the lessons of these verses. Ours is all the sin and failure. Ours is the doubting, the lack of understanding, and the unbelief. His is the redeeming, and the deliverance.

God still saves 'for his name's sake'. What does this mean? It surely means that it is in God's nature to save, that salvation shows his character and all that he is. The LORD still desires to make his mighty power known (v8).

Can we not turn to this same God, to our God, even on this day? Can we not bring to him, with tears, all our failings and disappointments, but come with fresh faith in his ability to save unto the uttermost? Let us pray with the words of this portion, and may we at length sing with thankfulness as we see his deliverance.

Day 260   Psalm 106:13-23

...But they soon forgot

There is a striking contrast between the last words of the previous portion and the first words of this one. 'Then believed they his words; they sang his praise', changes to 'they soon forgot his works'.

How often these words are true of us. Again and again in Israel, memorials were set up, again and again they were commanded to tell to their children; to bind his law upon their hand; to place it between their eyes; to write it upon the doorposts and gates of their houses ... lest they forget (Deut. 6:1-15). We need reminding, and reminding, and reminding of all that the LORD has done.

We must gratefully accept God's provision. Verse 15 is very solemn – 'He gave them their request; but sent leanness into their souls'. It is better to be denied what we want, if only our souls are blessed. Thomas Boston shows this truth very effectively in his book 'The Crook in the Lot'[1], by expounding Prov. 16:19. We should seek great things from God in prayer, and yet, at the same time, accept our lot if he humbles us, and in his wisdom withholds them.

The portion closes with a reminder of the power of prayer (v23). Let these words drive us to our knees in prayer for others in danger of wrath.

---

[1] Thomas Boston, *The Crook in the Lot, or a Display of the Sovereignty and Wisdom of God in the afflictions of men, and the Christian's Deportment under them,*

Day 261   Psalm 106:24-31

Then Phineas stood up

One of the differences between singing the Psalms and singing songs that are thought up by men, is that the Psalms contain teaching directly from God. Singing the Psalms leads us into new truth and new insight, rather than being a reflection of familiar truth. We are taught as we express the inspired word in song.

David Baron[1] states that this Psalm sets out the six great national sins of Israel in the wilderness:

1. Lust for food (v14,15 – Numb. 11 and 20)
2. Rebellion against Moses and Aaron (v16-18 – Numb. 16 and 17)
3. The golden calf (v19-23 – Exod. 32; Deut. 9)
4. Unbelief, not entering the land (v24-27 – Numb. 13,14; Deut. 1)
5. The sin of Baal-Peor (v28-31 – Numb. 25; Rev. 2:14,20)
6. The sin at Meribah-Kadesh (v32,33 – Numb. 20; Deut. 32:51)

In this portion we are introduced to Phineas, who is in some respects a type of Christ. He turned away God's anger and wrath [although by executing punishment upon another, rather than taking the punishment himself] and he was granted a continuing priesthood (v31; Numb. 25:10-13).

Let us be instructed by this Psalm.

---

[1] David Baron, *Israel in the Plan of God*.

Day 262   Psalm 106:32-40
Partial and pretended obedience

The Scriptures always speak plainly. We tend to romanticise about the past and to see things through rose-tinted spectacles. Not so the Word of God. Here the Holy Spirit shows the failings of the Israelites in all their ugliness.

The sin at Meribah-Kadesh was not the last of Israel's failings in the wilderness, but it was their climax. The meekest man in all the earth (Numb. 12:3) lost his temper. He was excluded from the land of Canaan. The Spirit of God was grieved (v33)[1].

This Psalm balances with Psalm 105 in showing human failure, whilst that Psalm shows God's mercy. These verses therefore pass over the glorious entry into the land, and turn again to the people's 'partial obedience', which let Canaanites remain there (v34-40). Let us ponder for a few minutes on this thought.

There is really no such thing as 'partial obedience'. We either strive to give full, total, and absolute submission to the LORD, or we choose our own way. We must take up our cross daily and follow Christ, or we will wander into ways of sin and failure. God knew the consequence of 'partial obedience' and therefore warned them in advance (Numb. 33:55). His commands to us are always for our good. God's way is the best way.

---

[1] Compare v7 and 43; Isa. 63:10; Ps. 78:40. See Dr Gill.
    However, De Burgh thinks the verse speaks of Moses' spirit.

Day 263   Psalm 106:41-48
They provoked, but he remembered his Covenant

The Psalm now tells that they were given into the hand of Gentiles (v41). After all the dismal events that are recorded, in the closing verses the writer raises his final prayer, 'Save us, O LORD our God and gather us from among the nations' (v47).

The Scriptures speak of 'the times of the Gentiles' (Luke 21:24). From the great world empires of Daniel's visions, through to the present time, Jerusalem has been trodden down. Not until the prayer of verse 47 is answered will the situation change. 'The Holy Place' - the Temple Mount - is still the site of a mosque. Jerusalem is still, in part, a Muslim Arab city. There have been repeated hopes of restoration, but the Lord Jesus said in Luke 13:35, 'Behold, your house is left unto you desolate: and verily I say unto you, you shall not see me, *until the time comes when you shall say, "Blessed is he that comes in the name of the Lord"*'.

The final verse calls on Israel to bless the LORD. This is the end of Book 4 of the Psalms. It is the concluding doxology. This one is so appropriate after verse 47.

Let us ponder the dealings of God with Israel. We see God's faithfulness to Israel despite all their failings. We can say, 'Amen' to that from our own experience.

Book 5

Psalms 107 – 150

Day 264   Psalm 107:1-9

O that men would praise the LORD for his unfailing love!

Although this is in a new collection of Psalms (Book 5), the closing prayer of the last Psalm, that God would gather Israel (106:48), finds its fulfilment in this Psalm (107:3). Bishop Horsley calls it 'A thanksgiving of Israel for their final restoration from dispersion'. This Psalm is therefore in the joyous context of Israel's redemption. The key to that redemption is 'crying to the LORD in their trouble' (v6; compare Zech. 12:10; Rev. 1:7).

Although the words are Israel's, we may appropriate them for our pilgrimage too as we wander, having no continuing city (v4; Heb. 13:14), beset by enemies, and hungry and thirsty. We look to the LORD to lead us by the 'right way' – to declare 'This is the way, walk in it' (Isa. 30:21). Let us learn the lesson of yet-to-be-redeemed Israel. Let us call upon him in the day of trouble.

Four of the five portions of this Psalm end with a call to praise the Lord's 'loving-kindness' or 'steadfast love' (AV 'goodness'). In today's portion this call is in v8. The last portion ends with a call to discern and understand his loving-kindness!

What a mighty God! His compassion is only equalled by his power, and his covenant mercy is over all. Let us praise him for it.

Day 265   Psalm 107:10-16

Out of darkness and out of prison

This section starts with people in a hopeless condition: sitting in a place of darkness and the shadow of death; bound in affliction and iron (v10); their heart brought down by labour; fallen, with none to help (v12). Worse still, their affliction is recognised as deserved affliction (v11). Therefore, they have no right to struggle to overcome their difficulties. They need to be careful in any attempt lest they should fight against God, because 'he brought down their heart' (v12).

Only one course of action offers any hope and any peace in such circumstances. It is to cry to the LORD. There is yet a door of mercy and help which stands open. We need to continue asking, seeking, and knocking - claiming the promises. We do not know how long Israel cried to God in their bondage in Egypt before the answer came, although he had already been preparing his answer by saving the infant Moses. We do not know how long Paul 'besought the Lord' before he got the answer 'my grace is sufficient for you' (2 Cor. 12:7, 8). The LORD hears, he delivers, he can break all bands asunder.

Only the LORD could break gates of brass, only he could cut bars of iron (v9). Only he could give release to the prisoner. Let us seek such deliverance for ourselves and for those we love. Then our response will be 'O that men would praise the LORD!' (v15).

Day 266   Psalm 107:17-22

Rescued from the gates of death

The affliction described here chiefly relates to sickness. Because of the way of life that was followed, those described here have brought affliction on themselves (v17). Those who turn to alcohol as a relief for depression find the depression deepening. Those who turn to drugs or immorality prove the word of the apostle, 'Be not deceived; God is not mocked: for whatever a man sows, that shall he also reap' (Gal. 6:7). These are empty, futile things that self-harm.

And yet there is a way out, even for those who have wilfully and foolishly brought trouble and distress upon themselves. It is to 'cry to the LORD' (v19). He is able to send his word and heal them (v20).

A.A. Bonar links the first three sections with the final gathering of Israel. He sees some coming from the prison house, and some coming sick and emaciated (the victims of the Holocaust returned to Israel in such a way), and so on. We long for Israel's final deliverance from all their distresses (v6). 'O that men would praise the LORD for his covenant mercy' (v21).

'Let us declare his works with singing', if not with shouts of joy (v22) – not just when we gather with other believers, but in personal praise and thankfulness.

Day 267   Psalm 107:23-32

Tempest tossed

These verses describe the experience of storm at sea. It is a dramatic account that calls to mind the shipwreck that Paul experienced (Acts 27), and the storm that the LORD sent after Jonah. Those passages could be profitably read alongside these verses.

Our God is one who speaks, and mighty waves arise (v23). Again, he speaks, and he makes the storm a calm (v29; Mark 4:39-41).

How is it with your soul? Are you buffeted and despairing because of the waves? Do you fear as the sea rises, or you go down into the depths, that this will be your final sinking? Remember, God commands the waves. It is for your good, as it was for Jonah's good, and for the good of those who travelled with Paul, that they might heed the Gospel. Remember too that the Lord Jesus' rebuked his fishermen-disciples for their little faith in their fragile boat. He has only to say the word; the storm will cease, and you will come to your desired haven (v30).

Bishop Horne likens the closing exhortation of this section to 'reaching our desired haven of glory where we shall praise him in the great congregation of saints and angels'. There the buffeted and troubled soul shall truly find rest and rejoicing with the saints of God.

Let us raise our voices in grateful praise.

Day 268   Psalm 107:33-43

The transforming power of God

This is a section of reversals. The LORD turns rivers into a desert (v33). He turns the wilderness into a fruitful place of pools of water (v35-38). He brings down the mighty, and lifts up the poor and afflicted (v39-41). The Psalm ends with the rejoicing of the righteous over what has happened, and the assurance that the wise will understand God's acts of mercy.

When the Lord intervenes, it is a time for reversals. In the days of the Christ's ministry it was the tax collectors, sinners, and prostitutes who found life, not the righteous Pharisees. When the Gospel was taken to the nations, the response was 'These that have turned the world upside down are come hither also' (Acts 17:6).

So it will also be at the last time, which is the subject of this Psalm. A host of parallels could be given to these verses. At that time ploughshares shall be beaten into swords. The weak shall say, 'I am strong' (Joel 3:10). Swords shall be beaten into ploughshares (Mic. 4:3). Fruitful Egypt and Babylon shall be destroyed (Joel 3:19; Jer. 50:35-40; Revelation 18). The desert will blossom like a rose (Isa. 35:1).

In this present confusing and discouraging age, in which 'all the foundations of the earth are out of course' (Ps. 82:5; Eccles. 3:16, 17), let us encourage ourselves that God's order will come (v43).

Day 269   Psalm 108:1-6

Waking the dawn

This Psalm combines 57:7-11 and 60:5-12[1]. It joins together the joyful and triumphant portions of these Psalms. It is titled in Hebrew and Greek 'a Psalm, a Song'. It is surely one of the 'Psalms, hymns and spiritual songs' that the apostle encourages us to use (Col. 3:16; Eph. 5:19).

The surpassing greatness of God in his attributes and in his person is declared, 'For your mercy is great above the heavens; and your truth reaches unto the clouds. Be exalted, O God, above the heavens: and your glory above all the earth'. Verse 2 is better translated, 'I will awake the dawn', this is either a powerful metaphor by the psalmist, or the words of Messiah himself who answers the cry of his people by bringing the 'morning without clouds' (2 Sam. 23:4).

Bishop Horne writes, 'He calls upon his tongue, with all his instruments of music, all the organs of the body, and affections of the soul, to unite their powers in sweetest harmony and concert and to awaken the sluggish morning with the voice of melody, sounding forth the glories of redemption'.

We can join in too. Let us 'awaken the morning' with songs of worship.

---

[1] In its origin v6 is from Psalm 60, we have included it in this portion as it gives the outcome of God's manifest exaltation in v5, which is the deliverance of those whom he loves.

Day 270   Psalm 108:7-13

With God we will gain the victory

This passage recounts the LORD saving and exalting his people, and putting down their enemies. We should discipline our minds to think of the Christian life as a warfare, in which we need the whole armour of God. We wrestle against principalities and powers, and spiritual wickedness in high places.

Whilst we can apply the principles of conflict and victory to ourselves, the passage refers to the land and people of Israel – 'over the land of Palestine I will in triumph go' (v9 Scottish Metrical Psalter). The whole land is included in the promises, Shechem to Succoth (v7, Gen. 33:17-20), i.e. on each side of the Jordan (Gilead and Manasseh, v8). This section should be read alongside Isa. 11:10-16, where we have Messiah's coming linked with possession of the land, and triumph over his adversaries. De Burgh[1] also helpfully links the reference to Edom here with Isa. 63:1-6, 'Where the Messiah, returning in "the day of his vengeance" from the slaughter of his people's enemies whose blood is represented as "staining his raiment", is described as coming "from Edom"'. Compare Isa. 63:6 with v13.

All the Lord's enemies, and all our enemies, will shortly be put under the feet of our blessed Lord Jesus, who shall reign from 'the throne of his father David'.

---

[1] Be Burgh commenting on Ps. 60:9 (108:10).

Day 271   Psalm 109:1-5

Hatred in return for my love

Acts 1:20 gives the key to the Psalm by quoting verse 8 as a prophecy of Judas's apostasy. In that context, we can understand the opening five verses as the words of the Lord Jesus in his feelings of grief, loneliness, and betrayal. 'When he was reviled, he reviled not again'. His tender heart was deeply wounded at his betrayal by his 'own familiar friend', who betrayed by the sign of a kiss.. He was not insensitive to the scoffing, mockery, and spitting, that followed.

There is a popular misconception of the patience of God, and of the meekness of the Lord Jesus, as though his forbearance and longsuffering can be taken for granted. We must always balance God's love with the words 'Be not deceived, God is not mocked, for whatever a man sows, that will he also reap' (Gal. 6:7). Mercy presumed upon will shortly call down coals of fire upon the head of those who are at ease in their sins (Ps. 140:10).

If we are opposed and abused by Satan and by wicked men, we should take the example of the Master in verse 4, 'But I give myself to prayer'[1]. We must turn our focus away from man and look to the LORD. There comes a point when we cannot, and should not, struggle against the wicked, but should look to the LORD alone to vindicate his own cause.

---

[1] Or 'I am prayer, nothing but prayer, - as it were, quite lost in, and identified with it' – Ewald, *Hebrew Syntax*.

Day 272   Psalm 109:6-15

Let him be condemned

These verses, which refer to Judas, are some of the most solemn in the Scriptures. The Lord Jesus emphasised this when he said 'Woe to that man by whom the Son of man is betrayed! Good were it for that man if he had never been born' (Mark 14:21).

Some have said that the words of this Psalm should never be spoken by Christians. Why then should we sing these verses? 1. This is a prediction rather than an imprecation. Bishop Horne translates most of the verbs in the remaining part of the Psalm in the future tense (compare Deut. 28) – 'his days shall be few...' etc[1]. 2. The verses demonstrate the hideousness of sin by showing its consequences. 3. We need to consider the author of the words. Although composed by David, the Holy Ghost spoke by the mouth of David (Acts 1:16). We must not disparage these words. 4. The prediction regarding Judas, the firstborn son of perdition, extends to Antichrist (2 Thess. 2:3 – compare John 17:12). 5. The sure word of prophecy should comfort our soul when the wicked prosper.

The words in the AV 'a wicked man' (v6) is better translated 'wicked one', i.e. Satan.

Sing these words soberly and thoughtfully and, 'knowing therefore the terror of the Lord, let us persuade men' (2 Cor. 5:11).

---

[1] v20 reads literally, 'This the reward of my adversaries' (there is no verb).

Day 273   Psalm 109:16-21
No mercy for the merciless

We have seen in the previous portions the identity of the person prophetically referred to – Judas - who is a type of the Antichrist. Here we have a list of the punishments that would fall on this wicked person. We are given the reason – 'because…' (v16). The punishment fits the crime. Such shall be the punishment of all the enemies of the LORD and of his Anointed (v20).

The phrase 'the wrath of the Lamb' (Rev. 6:16) is a strange one. He showed all the meekness and submissiveness of a lamb in his walk on earth when he was betrayed into the hands of sinners, but there is a time for his wrath, and that time is hasting on for all his enemies. He shall go forth with his vesture dipped in blood (Rev. 19:11-21). Let us urge all men to make their peace with the only Redeemer now. As Ps. 2:12 says, 'Kiss the Son, lest he be angry, and you perish from the way, when his wrath is kindled but a little. Blessed are all they that put their trust in him'.

We need not fear such dreadful retribution as is described in these verses, if we will but rest on his mercy. We can take v21 as our prayer, 'But you, O LORD, the Lord, deal with me for your name's sake: Because your mercy is good, deliver me'.

Day 274   Psalm 109:22-31

The Man of Sorrows

It has often been said that the Psalms take us beyond the Gospels in describing the inner spiritual life and prayer of the Saviour. So it is in these verses. His sorrow, his grief, and his agony were real. Therefore, he is able to sympathise fully with our infirmities.

The writer, giving words that Messiah could take on his lips, appeals to God for mercy. He is broken in heart and enfeebled in body. His sufferings are aggravated by the lack of sympathy and scorn of his enemies. De Burgh notes, 'When they looked upon me, they shook their heads' (v25) found its literal fulfilment in Matt. 27:39. A.A. Bonar comments on verse 23 that the declining shadow speaks of night closing in; and the locust being tossed up and down in the wind of the onset of the storm. Praise God, he endured both the night and the storm of God's wrath for our sakes.

Isa. 53:11 says, 'He shall see of the travail of his soul, and shall be satisfied'. Glory awaited him after his sufferings (Luke 24:26; Phil. 2:8). So at the close of this Psalm, after his sorrow is described, we have verse 30, 'I will greatly praise the LORD with my mouth; yea, I will praise him among the multitude'.

Let us think of our dear Lord Jesus as we sing and pray.

Day 275   Psalm 110:1-3

He is only waiting for the word

The New Testament quotes this Psalm more than any other portion of Scripture. We should therefore consider it carefully.

Its messianic character is declared by the Lord Jesus himself, who confirms the title - that it was written by King David (Mark 12:35, 36).

The opening verse is spoken by the LORD to the Messiah. He is given a place of authority at the Father's right hand, but is to wait not 'while his enemies are being subdued', but 'until the time that his enemies are made his footstool'. What is envisaged is not a gradual progress through Gospel preaching, but a dramatic intervention by the LORD himself. Then the call shall go out, 'Rule in the midst of your enemies!' The Deliverer, pictured as riding upon a white horse in Revelation 19:11-21, will go forth, and the cry will go up, 'The kingdoms of this world are become the kingdoms of our Lord and of his Christ; and he shall reign for ever and ever' (Rev. 11:15.

What a glorious day to look forward to! There are no 'ifs' or 'maybes' about the ongoing struggle. Our Lord Jesus is simply waiting 'until' the time appointed by the Father. How we look forward to his people (even Israel) being willing in the day of his power, in the beauty of true holiness.

Day 276   Psalm 110:4-7

Our Melchizedek Priest

This is a second proclamation, conferring upon Christ another office – a priest forever after the order of Melchizedek. De Burgh very helpfully points out that, although this priestly ministry commenced at Christ's ascension, these verses refer to an earthly ministry at his return. He will then truly be seen as the King of Righteousness (Jer. 23:5), the King of Salem (see Ps. 76:2 and Jer. 3:17), and the King of Peace (Heb. 7:1, 2; Psalm 72:7; Isa. 11:1-5). He will be a priest on his throne (Zech. 6:13). He goes on to say that Christ (as Melchizedek greeted Abraham) will meet and bless his people at their final triumph over the powers of this world.

Christ himself is shown as victorious over his enemies here. Verse 6 says that he will wound (or crush) *the head* [singular] over many nations, referring, no doubt, to Antichrist, whom he will 'consume with the breath of his mouth, and destroy with the brightness of his coming' (2 Thess. 2:8). De Burgh sees a further parallel between verse 7 and Samson's refreshment after a great victory (Judg. 15:18, 19).

There is much consolation and encouragement for the believer in these verses. Christ's power, offices, and glory are now hidden from those who do not receive them by faith, but the word will shortly go out 'Rule!'

We rejoice in this hope.

Day 277   Psalm 111:1-6

The works of the LORD

This is an alphabetical Psalm[1]. It is also a Hallelujah Psalm. It begins with 'Hallelujah' in the original. The opening verse gives the character of our worship - it is to be with our whole heart. The Psalm then goes on to give the place of our worship - it is to be in the congregation, and in communion with other believers. The remainder of the Psalm is then concerned with the object of our praise; first, God's care and providence; then, towards the end of the Psalm, in his saving work.

It is a song of Israel, who rejoice in God's continual faithfulness to his covenant (v5) and his giving them the heritage of the nations (v6), but the Church has much to share in this worship.

Although the works of the LORD are great, honourable, gracious, and powerful, we need to 'seek them out', and take pleasure in them, if we truly love him (v2). Do we 'seek them out'? Do we spend time in a rushed and godless world to think what the LORD had done for us personally and for our families? Are we diligent in praising him 'in the congregation'? Is our worship praise and thanksgiving to God, or something else?

There is a much for us in these verses if we will take time over them. Let us use these words thoughtfully and prayerfully.

---

[1] Lines start with letters in the order of the Hebrew alphabet.

Day 278   Psalm 111:7-10

The beginning of wisdom

This Psalm begins with 'Hallelujah!' (Praise the LORD) and ends with 'his praise endures forever'. This is, however, not just a hymn of praise. It has practical advice. A promise follows in the next Psalm.

God is faithful and just in all that he does (v7). His commandments are permanent and unchangeable (v8). Redemption comes from him (v9). He keeps covenant (v9). His name is holy and awesome (v9). Therefore (and here is the practical application) 'the fear of the LORD is the beginning of wisdom'. Everyone who acts in the light of this is wise, and shows understanding (v10).

Do we obey God's commandments? Do we accept all that he brings to our lives? In our darkest hours, do we cling to him as our covenant God who alone can redeem us?

When the world's wisdom is to keep our heads down, to deceive, to take the comfortable path, do we resolve to think, and speak, and act as those who fear God? (v10). It may not bring us 'success' in the world's terms ('good success have all they that do them', AV margin), but it will bring a crown of righteousness in glory.

Fear of God is not merely an emotion. As we are commanded to love (Deut. 6:5; Matt. 22:37). So here we are instructed to fear. Are we 'God-fearing'? If not, why not?

Day 279   Psalm 112: 1-4

Riches stored up at home

This Psalm is another alphabetical one[1], apart from 'Hallelujah' [Praise the LORD] - the title. The alphabetical sequence starts at 'Blessed'.

There is a strong link with the previous Psalm. In Ps. 111:10 we are told that 'the fear of the LORD is the beginning of wisdom'. In verse 1 of this Psalm the writer exclaims, 'How blessed the man who fears the LORD'. The psalmist explains to us what fearing the LORD involves in the second half of verse 1, for that man 'delights greatly in his commandments'.

Frequently in the Scriptures, the faithfulness of the parent leads to blessing upon the family (e.g. Ps. 103:17,18), and so it is here –'his children shall be mighty in the earth' – 'the generation of the upright shall be blessed' – 'wealth and riches shall be in his house'. We should love the LORD for his own sake, but can we not use this as an incentive to obey and serve God? Let us keep ourselves from sin for the sake of our children and for God's blessing on them.

Scripture speaks a great deal about 'headship', and how this affects those under that headship. The father is the head over the family, and the mother also has authority over the children. If Christian graces are sown by the parents, a good harvest will be reaped in the children. May all our ways be 'gracious, kind, and righteous' (v4).

---

[1] Lines start with letters in the order of the Hebrew alphabet

Day 280   Psalm 112:5-10

A fixed and trusting heart

This Psalm is well illustrated by Job – 'a blameless and upright man, fearing God and turning away from evil' (Job 1:1).

Job undoubtedly 'guided his affairs with discretion' (v5); his care for his children is shown in Job 1:5. The Psalm speaks of generosity to the poor (v5, 9); Job was able to say 'I delivered the poor that cried, and the fatherless, and him that had none to help him' (Job 29:12-16). The Psalm says 'He shall not be afraid of evil tidings: his heart is fixed, trusting in the LORD' (v7); Can any response compare to that of Job who, when he had lost everything, could say 'The LORD gave, the LORD has taken away. Blessed be the name of the LORD' (Job 1:21).

Consideration of the life of Job is also helpful, as it illustrates the mystery of God's providence, and shows that his blessings are not always evident or immediate. They are nevertheless sure. We will prove it, whether in the eventide of our lives, or when we pass into God's presence and know even as we are known. Paul confirms this in 2 Cor. 9:9, where he quotes verse 9.

It is not so with the wicked person (v10). He will not stand in the judgment. He will look on with remorse and lost hopes in the day when all God's ways are shown.

Day 281   Psalm 113

Praise the Name of the LORD

This Psalm commences the Hallel (Psalms 113-118).

The words of this and the five following Psalms were upon the lips of the Lord Jesus and his disciples in the hours before his betrayal and crucifixion. The 'hymn' they sang (Mark 14:26) was undoubtedly the required portion of the Hallel[1]. How precious then should these Psalms be to us. As they were to the Lord Jesus, so may they be a comfort to us, in suffering, and at the approach of death itself.

The longing of the psalmist's heart is for that time when the LORD will be praised from the rising of the sun to its going down (v3); we might say 'from the east to the west'. He waits for the time when the earth will be full of God's praise (Isa. 59:19-21; Mal. 1:11). His 'name' will be praised. He will be praised for all he has shown himself to be.

The LORD is worthy to be praised because he shows his mercy and kindness to those whose condition seems hopeless. The poor and the childless woman is spoken of here (v9). The song of Hannah (1 Sam. 2:1-10) is parallel to these verses. Our God is not just the God of the great and the good. He reaches out to helpless sinners. He desires that we too should do the same (Ps. 82:3).

---

[1] See David Baron, *Types, Psalms, and Prophecies*.

Day 282   Psalm 114

The sea looked, and fled!

The Hallel, of which this Psalm is a part, was sung at the pilgrim feasts of Israel. It is sometimes called The Egyptian Hallel. The words of Psalm 114 are particularly related to the Passover, when it was sung.

The depths of the Red Sea and the floods of the Jordan could not hold back the Exodus when God led his people. Although there were times it looked as though the outcome was fragile and in doubt (Exod. 14:10, 11; Numb. 14:11-20), Israel's return was unstoppable. God's purposes are unchangeable.

The LORD established Israel as a theocracy – 'Judah was his sanctuary and Israel his dominion' (v2). The theocracy ended when Nebuchadnezzar came. God gave him 'all the kingdoms of the earth' (Jer. 34:1, 2; Dan. 2:38; 4:18, 19). 'For the children of Israel shall abide many days without a king, and without a prince … Afterward shall the children of Israel return, and seek the LORD their God, and David their king; and shall fear the LORD and his goodness in the latter days' (Hos. 3:4,5).

And so it has been, and will be, until the time when 'according to the days of your coming out of the land of Egypt I will show you marvellous things' (Mic. 7:15-17). The throne of David, and Israel his sanctuary, will be the focus of the LORD's worldwide reign (Isa. 9:7).

'He has said and shall he not do it?' (Numb. 3:19).

Day 283   Psalm 115:1-8

They have a mouth, but they do not speak

The Psalms in the Hallel (113-118) are a connected series. 'Not unto us...but to your name give glory!' (v1) follows on from the preceding description of deliverance in Psalm 114.

As in Psalm 113, the LORD's name (v1, all that he has revealed himself to be) must be glorified, magnified, hallowed, exalted, and manifested. Unless we have a proper view of the LORD's character - mercy inseparably linked to truth - we will make a god in our own image (v2-8). Such a god may be approachable, easy to understand, and suited to what we see as our need, but it will be a false god. So are all the false gods of the 'great' world religions. So is the god of materialism and the god of pleasure. We must cling to the God of the Scriptures who has revealed himself to man: for he is a jealous God who will not give his glory to another (Exod. 20:4-6; Isa. 42:8).

An unbelieving and carnal world will not understand. They will say 'Where is their God?' (v2). This is not surprising, for the Scriptures teach that 'the world through wisdom did not know God' (1 Cor. 1:21). Jeremiah, in a chapter that describes the foolishness of gods that we make, says, 'Every man is stupid and is without knowledge' (Jer. 10:14).

We must return to the words that begin this Psalm. We must give glory to God's great name, not to ourselves or our vain ideas.

Day 284   Psalm 115:9-14
Trust: trust: trust

Three sets of people are spoken to in these verses – Israel, the house of Aaron, and 'you who fear the LORD' (so Ps. 118:2-4 as well). It refers to (1) God's covenant people, (2) the religious leaders (Dr Gill says 'ministers of the Word'!) and (3) all 'small and great' who fear God. Some Jewish commentators refer (3) to God-fearing Gentiles (compare Acts 13:16, 26 etc).

In contrast with those who trust in false gods, we are urged three times to trust in the LORD (compare Ps. 135:19, 20). We do not believe in a man-made god. "'For as the heavens are higher than the earth, so are my ways higher than your ways, and my thoughts than your thoughts", says the LORD' (Isa. 55:9).

It is through putting our trust in the LORD, and only in him, that we find help, protection, and blessing. Let us not go anywhere else, but only to our God. We either go through life relying upon our own strength and self-defence, or rely on the LORD as our only help.

The three-fold command to trust the LORD 'because he is our help and shield' is followed by a three times repeated promise of blessing. The promise is certain to those who will trust – 'he will bless us' (v12, 13).

We are thankful too for v14. These are covenant blessings. They are for us, and for our children (compare Ps. 103:17, 18).

Day 285   Psalm 115:15-18

Bless the LORD from now on ... forever

Some remarkable statements are made in these remaining verses. They refer to three places. (1) The <u>heavens</u> are God's dwelling place (2 Chr. 6:39). They are uniquely his, 'the heavens are the heavens of the LORD'. (2) He has given <u>the earth</u> to men (v15, 16). Is there not a modern echo of Gen. 11:4 in the urgent calls by Stephen Hawking to colonise other planets to safeguard the existence of the human race, and the plans announced by NASA in October 2010 to start a Martian colony towards the end of this century? (3) Verse 17 speaks of man's inevitable end, and, <u>a place of dreadful silence</u> where God's praise is not heard. 'This poor lisping stammering tongue' of the believer shall soon lie silent in the grave, until body and soul shall join again at the resurrection. But then, heaven will be a noisy place (Rev. 5:11-14)! All men should praise the LORD now. Our time here is unique and unrepeatable.

We are thankful that we have the comfort of the Psalm that follows 'For you have delivered my soul from death, my eyes from tears, and my feet from falling. I will walk before the LORD in the land of the living' (Ps. 116:8, 9).

O that we might commence the eternal song, and fill all our days with our thankful 'Hallelujahs' (v18). Let us not be silent, but sing God's praises 'from this time forth and for evermore'.

Day 286   Psalm 116:1-9

Return to your rest

These words are full of personal testimony and resolve to please God, because he is so good.

The Lord Jesus went to Gethsemane with these words on his lips. He endured Pilate's Judgment Hall and Gethsemane in the strength of them. He later said, 'Ought not Christ to have suffered these things and to enter into his glory' (Luke 24:26). How rich are the words of this portion when we read it as a testimony of our dear Lord Jesus! Though the 'sorrows of death compassed him', though 'the pains of Sheol got hold upon him', God 'delivered his soul from death' that 'he might walk before the LORD in the land of the living'.

And do we have no testimony to bring? We may at this time be going through great trial. Can we not command our souls 'Return unto to your rest, for the LORD has dealt bountifully with you' or rather 'For the LORD will complete his work in you' (v7)? Calvin discusses the believer's (and particularly David's) perpetual struggle with lack of trust during afflictions. He explains how we should deal with such doubts[1].

Let us return to our rest. He has given us the gift of faith, which will powerfully keep us in the fellowship of his Son and finally bring us to glory[2]. He will 'deliver my eyes from tears, and my feet from falling'.

---

[1] Calvin, *Institutes*, Book 3, Chap. 2, s.17
[2] Canons of the Synod of Dort, Chapter 1, Article 7. As
   translated in C.W.H. Griffiths, *Chosen – Called – Kept.*

Day 287   Psalm 116:10-15

My death is 'precious'

The remainder of this Psalm is taken up with thankful praise. As de Burgh says, affliction used rightly begets prayer, and prayer begets love to him who hears and answers it.

It is only faith that can sustain in trial, and the psalmist responds in this way in verse 10, 'I believed, therefore have I spoken', words which Paul quotes in connection with the suffering of the Apostles (2 Cor. 4:8-13). We must also say with the psalmist that 'all men are liars' [or, literally, 'a lie'], and put no trust in them. An old tract of advice to young Christians therefore says, 'Never take your Christianity from Christians and argue that because such and such people do so and so, that, therefore *you* may' (2 Cor. 10:12). 'Let God be true, but every man a liar' (Rom. 3:4).

'Precious in the sight of the LORD is the death of his saints' (v15) was the text at my father's funeral. Spurgeon says of this verse, 'They shall not die prematurely; they shall be immortal till their work is done; and when their time shall come to die, then their deaths shall be precious. The Lord watches over their dying beds, smoothes their pillows, sustains their hearts, and receives their souls'[1].

Let us therefore praise him while we live.

---

[1] C.H. Spurgeon, *Treasury of David.*

Day 288   Psalm 116: 16-19

Heartily willing and ready

The remaining verses of this Psalm confirm the writer's intention to publicly perform his vows, and to make public confession of his love to his Lord. He is determined to make it 'in the presence of all his people', 'the courts of the LORD's house', even 'in Jerusalem' (v18, 19). We may see the comfort of such words as these to the Lord Jesus as he sang this 'hymn' (Matt. 26:30) and went out into Gethsemane at night. Truly he paid his vows in full. In verse 16 the writer calls himself not just a servant, but a mere son of a servant (compare Ps. 86:16 and Luke 1:38). Those words are true, for 'he took upon him the form of a servant ... and became obedient, unto death, even the death of the cross' (Phil. 2:7).

He knows all our days, our birth day and our death day. He has called us to his service. Shall we not confess him openly, whatever the cost? We have been bought with a price; we have vowed to serve him. Let us take up that responsibility and publicly own him. Let us be found in the courts of the LORD's house, and let us serve him there.

May our testimony be the response of the Heidelberg Catechism, 'He also assures me of eternal life, and makes me heartily willing and ready from now on to live for him'.[1]

---

[1] *Heidelberg Catechism*, Lord's Day 1, Question 1.

Day 289   Psalm 117

The nations called to praise

This is the shortest Psalm. The psalmist calls out to all nations and all peoples to praise the LORD. The word translated 'nations' is the word that the Jews use to refer to the Gentiles. This call is to 'you Gentiles' (v1). The reason given for this call to praise is 'his merciful kindness upon us'.

As de Burgh points out, this does not relate to the time when Israel is cast off and God's mercy is therefore shown to the Gentiles, but rather to a time when believing and restored Israel is able to instruct the Gentiles on account of what he has done for them. The words may be translated literally 'his mercy has prevailed over us'. De Burgh notes the use that is made of verse 1 by the Apostle Paul (Rom. 15:8-12). Those 'promises to the fathers' which Paul quotes still await their ultimate fulfilment, as does, as, for example, Isa. 11:1; 'There shall be a root of Jesse, and he that shall rise to <u>reign over</u> the Gentiles; in him shall the Gentiles trust'.

The call for all the nations to praise God is not merely a pious hope; it is a command.

Let us now, whether Jew or Gentile, praise God for his great loving-kindness towards in the confidence that the truth of God stands fast for ever.

Day 290   Psalm 118:1-6

Everlasting mercy

Here we reach the last part of the Great Hallel. This was also sung to conclude of the Feast of Tabernacles. It is a rich and versatile Psalm.

The words of this Psalm have often been the solace of the heroes and martyrs of faith who have gone before us. The persecuted Huguenots frequently used it to open their worship. 'O give thanks to the LORD for he is good, for his mercy endures forever!'

The opening verse picks up the theme of Psalm 117 – the greatness of his enduring mercy. Nothing short of 'everlasting kindness', as William Gadsby calls it, would be sufficient to save guilty sinners, and to restore rebellious Israel.

We may indeed say, 'I called upon the LORD in distress (or 'confinement'}: the LORD answered me and set me in a large place'. 'If God be for us, who shall be against us?'; in the words of this Psalm, 'The LORD is on my side, I will not fear: What can man do unto me?' Well might Martin Luther write on his study wall, 'The 118th Psalm is my Psalm'. He wrote:

> *With force of arms we nothing can*
> *Full soon were we down-ridden,*
> *But for us fights the proper Man*
> *Whom God himself hath bidden.*

Let us then glory in the words of this portion, and place all our confidence in the mercy of our God.

Day 291   Psalm 118:7-14

It's better to trust in the LORD

Our last portion finished with 'The LORD is on my side; I will not fear; What can man do to me?' The psalmist continues in this confidence. He recognises and affirms that the LORD is on his side, helping him (v7). He therefore shrinks from putting trust in anyone but God. Man, princes, all the great and good of this world, may fail, so we do not put our confidence in them. He feels the isolation and threat of being surrounded by enemies – he cannot go backward or forward, this way or that way – it is like trying to get away from a swarm of bees (v12). And yet, each time he speaks of being surrounded, he goes forward in the name of the LORD (see too 1 Sam. 17:45-47). What a lesson for us!

On the comparison of his enemies to burning thorns (also v12) we may quote Calvin, 'They are quenched as a fire of thorns - which at first makes a great crackling, and throws out a greater flame than a fire of wood, but soon passes away'.

In our Christian warfare, we depend upon the LORD, but use the equipment for war that he has given to us (Ephesians 6). Then, in the spirit of dependence and gratefulness, we attribute all our victories to God (v13, 14). Let us encourage our hearts in the battle, for he is our strength, our song, and our salvation.

Day 292   Psalm 118:15-21

The right hand of the LORD

The psalmist was surrounded by enemies like a swarm of bees (v12), but his focus is not on man, but on the LORD. He is talking about 'the LORD' in these verses. He is the subject of worship in the dwelling places of his people (v15). His deliverance has been great (compare v15, 16; and Exod. 15:6, 12). The writer knows that he will testify to what the LORD has done for him (v17). He sees the severe, yet not destructive, chastening of the LORD in all that he has gone through (v18). He desires to praise God publicly among his people (v19, 20). He speaks in verse 21, not *about* God, but *to* him, in thankfulness for hearing his cry and saving him.

Can we not turn our eyes and ears from the hubbub, threats, and demands of a world in rebellion against God? Can we not, in the heat of the battle, focus our eyes upon our Commander, even the Captain of the LORD's host (Josh. 5:13-15)?

Dickson sees four reasons given for praise here (1) All the glory of his victory belongs to God, v14; (2) The certainty of our salvation purchased through Christ's sufferings and battles, v15,16; (3) The assurance of complete victory v17; (4) The LORD moderates all our chastisements, so that we are not destroyed by them (v18).

Is our tongue silent? Do we have no reasons for praise?

Day 293   Psalm 118:22-29

The Stone the builders rejected

We have so far considered this Psalm in the light of the believer's experience. However, the first verse of today's portion is considered by many to be a key to understanding the Psalm in a different light.

'The stone which the builders rejected is become the head of the corner', (v22) is applied to Christ repeatedly in the New Testament (Matt. 21:42; Mark 12:10; Luke 20:17; Acts 4:11; Eph. 2:20; 1 Pet. 2:4-7). The Gospels speak of Israel's stumbling, and their consequent rejection. They would not have Christ to reign over them (Luke 19:14).

But, verse 26 indicates that their rejection will not be final. A day will come when they shall say 'Blessed is he who comes in the name of the LORD' (see Matt. 21:9; 23:39; Mark 11:9; Luke 13:35; 19:38). They add 'we have blessed you', which is plural. We are told his believing people shall welcome the Lord with this verse at his coming with his angels and glorified saints (Matt. 25:31; Jude v14).

It is clear from these references that this Psalm refers to both Christ's first and his second coming: the stone's rejection and its final glory.

Should not these words be on our lips also, in gratitude and thankfulness for all he has done for us, and for the joy that is therefore set before us? For 'he has made his light to shine gloriously upon us' (v27; 2 Cor. 4:6).

Day 294   Psalm 119: 1-8.   1st Part

Walking in the law of the LORD

Psalm 119 is the great alphabetical Psalm, which has 22 eight-line sections. The lines in each section begin with a letter of the Hebrew alphabet – aleph, beth, etc. See the further notes on Psalm 119 in Appendix 7

Its great subject is the Torah. To translate the word as 'the law' suggests a legal system. The root meaning of the word is 'teaching', 'guidance', or 'pointing out'. The theme of the Psalm is accepting, and submitting to, God's revealed will for our lives. At the beginning our study, let us learn that 'no man shall ever have cause to repent of a sincere endeavour to obey God's revealed will' (David Dickson)[1].

The first half of this portion looks with longing upon those whose way is blameless, who walk in the law of the LORD, keep his testimonies, and seek him with all their hearts. Such purity and obedience were truly only evident in one Man, the man Christ Jesus. For him, acceptance of God's direction was his delight.

How can we attain such holiness? We know that our way is unsure and we are prone to slip, but God has given us his instruction (v4). Should we not ask for grace, and endeavour to obey (v5, 6)? We do not obey in pride or trust in ourselves, but confess our dependence upon God. Unless the LORD is with us, there is no hope of success (v8).

---

[1] David Dickson, *A Brief Explication of the Psalms.*

Day 295   Psalm 119:9-16.   2nd Part

Hiding the word in our hearts

This is the young man's (or young woman's) portion. It recognises the sullying of a life that can come in the time of youth, where things can be done that are long afterwards regretted. How can such things be avoided, or dealt with when they occur?

The answer is in verse 9. It is by governing all our actions by God's word. How important it is then to train up our children in the way in which they should go (Prov. 22:6; 2 Tim. 3:15). We cannot make them take the right paths, but we can ensure that they know the way they should go.

Verses 9-11 advise this sort of preventative action. The psalmist has taken certain steps, followed by an expectation that the LORD will confirm his desire and answer his prayer.

The remainder of the portion is taken up with the writer's delight in the ways of God. How close we need to be to Him before these words become our words! We need to spend time with God; we need to spend time meditating upon his Word and his paths; we need to praise and rejoice in his presence, before we can share the heart of the psalmist.

And it is not just the heart of *the psalmist*. It is the heart of him who said 'My food is to do the will of him who sent me, and to accomplish his work' (John 4:34; Heb. 10:7). May it be ours too.

Day 296   Psalm 119: 17-24.   3rd Part

Open my eyes that I may see

Can any one of us say, 'My soul breaks for the longing it has unto your judgments - what you ordain - at all times' (v20)? Do we have such a burden of affection to know and obey God's word that it threatens to break, not our back or our hearts, but our very soul? If, perhaps, we can say that we know what the psalmist means, can we say that we know what it is to have that longing constantly at all times? So it was for the Son of God, who rose up in the darkness before dawn to pray (Mark 1:35) and who, in the agony of the Garden, as he sweated great drops of blood, nevertheless lisped the words, 'not my will, but your will be done'.

Pray, pray, pray with the psalmist, 'Open my eyes that I may behold wondrous things out of your law' (v18). O to have such an enlightening touch, to have the veil lifted upon the delightfulness of knowing and doing God's will. We would then go out into a fallen world aware that we are strangers and pilgrims here (v19). How futile it is to try to ameliorate the world through social action when it is under God's wrath and at enmity to him. We should certainly not make it worse, but politicians, and those who use carnal means, cure one ill, but often make way for a far worse state of affairs (Luke 11:26).

We can only briefly touch upon the pregnant words of this portion, which yield fruit a hundredfold to those who will take time to meditate upon them.

Day 297   Psalm 119: 25-32 4th Part

A big heart for God

There are two parts to almost every statement made in this short section. Each step leads to another step. It is as though the writer is climbing a mountain. He is exhausted and therefore needs to be revived (v25). He has a problem with the route that he has taken and therefore needs fresh instructions (v26). He receives the LORD's directions; but he needs to understand them (v27). He is almost exhausted with his effort; therefore he desires fresh strength to stand (v28). He realises there are false and misleading paths; therefore he desires to be kept from them (v29).

He knows that there is no turning back (v30). He depends completely on the directions of his Guide (v31). He wants to speed forward if only he can be set free from his present difficulties (v32).

The psalmist is not proud and self-confident. He has a good conscience towards God and declares his sincerity. He is not pleading his own merit, but is asking God to vindicate his Name. If we depend upon God only, we leave the support that the world gives, and walk by faith. Such a path draws out the cries for help that we find in this passage. 'I will run the way of your commandments, when you enlarge my heart'.

We need 'larger expectations of God if we would receive more from him' (Thomas Manton. Compare 2 Cor. 6:11-13).

Day 298   Psalm 119:33-40 5th Part

The enabling God

The world speaks much of 'the rights of man', but nothing of 'the rights of God'. It praises the abilities, the achievements, the independence, the self-sufficiency of 'great' men and women. The world loves to proclaim 'I did it _my_ way', '_I_ am the captain of my soul'[1].

For the believer it should be different. His or her path is one of dependence. It is one of constant recognition of inadequacy for what is required of him or her. The paradox is that this is strength; for the true believer does not rest upon another weak mortal, or even upon religious traditions and forms. By resting upon the Almighty and All-knowing God, the believer can echo Paul's words, 'If God be for us, who shall be against us?'

Dependence upon God is the theme of today's portion. The psalmist pleads, 'teach me', 'give me understanding', 'make me to go', 'incline my heart', 'turn away my eyes', 'revive me', 'confirm your word to me', 'turn away my reproach'. In all the uncertainties of our lives, in all the unknowns, our position of greatest security is to be where God wants us to be, and doing what he wants us to do – 'in the way of his statutes/ decrees'.

Let us cultivate this attitude of dependence today. Let us learn from the psalmist as we sing his words.

---

[1] _Invictus_, poem by W.W. Henley

Day 299   Psalm 119:41-48. 6th Part

Able to answer

This portion is about speaking for God. In verses 41 and 42 the psalmist desires to give an answer to those who are reproaching him. He therefore asks for real experience of God's mercy and salvation. We have no answer to those who scoff and mock if our faith and walk with God is not real.

In verse 43, he wants to be able to keep giving testimony to the word of truth. He does not want his perplexity to silence him (cf. Jer. 20:9). Confession of truth is necessary to oppose evil and to build up fellow-believers, but it is very difficult to give in time of personal crisis.

Forgotten, unknown, young, and unlearned people, when God has met with them, have spoken boldly without fear (Exod. 3:10; 1 Kgs. 17:1; Jer. 1:4-10; Acts 4:5-20). So the psalmist says confidently, 'I will speak your testimonies before kings' (v46: compare v23).

If we have a vital and personal experience of God (1 Pet. 3:15, Isa. 50:4), then 'we cannot but speak the things that we have seen and heard'. Paul pleaded for God's help, but he also sought the prayers of the Church that he might speak - even as he [and we] ought to speak (Eph. 6:20; Col. 4:3, 4).

This portion is a prayer for singing. Let us pray and sing it now.

Day 300   Psalm 119:49-56. 7th Part

Remembering

In this portion 3 of the 8 lines commence with the Hebrew verb '*zakar*' - 'remember', 'recall', 'be mindful of', 'keep in mind'.

Firstly, the Psalmist asks God to 'recall' (v49) – not that God could ever forget, but part of the work of prayer is to bring promises before God, as though we would remind him of what he has promised. We are not told what it was that had 'caused him to hope'. We may have many things that give us cause to hope when we look back to a time when God met with us. We should bring such tokens before the throne of grace when things become difficult.

Secondly, we need to constantly remind ourselves of what the LORD has done (v52). Moses does this for the people of Israel in the early chapters of Deuteronomy. The name 'Deuteronomy' means 'the law a second time'. Augustus Toplady wrote, 'His love in time past forbids me to think in trouble at last he'll leave me to sink'. Keeping a diary of our spiritual walk with God is a good discipline. Re-reading such an old diary can be very helpful in keeping such incidents fresh in mind.

Thirdly, it is particularly profitable at night time for us to remember and meditate upon God and all he is, as we wait for sleep (v55). The confident prayer of Ps. 4:8 can then be ours.

Day 301   Psalm 119:57-64. 8th Part

My Sure Portion

We are often shown in the Book of Psalms a very personal walk and relationship between a man and his God. That is its glory where the speaker represents Christ. We are thus shown his hidden walk of communion in a way that is not often found in the New Testament, apart from occasions such as described by John in his Gospel. The words of this portion are very personal and almost every sentence begins with 'I'. In their fullest meaning, they can only apply to Christ. They are words of unparalleled personal devotion and commitment.

The opening line here is simply 'My portion, the LORD'. We may reflect on the dividing up of the land of Canaan to the Israelites, where each was given his portion of land. The story of Naboth shows how precious and inalienable that portion was to an Israelite. All that follows in this section stems from this opening statement. He is most precious.

We should desire unity and fellowship in the Church, in our homes, and in our marriage relationship, but we must, at all costs, maintain our one-to-one relationship with God. We cannot rest on anything else. Vain is the help of man! There is no substitute for a personal walk with God. Let us take for ourselves the words of this Psalm.

Day 302   Psalm 119:65-72. 9th Part

It is good that I have been afflicted

Spurgeon says 'Often our trials act as a thorn-hedge to keep us in the good pasture; but our prosperity is a gap through which we go astray'. He then adds, 'Where there is no spiritual life, affliction works no spiritual benefit, but where the heart is sound, trouble awakens conscience, wandering is confessed, the soul becomes again obedient to the command, and continues to be so'.

The writer of this Psalm has again and again asked the LORD to teach him. Here is the evidence that the LORD has done that, although not in the way that he expected (v71). We learn very little of God's ways until they are worked out on the anvil of experience.

This is often not pleasant, and it will do us no good if we are angry at the hammer, whatever that may be. We must look beyond the trial to God's hand, and to his heart of love, in what he puts our way. Hebrews 12:11 teaches us 'No chastening for the present seems to be joyous, but grievous: nevertheless, afterward it yields the peaceable fruit of righteousness unto them which are exercised thereby'. All our trials, every crook in our lot, is there for our good.

If we have experienced v67, then let us share these words with others who have broken hearts.

Day 303　Psalm 119:73-80.　10th Part

God humbles us because he is faithful

These verses return to the theme of affliction (v75). There are two new thoughts. Yesterday he reflected on the good effect that affliction had had upon him. Today he considers it from God's side. Firstly, he says God's chastisements are not unfair, but are carefully designed and well deserved. 'I know, O LORD, that your judgments (the things that you ordain) are right'. Secondly, the psalmist says 'you have afflicted me out of faithfulness'. He acts as our dependable friend who does not leave us alone when we go astray.

In his covenant with the believer, the LORD is committed to bring him, or her, to glory. He uses all necessary means to do so. 'The sight of his justice checks murmurings, the sight of his faithfulness fainting and discouragement' (Manton). Even if we do not know affliction now, we must prepare so that we may view a change in health, or job, or family relations as intended for our good. God's dealings with us are always 'just' and 'faithful'; cf. Prov. 27:6.

This portion is not so intensely personal as verses 57-64. In verses 74 and 79 he desires the mutual encouragement of 'those who fear you'. He hopes that his good testimony may make them glad, and he desires that they might come to him. Let us encourage others as they pass through the valley of affliction. It is better 'to suffer affliction *with* the people of God, than to enjoy the pleasures of sin for a season' (Heb. 11:25).

Day 304   Psalm 119:81-88. 11th Part

Like a bottle in the smoke

In earlier parts of this great Psalm the writer speaks of affliction as God's plan and purpose for him.

Here he describes the painful experience it has brought. His soul faints – the very life-force within him seems to ebb away. His eyes become dim from constant watching and weeping. He is like a wineskin subject to the blackening and stinging smoke as it hangs in the tent of the wandering tribesman, disfigured and maybe useless. He feels his mortality, and death following him, and asks, 'How many are the days of your servant?' The pathway that he treads is unsure, and evil men conspire to make him fall. He has a clear conscience and yet he is persecuted for things of which he is not guilty, 'They persecute me wrongfully' (v86 AV).

Yet, in all this, there is the confidence that God can reverse his circumstances – that he can be quickened and revived – and there is a resolute determination to be faithful to the end, 'so shall I keep the testimony of your mouth'.

These words speak of the life and experience of the Man of Sorrows. If we are called to walk in his path, it will comfort us that he has been there before.

Let us cast ourselves upon our faithful God to bring us through all our trials.

Day 305   Psalm 119:89-96.   12th Part

Fixed and settled in heaven

The theme of this portion is the continuance and perpetuity of everything that pertains to God. It is in sharp contrast to all that the previous portion said about the frailty, and precarious state, of the writer.

God's word – all that he has revealed to us – is fixed and unchangeable, established in heaven. There is no inner light, no insights from other religions. God's written revelation is fixed and final (v89). God himself continues, changeless, through all generations, always remembering to be faithful to his covenant (v90). The earth and heavens continue, because they are sustained by God's appointment and decrees (v91). The continuance of the writer under affliction has been due to the sustaining power of adherence to God's law (v92). The writer always remembers God's precepts, for by them he has found life. Casting his eye around him, he can see the limit of all perfection here - but God's commandment is limitless in its scope and effect (v96).

In his affliction the writer cries, 'I am yours, save me' (v94). The security of the believer does not rest upon human choice or decision, but upon the eternal decrees of God in election, which are 'forever settled in heaven'. Nothing shall separate us from the love of God (Rom. 8:35-39).

Day 306   Psalm 119:97-104.   13th Part

Through your precepts I understand.

This section lists the blessings the writer receives from God's word. The benefits are in the first half of each of the verse from 97-102. The means to these benefits are in the second half of each verse. The aim is 'to understand' (v104). The LORD's instructions (law, Torah, precepts, judgments, word, commandments or ordinances) enable us to be wise, and understand things.

Daniel was a man to whom the LORD gave wisdom and understanding, and some consider he was the author of this Psalm[1]. Certainly, as a young man, he sought to guard his way according to God's word, and the LORD gave him understanding (v9; Dan. 1:4, 17)[2]. Daniel was a great statesman, as Cromwell, Shaftesbury and others were. Our politicians are dangerously unwise if they do not live in obedience to God's commands.

Is this 'law' legalistic? Surely not! We obey God because we love him, because his word is the best guide through life – not to earn reward, or to escape punishment. 'How sweet are your words to my taste; sweeter than honey to my mouth', v103.

---

[1] See John Douglas, *Psalm 119: The Complete and Full Orbed Alphabet of Heaven*.

[2] We may helpfully compare what is written of Daniel with the words of this Psalm, as suggested by *The Newberry Bible*: v1 & Dan. 1:8; v11 & Dan. 6:4,5; v23 & Dan. 6:1-8,11-15; v95 & Dan. 6:4-6,11-13,15-17; v98-100 & Dan. 17:19,20; v110 & Dan.6:10; v121 & Dan. 6:4; v137 & Dan. 9:7; v153-168 & Daniel 6.

Day 307   Psalm 119:105-112.   14th Part
A lamp to my feet and a light to my path

This passage speaks of the believer's commitment, and determination to serve God faithfully all his life. It is about the surrender of our will to the LORD; a recognition of our covenant obligations to him.

When a covenant was made, a solemn oath was taken and confirmed by sacrifice (see Gen. 15). The psalmist refers to his solemn vow to serve God and his determination to fulfil it – 'I have sworn, and I will perform it, that I will keep (observe) your righteous judgments (what he righteously ordains', v106).

This is not a gilded path of easy and prosperous service – it is a relentless struggle amidst affliction (v107). And yet all is on the altar for God – not as a mere duty, but as a freewill offering (v108). He brings God's law continually to mind in his daily struggle (v109). Like Pilgrim, he is tempted to go into bypath meadow, but he does not stray from God's commands, even though that may make a difficult path. He sees his struggle as lifelong (v111, 112) 'I have inclined my heart to perform your statutes. Forever, even unto the end' (compare Matt. 10:22; Rev. 2:26, etc).

This is not just the pathway of a driven and strong-willed man. It is the pathway of every true believer; but it is with the constant help of the Lord – guiding our feet, enlightening our path, reviving and quickening, teaching, and causing our hearts to rejoice in his Word.

Day 308   Psalm 119:113-120. 15th Part

Not double minded

The focus of this portion is the relation of the psalmist to the wicked, who are double-minded.

The AV translates I hate 'vain thoughts' (v113), but Gesenius 'those who are double-minded'. The psalmist is utterly single-minded for God (v112). God is his refuge and defence against the ungodly (hiding place and shield v114). He rejects the company of evildoers (v115 compare Ps. 1:1).

He sees God's judgment on the wicked, and so makes God's verdict his own – for God rejects, treads down, and spurns those who wander from his statutes (v118). They cannot fool God. Those who stray will be separated from the godly like dross in the refining process (v119 compare Isa. 1:24,25; Zech. 13:9; Mal. 3:2,3; 4:1; Matt. 13: 49; Rev. 21:27).

In all this, he acts in the fear of God (v120). It is this fear of God, this awareness of God's holiness and just judgment, which should drive us from evil company (Prov. 1:7-19).

We are in the world, but not of it. We must always keep ourselves aware that we are the elect of God. We cannot go in the way of ungodly men. We have been bought with a price.

Day 309   Psalm 119:121-128. 16th Part

It is time for the LORD to work

How do we respond to the apostasy of our day - to the ascendancy of wicked men who seem to succeed in their opposition to Almighty God? Do we allow the prevailing evil to undermine our faith and commitment to God's Word? Alas, this has happened to so many who once stood for God's truth.

The psalmist reacts in the opposite way. Sure enough, he feels oppressed by proud ungodly men (v121), but he pleads for deliverance from that oppression. He prays to the LORD for a token (a pledge, a surety) upon which to rest his hope for better days (v122). He no doubt has head knowledge of God's word, but he desires to be taught (v124). He wants the LORD to be his Teacher. He prays for this 8 times in Psalm 119.

For him, apostasy and wickedness have gone far enough. He cries, 'It is time for you to work, for they have made void your law' (v126). Today men make God's law 'void' by acting as libertines, by demanding 'human rights', as if they were wiser than God. They deny God's authority, and the truth of the Scriptures (compare Exod. 5:2). Whether in revival or judgment, it is high time for God to work (Gen. 15:16).

These things drive the psalmist to God, not away from him ('Therefore…' v127), and to a resolute determination to honour God by declaring that 'God's precepts are right concerning everything'.
Can we say, 'Amen'?

Day 310   Psalm 119:129-136.   17th Part
Rivers of waters and streams of tears

In yesterday's portion the psalmist's cry was that the time had surely come for the LORD to work, because proud people had made void God's law (126). He ends today's portion with 'rivers of waters run down my eyes, because they do not keep your law' (v136). This may also be what he refers to in verse 134.

What can we do when faced with a similar situation, surrounded by godless people? We should start by meditating on, and living by, God's word (v129). We can seek more light and understanding on our present situation from God's word (v130). We should continue to be receptive to his commands (v131). We should recall God's covenant commitment to us, and plead it as our ground of hope (v132). We should keep ourselves in purity, so that sin should not have dominion over us (v133). We should pray for deliverance from this oppression (v134). We should seek a deeper personal communion with God, that he may 'make his face shine' upon us, and personally instruct us in his ways (v135). Lastly, there is a place for intercession – Oh that God would give us tears for his honour, and for the lost and disobedient (v136).

The response that the psalmist makes is not bitter or judgmental: he turns to God with a broken and a contrite heart. The LORD delights to answer prayers that grow from that soil.

Day 311   Psalm 119:137-144. 18th Part

Everlasting Righteousness

Three times in this portion, the verse starts with a word derived from the Hebrew word *tsadaq* – 'righteous'. God is infinitely righteous in himself (v137). His righteousness is unalterable and unswerving at all times, and in all circumstances ('everlasting righteousness' v142). His 'testimonies' – which witness to his righteous nature, attributes, and demands - are therefore permanent and unchanging (v144). He is in every respect righteous.

This view of the surpassing excellence and perfection of God and his word has a profound effect on the psalmist. In verse 139 he says, 'My zeal has consumed me'.   He feels the utmost grief at sinners who disregard God's word. All his desires, aspirations, and ambitions are set on 'glorifying God and enjoying him for ever'. His mortal frame, inadequate for such a task, is consumed in the undertaking. The burning purity of God and his word draws out his admiration and affection (v140). Despite his low outward condition, he continues to be conscious of God's holy commands (v141). Even in trouble and anguish where there is no outward comfort, God's commandments are his delights (v143).

Oh, for such an understanding, such a sight, such an acquaintance with God, that this might be our experience. Such a burning zeal was the character of the Son of God (Ps. 69:9; John 2:17).

Day 312   Psalm 119:145-152. 19th Part

Calling upon God

The theme of this section is calling upon God. The psalmist calls upon God with all his heart (v145). Such pleading can be costly and sacrificial. If we are to speak like this, the consuming passion of our whole heart must be for God and for his glory.

This is not routine or formal prayer. It is a cry to the LORD for his personal intervention, and for him to hear and answer with clear results. It is the prayer of Jacob, 'I will not let you go, except you bless me'. It is prayer with urgency and zeal – the psalmist is found in prayer before the twilight of the dawn (v147, compare Mark 1:35). Last thing at night he is filling his mind with thoughts of God (v148; compare Matt. 14:22, 23). These are not prayers in his head, but with his voice - strong cryings – because he wants God to hear (v149). In his entire tryst he feels the nearness of wicked men, and the nearness of his God.

The Son of Man wrestled in prayer as no one else has ever done, and these words are supremely applicable to him. He often prayed all night, or got up a great while before dawn, and what shall we say of the time when he sweat as it were great drops of blood in Gethsemane, or when he cried out in the noonday darkness of Calvary?

As we sing these words, let our prayer be 'Lord, teach us to pray'.

Day 313   Psalm 119:153-160. 20th Part

A prayer for Revival

The psalmist asks the LORD to 'quicken', 'revive' or 'make alive' three times in these verses. His first plea for revival (v154) is grounded on the LORD's word to him. We saw yesterday how the psalmist spoke to the LORD, and the LORD apparently spoke to him too (although not with audible voice). Our communion with God should be two-way. His word to the psalmist had caused him to hope (v49). For us, this will usually be through the written word (v25, 107).

The next plea for revival depends upon the LORD's pre-determined will (v156). We take this as an appeal to the LORD's order in the preservation of the believer to life. Compare Jer. 26:11, 16, where the Hebrew is literally 'the judgment of death'. AV translates 'according to thy judgments' here, but the word is used in a wider sense of a judge or ruler making a fixed decision (see v132 and v149, where the same word is used).

Above all else, our spiritual life and revival depends upon God's 'loving-kindness', or 'mercy' (Hebrew *ḥeṣed*, v88, 159) - 'shows mercy to thousands of them that love him and keep his commandments' (Deut. 5:10).

We cannot revive ourselves. God alone gives natural and spiritual life. Let us join our prayers with those of the psalmist. We too need a fresh touch of his Life-giving Spirit.

Day 314   Psalm 119:161-168. 21st Part

More than words can express

We may summarise this short passage as:

1. Great possession – found in God's word.
2. Unceasing praise – for all the LORD's righteous acts.
3. Great peace – to all those who love God's law.
4. Consuming passion – for the person and work of God.

This is a portion of superlatives. The psalmist rejoices in God's word as one who has found great spoil (v162), the warrior's prize on the battlefield. One version translates, 'a vast treasure'. The psalmist's praise is superlative. He praises the LORD 'seven times a day' (v164 compare Ps. 34:1). He, and all those who love God's law (his way and direction), have great peace (v165). The LORD's testimonies (his declarations about his person and character) are 'loved exceedingly' by the psalmist (v167, compare Song of Solomon 5:10-16).

The result of such a view of God, and of his word, is obedience (v163, 166, 167, 168). The psalmist walks with God. He can say 'All my ways are before you' (v168).

If the psalmist had such a view of God, and such stirrings of his heart, under the Old Covenant of types and shadows, how should we respond who have the fullness? Let us use these words to lift our hearts to God.

Day 315   Psalm 119:169-176. 22nd Part

Let your hand help me

These are words of one who desires communion with his God, and yet is conscious of all his weakness. He wants the LORD's hand to help and uphold him (v173). He desires that God would teach, revive, protect, prolong his life, and rescue him from persecutions and trials; that his lips should pour out praise (v171; that he may speak and witness[1] for God (v172). How many years do we have left of our lives? Do we desire to do greater things for God? Do we want the Lord to still give opportunity for service (1 Cor. 16:9; 2 Cor. 2:12; Col. 4:3; Rev. 3:8)?

David Dickson writes, 'If God delay to answer us in this petition or in any other, or seem to hide himself from us, let us follow hard after him with earnest supplication, as the psalmist teaches us – "let my cry come near before you, O LORD". The promises of God's word are sufficient to give us breath in crying, hope to have a good answer, and patience till it come – "Give me understanding according to your word"'

As we close this great Psalm, may our experience be that of Henry Martyn, who once wrote in his diary 'in the evening I grew better by reading Psalm 119, which generally brings me into a spiritual frame of mind ... by reading some of
Psalm 119, and prayer, I recovered'[2].

---

[1] Hebrew lexicons, followed by modern versions, translate 'sing' here, as the primary meaning of the Hebrew word.

[2] Henry Martyn, *Journal*.

Day 316   Psalm 120.
Song of Ascents (1)
Too long with those who hate peace

Commentators give different explanations of why these fifteen Psalms were given the title 'Song of Ascents'. The most likely (confirmed by internal evidence, e.g. Ps. 122:4) is that they were on the pilgrim journeys of the Jews to Jerusalem for their great annual festivals.

'There is a strong prophetic vein running through this "Little Psalter" – that they speak chiefly of a time yet future, and describe some of the steps by which Israel will *ascend* out of the valley of national apostasy and humiliation up to the Mount of God in order to catch his glory and reflect it on the nations around'. [1]

In this first Psalm of Ascents, the writer sorrows that he sojourns in the distant regions of the North (Mesech) and lives an unsettled life in the far South (in tents in Kedar). He seems to be expressing sorrow at Israel's dispersion from their land and Temple. He does not find himself in friendly company, but where lying, deceitful, false, and piercing words are the order of the day, and where, although he seeks peace, those he dwells with are bent on depriving him of peace.

Such has been the lot of the Jews down the centuries. Let us pray for the peace and salvation of that troubled nation as we take up this refrain. As believers we are all 'strangers and pilgrims'.

---

[1] David Baron, *Types, Psalms, and Prophecies*.

Day 317 Psalm 121.

Song of Ascents (2)

Kept by the power of God

Almost every line of this short Psalm breathes an awareness of the all-embracing protection of the LORD. The Hebrew word 'preserve' is used six times in this Psalm[1]. The Psalm starts as a personal prayer. It then gives encouragement and teaching – verse 3 changes to the second person singular ('your' = 'thy'). The description of the LORD as 'He who keeps Israel' (v4) indicates that these verses are addressed to Israel as a nation, although we may take them for our comfort.

The LORD sends help to those who look to him for aid. He is all-powerful as the Creator of heaven and earth, and yet his care is personal and tender – 'He will not allow your foot to be moved'. He does not slumber, nor grow weary from his constant personal care. He is beside us, even to protect us from the burning sun or the glare of the moon. He guards us from the unimaginable malice of the Evil One. All our movements and actions are within the safety of his constant, tender watchfulness. I recall that, in the entrance hall of my parents' house, there was an old, framed, silk-embroidery of verse 8 – a comfort to them, and a warning to burglars!

Let us take comfort from these words.

---

[1] Hebrew *šamar*. *Young's Literal Translation* translates the word uniformly.

Day 318   Psalm 122.

Song of Ascents of David (3)

Going up to the house of the LORD

After the initial encouragement to worship in verse 1, 'Jerusalem, the city of God' is the focus of this Psalm. 'For there are set thrones of judgment, the thrones of the house of David' (v5). This does not refer to a court, dealing with legal issues, but to the whole administration and the exercise of righteous judgment that is ascribed to the Messiah[1].

The use of the plural *thrones* is instructive. David may have had seats or thrones of justice for his kinsmen to assist him in his work as chief judge (2 Sam. 15:1-4). However, we look forward to the time when the saints will judge the world and reign with Christ (Matt. 19:28; Rev. 3:21 and 20:4)[2].

Since Augustine, the Church has applied this Psalm to itself as 'the City of God'. The joys of fellowship, and the kingship of our Saviour, render it easily applicable, but the Church lacks the unity, prosperity, and peace spoken of here. The misinterpretation fed the Popes' delusions of grandeur. The correct interpretation is to Jerusalem's promised blessing (see Isa. 60).

We will share Israel's blessing, and the fulfilment of these things in the age to come.

---

[1] Ps. 9:7,8; Isa. 9:7; Jer. 23:5. Hebrew *mišpaṭ*, 'judgment', is paraphrased here by Bishop Horsley as 'The settled plan by which God will finally judge the world'.

[2] See de Burgh on this Psalm.

Day 319   Psalm 123.

Song of Ascents (4)

Lifting up our eyes to God

In this Psalm, the writer gazes expectantly to the LORD, longing that he may show mercy to his people. He is looking for the least indication of the LORD's response to his heartfelt longing. The picture is of a domestic servant who waits for the slightest gesture of his master – it is not even necessary for him to say a word – just to demonstrate his favourable response. The servant is in entire submission to, and dependence on, his master.

In outward condition, the believer is often in great difficulty and contempt. The scorn of the last days will be 'Where is the promise of his coming?' Twice the writer says that he, and his people, are 'filled' with the scorn of proud men who find life easy (v3, 4). He could not take any more. He had had enough. Often, we do not pray real prayers until we reach this point; the point at which we acknowledge that we are at an end of ourselves.

We should not pray, and then forget our prayers. Our eyes should be lifted up. Our eye should be upon the hand of our Lord *until* – that is persistence – *until* the LORD gives answer and relief. We will then say with thankfulness 'my cup runs over!' – I am 'filled' - with good things. Let us so wait upon him.

Day 320   Psalm 124.

Song of Ascents of David (5)

If God be for us, who can be against us?

This Psalm of David bursts forth in a joyous celebration of the LORD's deliverance from impossible difficulties, when all seemed lost. We would place this, as a prophecy, with the closing chapters of Zechariah, when the spirit of grace and supplications is poured upon Israel, and the nation is restored and delivered.

Vivid metaphors are used here to describe the desperate state of the people of God:

5. Threatened as by murderous cannibals (v3).
6. Drowning in floods of waters (v4, 5).
7. Hunted by savage animals (v6).
8. A bird caught in a hunter's trap (v7, 55:6-8).

This Psalm was used annually at Geneva in Reformation times to celebrate God's deliverance, (the Scottish Psalter gives a version to the Genevan tune). This, and Psalm 125, were set Psalms for an annual thanksgiving service that used to take place in all Church of England Churches on 5th November to celebrate the failure of the Gunpowder Plot and the arrival of King William on that day[1]. Let us sing it celebrate our deliverance from the Evil One's power.

O for a further deliverance in our day.

---

[1] The Psalm was the subject of an exposition by the puritan Daniel Dike entitled, *Comfortable Sermons upon the CXXIIII Psalme. Being thankefull Remembrances for God's wonderful deliverance of us from the late Gunpowder-Treason.*

Day 321   Psalm 125.

Song of Ascents (6)

As firm and secure as Mount Zion

The previous Psalm describes the grave dangers that Israel had faced. This Psalm speaks of them having arrived to a place of safety and security. The LORD's protection of them, like the mountains around about Jerusalem, is 'for ever' (v1, 2). It proclaims the 'Peace-upon-Israel time' (v5). There is no verb in the Hebrew (see Psalms 122:6-8; 128:6).

David Dickson, the puritan, helpfully suggests that the psalmist gives four arguments 'to confirm the faith of the believer, persecuted and oppressed by the wicked, that he may hold out, walking in the straight way of God's obedience'[1]. These are:

1. The preservation of the believer and the stability of his blessedness depend upon God (v1, 2).

2. Our time of trouble is short, and limited by God (v3).

3. However it seems now, it will appear afterwards that God is doing good to us and for us (v4).

4. God will judge hypocrites who seek to free themselves from troubles by unlawful means (v5).

Let us reflect on these things.

---

[1] David Dickson, *A Brief Explication of the Psalms*.

Day 322   Psalm 126.

Song of Ascents (7)

The LORD has done great things for us!

We continue upward with the Songs of Ascents, which the Latin Vulgate calls 'stair songs'.

This is a joyful and exultant Psalm. At first sight it may seem to be about the return of the Jews from Captivity in the time of Ezra and Nehemiah, and therefore a late post-Exilic Psalm. We must however bear in mind the prophetic nature of these Songs of Ascents. In this light, we see the final and joyful restoration and return of Israel (Compare Deut. 30:3). The cry of this Psalm is 'Turn again our captivity as the streams of the South' (v4). The autumn rains result in a radical change to the arid Negev.

The Scripture assures the believer that 'eye has not seen, nor ear heard, neither have entered into the heart of man the things which God has prepared for them that love him' (1 Cor. 2:9; see Isa. 64). Let us not listen to the voice of scoffers and doubters. Let us believe, for one day the reality will be beyond our wildest dreams (v1).

Good seed must to be sown with tears. The Lord's parable of the Sower shows that it will not be readily received - but there will be a day of harvest. Let us sing these words, in tears maybe, but with this joyful hope.

Day 323   Psalm 127.

Song of Ascents for Solomon (8)

House-building with God

This Psalm is titled 'for', or 'of', Solomon. The writer's reference to the vanity of human effort without God (v1) echoes the constant refrain of the Book of Ecclesiastes. If it is associated with Solomon, we may conclude that the building of the LORD's House (v1) refers to the task of building the Temple, which was committed to him[1].

Without God, man's best efforts and achievements are all doomed to failure (v1, Gen. 11:1-9 – Babel; Revelation 18 – Babylon). 'God's work' can only be carried out in accordance with his will (2 Sam. 7 – David could not build the Temple). However weak his servants may be, God's work must only be done in his way (Ezra 4:1-3 – rebuilding after the Exile).

We may apply what this Psalm says about 'building the house' to our home life. 'House' is more than bricks and mortar (Josh. 24:15). True family worship is essential as we build. As we build families that love and obey the LORD, we must confess our inability to achieve anything unless the LORD works. We must cast our anxious care upon him (v3). Just as the natural birth of our children is God's gift (v4), so is their spiritual birth. We must depend on him, and claim his covenant promises (Ps. 103:17, 18; Acts 2:39)

---

[1] Note v2, his beloved (Hebrew *yedido*). Yedidiah (Beloved of the LORD) was the name given to Solomon (2 Samuel 12:25).

Day 324   Psalm 128.

Song of Ascents (9)

Blessed is each one that fears the LORD

This Psalm declares the happiness of the man who fears the LORD and who walks in obedience to his commands. It makes a direct link between the obedience of the believer and domestic contentment. This Psalm was sung at the end of marriage services at Geneva in Calvin's time.

Whilst the God-fearing believer should indeed seek first the Kingdom of God and leave other cares safely with the LORD, the promise of this Psalm is not always fulfilled for him. Indeed, he is warned in the New Testament that he may need to leave wife, children, and home for the Gospel's sake (Matt. 19:29), and that children may deliver up their faithful parents to suffer under the ungodly (Matt. 10:21). This was the experience of the godly Scottish Covenanters during 'the killing times'.

De Burgh gives the prophetic key to understanding this Psalm. It is in verses 4 and 5, with their reference to the blessing of Jerusalem. It will be fulfilled in its literal sense by Israel when they shall be restored (compare Isa. 65:18-23; Zech. 3:9, 10; 8:4, 5).

It is a good thing to fear the LORD and to walk in his ways. Let us seek this with all our hearts, and leave the outcomes with him who loves to bless us - his children.

Day 325   Psalm 129.

Song of Ascents (10)

The wicked will not win

The psalmist speaks for afflicted Israel. He begins suddenly, and abruptly, overburdened with more afflictions than he can number, but the glorious truth is also here – 'Yet they have not prevailed against me!' The 'youth' of Israel, and of the Church, were years of severe trial. The hatred and malice of the wicked have been against God's people 'many times' – too many to number – and yet the Lord at length cuts asunder the cords that bind the victim. As Spurgeon says, 'Never has God used a nation to chastise his Israel without destroying that nation when the chastisement has come to a close'[1].

We do not find the expression 'them that hate Zion' (v5) anywhere else in Scripture. We believe that it represents that quintessential hatred for God's people that will show itself in the last times (see Ps. 83:4; Mic. 4:11-13; Rev. 20:9).

Dear believer, are you at this time bowed down, with the furrows of affliction deep and long upon your back? Look to him who will preserve you. May you yet say the triumphant 'But yet they have not prevailed!' (v2). Let us sing these words in confident hope.

---

[1] C.H. Spurgeon, *The Treasury of David*.

Day 326   Psalm 130.

Song of Ascents (11)

A cry from the depths

Psalm 129 and 130 are a pair. The Psalm 129 speaks of Israel's outward deliverance and Psalm 130 speaks of Israel's inward deliverance[1].

This Psalm very movingly expresses hope in the LORD's forgiving love. It rises 'from the depths of anguish to the heights of assurance': 'faith pleads in the face of conscious unworthiness' (Spurgeon). The writer speaks to himself about his longing for the LORD to come and meet his need. Then he shares his faith and trust with others, particularly with Israel.

Dr Gill comments on verse 4 that, if there were no forgiveness, men might have dread of God, like devils, but would have no godly childlike fear grounded on a hope of forgiveness[2]. As we seek forgiveness, let us walk in his fear.

Martin Luther loved this Psalm. It is one of his four 'Paul's Psalms' i.e. Psalms that taught Paul's Gospel of free grace[3]. Luther's hymn 'Out of the depths I cry to you' mingles his own longings with those of the psalmist. John Owen's conversion was through the LORD powerfully applying verse 4 to his heart.

---

[1] David Baron, *Types, Psalms, and Prophecies*. He notes the emphasis of v4 - with you is the forgiveness - the great forgiveness, which is promised to Israel.

[2] See too Luther's comments on this, quoted by Perowne.

[3] The others are 32 ,51, and 143.

Day 327   Psalm 131.

Song of Ascents of David (12)
As a weaned child

This Psalm of David shows a childlike trust in the LORD. His humility and submissiveness are born of experience. He has 'composed and quieted his soul', and has been weaned from the vanities of this life (v2).

Thomas Manton, the puritan, comments, 'Though the weaned child has not what it would have, or what it naturally most desires, the milk of the breast – yet it is contented with what its mother gives – it rests upon her love and provision'. 'Children are in no care for enlarging possessions, heaping up riches, aspiring after dignities and honours: but meekly take what is provided for them'.

We think of the compliant spirit of David, the anointed king. He waited, tending his flock of sheep; defeated Goliath, yet slipped back into obscurity; persecuted by Saul, yet left his cause in God's hands until God's time; anxious to honour God by building a Temple for him, yet quietly conceding that honour to his son at the command of the LORD. And was not the same spirit in 'David's greater Son'?

O for the time when Israel too shall leave their self-sufficiency, and their salvation by works, to rest wholly upon their God (see Isa. 66:10-14). O that we too may be able to utter these words in childlike trust, and abandon the lust of the flesh, the lust of the eyes, and the pride of life (1 John 2:16).

Day 328   Psalm 132:1-10
Song of Ascents (13)

Unfulfilled desires

Alec Motyer[1] divides the Songs of Ascents into 5 groups of 3. These last three describe the pilgrims safe at home in Zion. Psalm 132: Zion is the city of the LORD and his anointed King. Psalm 133: Sweet unity is enjoyed by the Lord's people there. Psalm 134: The LORD's people are safe at last, blessing the LORD and being blessed.

This is a Psalm of David (Acts 2:29, 30). His 'afflictions' (v1) come from his desire to please and serve the LORD. David longed to see the ark restored, and a fixed place of worship (v3-6), where God would dwell. But those desires were not fulfilled, and the work he longed for was not completed until Solomon's day. Verses 8-10 were on the lips of Solomon in 2 Chr. 6:41, 42, and then, with the work completed, the fire fell from heaven.

Dear reader, there may be lost hopes in your life over which you mourn, and over which you could continue to mourn until the grave. Let us accept with joy the lot and task that the LORD has committed to us. Even though we may not see the outcome, let us still trust and pray. The LORD will surely complete the work he has begun, whether we see it or not.

---

[1] Alec Motyer, *Journey. Psalms for Pilgrim People: An Exposition of Psalms 120-136.*

Day 329   Psalm 132:11-18.

Song of Ascents (13)

Two unchangeable purposes

Two of the LORD's purposes are set out in these verses, confirmed by promises. A stream of 'I wills' demonstrate his sovereign power and confirm:

1. His sovereign choice of David to be, not only king, but the sire of all the kings of Judah, and of Messiah himself (v11, 12).

2. His sovereign choice of Mount Zion as his habitation (v13-18).

Our Jesus is spoken of in verses 17 and 18. 'Crown' and 'flourish' (AV) have precious richness in them. This Hebrew word for 'crown' (*nezer*) means not just a diadem, but the mark of kingship (2 Kgs. 11:12); part of the High Priest's head covering (Exod. 29:6); the head of hair of the separated nazarite (Numb. 6:4 etc, 'separation' AV); and holiness itself[1]. The Hebrew word 'flourish' is probably associated with the victor's laurel wreath. It has the meaning of flowering, and of shining[2]. These are evocative words.

He no longer wears the cruel crown of thorns (Rev. 19:12). Come, victorious, holy, Lord Jesus! Come, and reign!

---

[1] The Old Greek translates this phrase as "he shall burst forth (as a flower) with holiness".

[2] The New Testament also uses two words for 'crown', the kingly crown (*diadema*) and the victor's crown (*stephanos*).

Day 330 Psalm 133.

Song of Ascents of David (14)

Brotherly unity

These Psalms have indeed been ascents into heavenly places. In Psalm 120 God's people were scattered and mournful in distant regions. Here we find them together in blessed unity where the high priest and Zion's hills are, and where the oil and the dew of blessing are bestowed.

The blessed, brotherly unity of this Psalm will at length come for Israel, as prophesied by Ezekiel (Ezek. 37:15-28). Then Israel, returned and restored, will at last be one again.

The Church at Pentecost knew the sweet bond of unity as the oil and dew of the Spirit descended. Alas, as de Burgh says, 'division, not union is the characteristic of the Church'. Even the glorious Reformation began a period when division has been multiplied.

Sadly, the unity of natural brothers and sisters is not always constant, even in a Christian home. It is a source of sorrow when it is absent, but 'How good!' when it is present.

How our hearts must long for that united anthem of all nations and peoples and kindreds and tongues, of all the angels, when all creation joins in worship of our God (Rev. 5:11-14). Till that time comes, let us sing this Psalm in thankfulness for the fellowship that we do enjoy as families, and as assemblies of God's people.

Day 331   Psalm 134.

Song of Ascents of David (15)

Blessings from Zion

The ascents, which began in faraway places in Psalm 120, conclude here, not just in Zion, but in the Sanctuary. The weary pilgrims enter God's house after evening has fallen. They call to the priestly ministers of the Temple to bless the LORD. The reply comes back in verse 3 with a blessing, not given generally upon a host of worshippers, but personally - as a word from the king – 'The LORD that made heaven and earth bless you [thee] out of Zion!' O to experience that personal, hand-picked blessing, even in the midst of a company of God's worshippers!

It is a millennial picture. The writer does not say 'The LORD that made heaven and earth bless you out of heaven', but 'out of Zion'. B.W. Newton links Psalms 133 and 134 together as speaking of Israel. He declares, 'They will be one – one in thought and one in testimony; one in service; and one in praise'[1].

But these blessings do not just apply to forgiven Israel, for "Many nations shall come and say, 'Come, and let us go up to the mountain of the LORD, to the house of the God of Jacob; and He will teach us His ways, and we will walk in His paths'. For the law shall go forth of Zion, and the word of the LORD from Jerusalem' (Mic. 4:2).

---

[1] B.W. Newton, *Babylon and Egypt* p133.

Day 332   Psalm 135:1-7

Stirred up to praise

Although the word 'Hallelujah' is confined to Revelation 19 in the Authorised Version, it appears in the Old Greek version in the title of 20 Psalms, including this one. The first three verses of this Psalm are one long Hallelujah, as the psalmist is carried away with the delightfulness of praise. The Septuagint translates the Hebrew literally, 'sing Psalms to his name, for it is delightful' (v3).

'Praising his name' shows that we must carefully take note of what is spoken or manifested by God, that he may be praised out of knowledge – 'for he will not have praises, but as his word directeth'.[1]

The writer hardly stops to give reasons for praise until v4, where God's sovereign election is in focus; followed by his peerless excellence (v5); and his omnipotence in creation (v6,7).

David Dickson applies 'servants of the LORD' and 'those who stand' to ministers. They should 'stir themselves up to this work of praising God' 'whatsoever may be their private condition, sad or joyful'. The presbytery meeting, the classis, and the ministers' fraternal, should all be occasions for praise!

We should never neglect to praise God. We should bless the LORD at all times (Ps. 34:1).

---

[1] David Dickson, *A Commentary on the Psalms.*   Quoted here and below

Day 333   Psalm 135:8-14
Remember your deliverance

Alec Motyer[1] links Psalms 135 and 136 with the 'Songs of Ascents' as 'a grand, concluding shout of praise' and as 'songs of the homeland'. He links these verses with the Passover as 'out of Egypt' (v8, 9) and 'into Canaan' (v10-12).

The psalmist here delights in the LORD's remarkable deliverances (v9-11), the gifts he bestows on his people (v12), his constancy towards them (v13) and his tender care and compassion for them (v14).

Though these are words given to Israel, for whom these things are a famous memorial (v13) till the latter day when the LORD shall again shall work for them, we may make good application of them to ourselves.

Do we forget so easily what a mighty deliverance it took to bring us out of the kingdom of darkness? How many giants and Appollyons withstood us on the way? Have we not known God's grace abounding to us as the chief of sinners? Is his changelessness in the face of all our waverings not a reassurance that he will see us right through the race we run? Do we not see his ordering and comforting us in all our circumstances as a cause for great consolation?

O for a fresh sight of these things. O that the LORD might surprise us with stirrings in our heart.

---

[1] Alec Motyer, *Journey, Psalms for Pilgrim People*.

Day 334   Psalm 135:15-21

Praise the Living God

We began this Psalm praising God for all that he has revealed himself to be – 'singing praises unto his name'. Today's portion begins by warning of the danger of making a god after our own image.

Five times the writer urges his people to praise that peerless name by which he has chosen to be known - 'the LORD - Jehovah', which Judaism will not utter, calling him simply *Ha Shem* - the Name. He then concludes the Psalm as he began, with 'Hallelujah!' O that the matchless wonders of our God might be fully known to our heart. O that this mortal frame might even be able to contain such knowledge. O that our hearts, our minds, and our wills might be yielded to offer him true and acceptable worship!

A.A. Bonar applies this passage to our Saviour in the days of his flesh. The final verse would have been very precious to him then. 'For he was Jehovah, come to fulfil all the types and shadows, being himself the incarnate God inhabiting Jerusalem. And then he would look forward to the future, when his throne shall be as a canopy over Jerusalem, and when in glory he shall inhabit it as the City of the Great King, while out of Zion issues forth such praise as makes the earth wonder – the joy of Jerusalem heard afar off. We too may share it with such thoughts, joining Israel and Israel's King'[1].

---

[1] A.A. Bonar, *Christ and His Church in the Book of Psalms*.

Day 335   Psalm 136:1-9

His Loving-kindness is forever

In the verses before us today we are urged to consider how 'good' his greatness is, and how 'good' his power is, manifested in creation. The point of reference for all 52 lines of the Psalm is four Hebrew words at the beginning, and one word in particular. 'Give-thanks to-the-LORD because [he is] good'. We know this, but we need to reflect upon it. We need to 'stir ourselves up to the work of praising God'. It is also possible to read the opening verse as a declaration of the 'goodness' of praise – 'for it is good'.

The repeated response of the Psalm, 'for his loving-kindness is for ever', was often used in Israel at great public events[1]. The setting of this Psalm may have been when the Ark was brought to Jerusalem (see 1 Chr. 16). The Hebrew word used for 'to give thanks' involves a public profession of thankfulness.

The word translated 'mercy' is the Hebrew word *ḥesed*, often translated 'loving-kindness'. It is used 127 times in the Psalms, and in every verse of this Psalm (26 times).

Matthew Henry writes, '"God's mercy endureth for ever" is magnified above all the truths concerning God'. This should make us love to sing this Psalm. Those whom he has chosen will never be lost, for his mercy to them was before all worlds and is 'forever'.

---

[1] Compare 1 Chr. 16:34, 41; 2 Chr. 5:13; 7:3; 20:21; Ezra 3:11.

Day 336 Psalm 136:10-20

Remembering God's mercy

These verses speak of the awesome power of God in delivering his people from Egypt, and throughout their journey to Canaan. At first sight it seems strange to sing 'To him who smote the Egyptians in their firstborn, for his mercy endures forever' (v10). The LORD's elect people are the particular objects of his mercy: 'The mercy of the LORD is from everlasting upon them that fear him' (Ps. 103:17). God is sovereign in all he does, (Rom. 9:15).

The use of words in verse 15 is vivid. It is literally, 'the LORD shook off the Egyptians in the midst of the sea' (as in Exod. 14:27), just as though the LORD was shaking crumbs from off a tablecloth. Thus, he destroyed the might of Pharaoh.

We must have confidence in God's goodness and mercy. This starts with the general appreciation of God's goodness in the opening verses of the Psalm. It then enables us to see God's hand in particular events throughout the Psalm.

We often forget how God has dealt with us in our lives, and fail to give thanks. Jews constantly give thanks for the deliverance from Egypt, particularly in their annual Passover. How much more should we give thanks for our deliverances! We have passed from death unto life, and from the power of Satan unto God.

Day 337   Psalm 136:21-26

God's giving love

Yesterday's portion was concerned with deliverance out of Egypt, and from the peoples of Canaan. Today's portion is concerned with the positive blessings that followed.

1. The provision of a land flowing with milk and honey, undeserved and unmerited (v21, 22).
2. Thanksgiving for God's final deliverance from adversaries (v24).
3. God's bounty in giving food to all living things (v25).

The emphasis of point 3 is God's indiscriminate giving to all of his creatures, from the lowliest worm and ant. We should thank God for his kind provision, even to the ravens - unclean birds! (Luke 12:24).

God's material largesse is indiscriminately given but is unequally shared (Matt. 5:45). We look for that time when all shall benefit, 'when the ploughman shall overtake the reaper, and the treader of grapes him who sows seed. The mountains shall drip with sweet wine, and all the hills shall flow with it' (Amos 9:13). We look for a time when men 'shall beat their swords into ploughshares and their spears into pruning hooks', and shall learn war no more (Mic. 4:3).

We have seen in this Psalm a God who 'delights in mercy' (Mic. 7:18-20). We should show that characteristic in our own behaviour too. 'Blessed are the merciful for they shall obtain mercy' (Matt. 5:7).

Day 338   Psalm 137

Without a song in Babylon

The context of this Psalm makes it the most recent of the Psalms; it was written after Israel had gone in captivity to Babylon.

It has been said that there are two cities in Scripture – Babylon and Jerusalem (or Zion). All the longing of the exiles was for Jerusalem, but they found themselves in Babylon. They were in a wonderful city which even Nebuchadnezzar marvelled over (Dan. 4:29, 30). They were by great rivers of water and shaded by luxuriant willows[1]. They were surrounded by people who were urging them to sing and be joyful (we need not take their words as mockery). And yet they wept (v1). They set aside their instruments of joy (v2). They reminded themselves of the true character of their circumstances ('How shall we sing...' v4). They set all their affections and desires on Zion (v5, 6). They passionately desired the vindication of God's cause in words that shock (v8, 9), but fulfil the prophecy of Isaiah (13:16).

Dear reader, how is it with your soul? We should not go about mournful all the time. In the company of God's people we may worship him in spirit and in truth, in a way that ancient Israel could not, but we must always remember that we are but strangers and pilgrims here.

---

[1] Elsewhere in Scripture these are not associated with sorrow as "weeping willows", but with joyfulness (Lev. 23:40) and blessing (Isa. 44:4).

Day 339   Psalm 138:1-5

Even kings will sing

This is a Psalm of quiet communion and reflection. It lacks the anxious cries and evident distress of some of the Psalms. David is able to say, 'In the day when I cried you answered me'. He alternates between speaking to God and speaking to his own soul. He starts speaking to the LORD straight away. He assumes we will know to whom he is speaking. He is so taken up with God that he does not formally address him!

We could translate the first verse, 'In the presence of the angels I will sing Psalms to you'[1]. If so, in Christ the lowly state of man is brought into association with the praise of the highest unfallen creatures. Calvin comments 'one reason why the cherubim overshadowed the Ark of the Covenant was to let God's people know that the angels were present when they come to worship in the sanctuary' (see 1 Cor. 11:10). In the same verse, 'You have magnified your word above all your name' may be paraphrased 'the revelation God has now made of himself to the psalmist exceeds all that he had known of him before'. So 'all kings of the earth shall praise' (v4).

These words will have their fulfilment in great chorus of praise that will surround the throne of God, and continue until its sweet strains mingle with those of the angels, the martyrs, and all his elect.

---

[1] So Calvin, and the Septuagint.

Day 340   Psalm 138:6-8

Refreshed in the midst of trouble

These words speak of David's dependence upon God. He sees himself as lowly, walking in the midst of trouble, appealing to his Maker. The portion ends with the lovely expression of one resting on his God, 'the LORD shall perfect that which concerns me', or as Bishop Horsley translates it, 'Jehovah shall bring things to a conclusion for me'. Whatever is important to our needs, the LORD will bring to its rightful conclusion.

David Dickson refers v8 to the believer's perseverance.

1.   The believer's heart cannot be quiet until it is sure of perseverance, and it can be sure.
2.   The believer's hope of perseverance is not built any of his own strength or constancy, but upon the unchangeableness of God's everlasting mercy.
3.   True assurance of perseverance is joined with the sense of human weakness.
4.   Faith must rest upon our relationship with God as believers

We may confidently rest on the words of verse 8 because 'His counsel cannot be changed, nor his promise fail, neither can the call according to his purpose be revoked, nor the merit, intercession and watchful keeping of Christ be rendered ineffectual, nor the sealing of the Holy Spirit fail, or be removed'.[1]

---

[1] Canons of the Synod of Dort, Chapter 5, Article 8. Quoted from C.W.H. Griffiths, *Chosen – Called – Kept.*

Day 341   Psalm 139:1-6

He knows all about me

Each Psalm of this short section (138-145) is attributed to David. He extols the LORD's omniscience, but not in an abstract, theological, way. He speaks of God's knowledge of every action, every part of our life. These thoughts are indeed wonderful, but they are also very sobering. They remind us that God views everything that we do, and weighs all our secret thoughts. How we should tremble, and walk humbly, before such a God! At the same time, walking with an all-knowing God should be our solace in all the changes of life.

Scripture frequently warns us to guard our speech. Verse 4 gives a powerful reason for this. We should not just avoid blasphemy and swearing. We should be careful of speaking any idle word (Matt. 12:36). As Bunyan picturesquely writes in his book *The Holy War* of the city 'Mansoul', 'Let us defend Mouth-gate with good words, prayer, and melodious Psalms'.

Verse 5 teaches that God there is no escaping God's presence. The Book of Hebrews reminds us that God's word discerns the thoughts and intents of our heart. 'All things are naked and opened unto him with whom we have to do' (Heb. 4:12-13).

May we sing these words under the deepest impression that God's eye is upon us. 'He knows the way that I take' (Job 23:10).

Day 342   Psalm 139:7-12

The LORD is always there

As the opening verses spoke of God's omniscience, the verses of this portion particularly speak of his omnipresence and immanence. 'Heaven and earth cannot contain him, and at the same time he fills both, and is a God at hand'[1].

What a comfort these words are to the believer who is walking humbly with his God. They were evidently a comfort to David, who could lean upon God's right hand wherever he found himself. And yet what a terror the words of this Psalm are to the awakened conscience of one who realises his guilt and sin. 'This makes it dreadful work to sin; for we offend the Almighty to his face, and commit acts of treason at the very foot of his throne'[2].

God met Jacob with kind reassurance, and yet, when he realised that 'God was in this place and I knew it not', he feared, and cried out 'How dreadful is this place!' (Gen. 28:16, 17).

May these words be a comfort and a delight to us, and may they guard us from sin this day.

---

[1] Louis Berkhof, *Systematic Theology*. His proof texts for this statement are Psalm 139:7-10; I Kgs. 8:27; Isaiah 66:1; Acts 7:48, 49; Jer. 23::23,24; Acts 17:27,28.

[2] C.H. Spurgeon, *The Treasury of David*.

Day 343   Psalm 139:13-18

Fearfully and wonderfully made

The psalmist develops his theme of the LORD's intimate knowledge of us in these verses. He knows us perfectly because he made us. Nothing is hidden from God.

David wonders at the marvels of his human body, and how God has sustained him from his earliest existence in the womb. This Psalm should give great pause for thought to those who speak of simply 'terminating a pregnancy', and a woman's 'right' over her body.

The word 'wrought' (AV v15) is translated 'embroidered' in the making of the Tabernacle (compare Exod. 35:35). Can this tender shaping and forming of a baby - can all that this Psalm says of the omniscience and immanence of God - be at all compatible with the murder of unborn children?

The wonders of the human body are still being discovered by scientists. Would that it might provoke the response of the shepherd king of Israel in every heart, 'I am fearfully and wonderfully made. How precious also unto me are your thoughts, O God! How great is the sum of them!'

Let us reflect on the wonder and frailty of our mortal bodies and marvel, for when we at last awake (v18) 'it does not yet appear what we shall be'! (1 John 3:2).

Day 344   Psalm 139:19-24

Search me, O God

In these verses, a fourth aspect of the Almighty God is seen. David has described him as the Omniscient One, the Omnipresent God, and as our Creator. These verses follow logically from those thoughts. To such a God we must give account. He is the Judge of all the earth. David, 'the man after God's own heart', fully identifies with God's hatred of sin. Even if a person has done him no harm personally, the wicked man is his enemy if he is an enemy of God (v22).

In our day it is considered a virtue to 'value diversity', even if it honours those who despise and flout God's law. The centre of gravity of our legal systems has shifted from the laws and rights of God to the rights of man. Are we not followers of him of whom it was said, 'The zeal of your house has eaten me up' (John 2:17)? We do not hesitate to defend our own interests. Will we be cowards when God's glory is at stake? Yet in all this, we hate the sin and seek to recover the sinner. We were all once children of wrath and at enmity to God.

In verses 23 and 24, David expresses a desire for the LORD to secure for him a practical holiness that goes beyond his own ability to understand or to do. He yields as clay in the hands of the Potter (Jer. 18) – 'Search me, O God, and know my heart; Try me and know my thoughts; See if there be any wicked way in me, and lead me in the way everlasting'.

Day 345   Psalm 140:1-7

The helmet of salvation

There are three ways of considering the words of this Psalm. (1) As our response to the enemies of God in all ages. (2) As the words of Christ during his earthly ministry. (3) As a response to the Antichristian persecution.

(1) We must see things through God's eyes and accept his verdict upon sin. What is presented here is not the hostility of David to his personal enemies, but a desire to see God's righteousness vindicated. The wickedness described here goes beyond the malice that evil men have for Christ's Church. It is more like the wickedness that crucified the Son of God.

(2) A.A. Bonar considers these words to be used prophetically by Christ and so introduces it, 'Another Psalm 'of David', to be sung by all saints, even as it was used by their Head, David's Son'[1].

(3) We may also view this Psalm as a response to the quintessential wickedness that will characterise the last times[2]. The Psalm is thus a cry of the saints, as in Rev. 6:10 'How long, O Lord, holy and true, do you not judge and avenge our blood on them that dwell on the earth'.

Thanks be to God who 'covers our head' in the warfare against all the forces of evil (v7, cp. Eph. 6:17).

---

[1] A.A. Bonar, *Christ and His Church in the Book of Psalms.*

[2] So de Burgh and Bishop Horsley.

Day 346   Psalm 140:8-13

The goodness and severity of God

We see the goodness and severity of God in these verses (Rom.11:22): on the wicked, awful punishment, but upon the poor and the afflicted (v12), God's merciful kindness.

This is a cry against intense wickedness. It seems as though the cause of truth hangs in the balance. The psalmist cries out 'Grant not, O LORD, the desires of the wicked [singular]; further not his evil device'. This person is 'The chiefest of those who compass me about' (v9). Scripture speaks elsewhere about such a Satanic and Antichristian rebellion. The sentence that the Lord of Heaven has passed will at length be executed (v10; compare Rev.19:20, 21).

The reference to coals of fire falling upon the head of the wicked (v10) is surely a reference to Sodom and Gomorrah, which is a type of that end-time judgment. Their wickedness was 'before the face of God' and had to be punished (Gen. 19:13). By contrast, we hunger and thirst after the living God and long to be 'before God's face' (Ps. 42:2). Our Psalm here tells us that we shall not only see God and appear before him, but *dwell* 'before his face' (v13; John 14:2, 3).

The joy of verse 13 will come when the storm is past. O the delight of confessing and giving thanks to God for all that he has revealed himself to be ('his name'), and in endless ages being in the company of our Redeemer.

Day 347   Psalm 141:1-4

Watch over my mouth

David here pleads urgently that he might have ready access into God's presence. There is something almost irreverent in his prayer. He uses the imperative. He is telling God to 'hurry up'. This is not a lukewarm 'saying prayers', but a burning desire to know and experience the presence of God. How often we have heard such requests in the Psalms! May the LORD give us urgency and a holy impatience in our prayers.

David longs to commune with, his God. The outward forms may be there. He thinks of the rising of the incense – the lifting up of hands – the evening oblation – but he desires the kernel, not the shell.

At the same time, he desires that he may be shut off from conversation, communion, and partaking pleasures with the wicked. He longs that the LORD will 'Set a watch before my mouth' and 'keep the door of my lips'. Alas, how often we find time to talk and say things that we have cause to regret, but when we are alone with God our words are few. William Cowper wrote

> *Were half the breath thus vainly spent,*
> *To heaven in supplication sent.*
> *Your cheerful song would oftener be,*
> *'Hear what the LORD has done for me'*

Let us think upon and pray this portion, seeking the LORD for a real heart-experience of his presence and keeping.

Day 348   Psalm 141:5-10

Wounded by a friend

David accepted the rebuke of the prophet Nathan concerning his sin with Bathsheba in 2 Samuel 12. In these verses he confesses that 'faithful are the wounds of a friend' (v5; Prov. 27:6). May we learn in our daily walk with God to accept reproof, and not to defend and justify ourselves when we are at fault. Such correction shall then be as oil upon our head. We should not refuse it. Let us most of all learn to accept the rebuke of the LORD.

The context and meaning of some of the statements of verse 6 are difficult. Many seek the meaning in David's personal circumstances, which they reconstruct by guesswork. It would be better to prayerfully seek the Holy Spirit's purpose in giving it to us. It may be that the LORD will cause fresh light to shine upon these verses when the time of the end approaches.

We consider David's 'prayer' at the end of verse 5 to be against the wicked of verses 4, 6, and 10. The LORD's people are the subject of verse 7[1].

David ends in quiet confidence that the LORD will deliver and preserve him.

---

[1] B.W. Newton, *Dark Sayings upon the Harp*, from notes of his addresses.

Day 349   Psalm 142

Meditation in a cave

The title of this Psalm is 'A Maschil of David. When he was in the cave. A Prayer'. 'Maschil' is derived from a word meaning to ponder, or to have insight. In verse 2 David's 'complaint' (AV) is a 'meditation', as in Ps. 104:34, or an expression of concern.

David is hardly well placed to meditate. He hid in caves at Adullam (1 Sam. 22) and En Gedi (1 Sam. 24), when he fled from Saul. However, the contents of this Psalm closely reflect the title. David speaks as a hunted man. He was not in control of his circumstances. His life was unsettled and uncertain.

He constantly had to run away. He speaks of his 'path' and his 'way' in verse 3. He speaks of a hidden trap being set in that path by his enemies (compare Ps. 141:9, 10). He looks around (v4), but no-one wants to know. The way of escape (AV 'refuge') is closed to him (v4).

He claims the LORD to be his refuge (v5 – a different word, with more emphasis on protection than escape). He cries to the LORD to deliver him from his persecutors (or 'pursuers', v6). He yet feels himself in prison (v7 – perhaps shut up in the cave).

However low, harassed, hunted, and perplexed we feel today, let us draw on these words of comfort. Our God is our refuge, our escape from prison. We await the everlasting rejoicing righteous.

Day 350   Psalm 143:1-6

Outstretched hands

This is a penitential Psalm of David, one of the Psalms Luther called 'Pauls Psalms'. The title in the Old Greek and other ancient versions suggests it was written when Absalom, his son, pursued him. David recognises this as God's judgment upon him, as Nathan had prophesied (v2; compare 2 Sam. 12:9-14; Ps. 51:4).

Here is a man wholly taken up with his God. His confidence in God is total. His dependence is absolute. He seeks no succour from man. He is confronted with a major crisis. Inwardly he feels persecuted, smitten to the ground, dwelling in darkness, his spirit overwhelmed, his heart desolate. And yet, in all of this, he reaches out to God and longs that God should draw near to his soul (v6).

The 'answer' is left in God's hands – whatever that answer should be. He does not tell the LORD what to do, although he does think upon what God has done, and what he is able to do (v5). He simply expresses his desire that God would be with him in his trial. 'My soul longs for you like a thirsty land'. The Prayer Book Version (Coverdale) translates, 'My soul gaspeth unto thee as a thirsty land'. He is desperate for the LORD.

As a child stretches out hands to be picked up and comforted by father or mother, so may we extend our hands to God in prayer this day.

Day 351   Psalm 143:7-12

The servant's prayer

We are privileged here to read the heart-cries of David as he pours them, one after another, before the LORD. The prayer of the Lord Jesus in the Garden of Gethsemane must have been a twin with this one. If we had overheard David praying, we would have quietly slipped away, rather than intrude into this intimate communion of a man with his God. But it has been recorded for our instruction and encouragement.

He gives a reason for every request. This is powerful, effectual praying. Count the nine petitions that David Dickson finds in these remaining verses. Consider the reasons why God ought to answer; why he needs to answer. Then bring your prayers before the LORD. See if you can plead those reasons too. Plead them feeling your own helplessness. As Calvin says in connection with verse 10, 'the passage teaches us what we are to think of free will; for David here denies the will has the power of judging rightly until our hearts are formed to a holy obedience by the Spirit of God'.

The key to all that we read here is in the last phrase, 'for I am your servant' (v12). This accounts for his willing submission in difficult circumstances. This gives the reason he wants to know his Master's will. This explains his desire for life and revival (v11) – that he might serve better. This is the prime warrant he brings for God to speedily answer his prayer.

Day 352   Psalm 144:1-8

Come down, O LORD!

This Psalm speaks of the dangerous, but triumphant, warfare of the man of God[1]. This is not warfare in the strength of the flesh, but in reliance upon God to secure a successful outcome (1 Sam. 17:45). We stand today against the strong armies of false religion, atheism, and liberal politics, without number as the hosts of Midian. In such a day, we need to be like Gideon, 'a mighty man of valour' (Judg. 6:12).

Verses 1 and 2 speak of how God empowers his people. In verses 3 and 4 David declares how weak and short-lived man is. Verse 4 and Psalm 102:11 used to be written on sundials to give the solemn lesson of the passage of time.

David makes a series of appeals to God to manifest his power. His calls are like the steady blows of a battering ram: 'Bow the heavens, O LORD, and come down; Touch the mountains and they shall smoke; Cast forth lightning and scatter them; Shoot out your arrows and destroy them; Stretch down your hands from above'. His heart echoes Isaiah's cry 'O that you would rend the heavens and come down' (Isa. 64:1).

Let us join our appeals with David's. 'It is time for you, LORD, to work: for they have made void your law' (Ps. 119:126).

---

[1] The title of this Psalm in the ancient versions links it to the defeat of Goliath, or Goliath's brother (1 Chr. 20:5).

Day 353   Psalm 144:9-15

Happy is that people whose God is the LORD

Our passage today moves from the noise of battle to deliverance, victory, and peace. So it will always be to those who are on the LORD's side - those who can say 'if God be for us, who can be against us?' For this victory David sings a new song (v9), and so shall we (Rev. 5:9). The transformation in verses 12-15 suggests the circumstances of millennial blessing[1].

Notice, contrary to the attempts of our age to blur the distinctions between male and female, the separate blessings of the boys and girls in verse 12. The boys are as plants grown up in their youth. Calvin comments, 'Trees rarely come to any height if they do not grow large early'! The girls adorn the house by their comeliness and elegance. The RV translation is surely unfortunate, 'after the fashion of a palace'!

We know, and serve, a great God who blesses us, and will bless us. Even now we may sing 'Happy is that people whose God is the LORD'.

The Psalm is sung by the Jews at the close of the Sabbath. So we end with thoughts of that time of the eternal Sabbath which shall never end, when we shall know the uninterrupted peace of God (Heb. 4:1-13).

---

[1] So A.A. Bonar, *Christ and his Church in the Book of Psalms*; William de Burgh, *Commentary on the Psalms*; B.W. Newton, *Prophecies respecting the Jews and Jerusalem*.

Day 354   Psalm 145:1-7

The king's King

Psalm 145 introduces the final group of Hallelujah Psalms. In Hebrew the Book of Psalms is 'The Book of Praises', but this is the only Psalm with the title 'Praise'. It is a fitting doxology to head up the remaining Psalms. We are entering the Beulah land of Pilgrim's Progress, where 'they had more rejoicing than in parts more remote from the Kingdom'. These closing Psalms are like the end of the Lord's Prayer, 'for thine is the kingdom, the power and the glory, for ever and ever'.

Verses 1 and 2 set the theme for the Psalm. The key phrase is literally 'my God, the King' which is elaborated in verses 11-13. 'King' David refers to the LORD as his King. All human Government is held in proxy by kings and rulers. They are accountable for their actions. It follows that 'avowed rejection of the Scriptures or any part thereof, is a moral disqualification for legislative authority'[1]. Some have gone further, 'We must take no part in governing or legislating on principles which exclude our Lord's rights over our nation's constitution, legislation and administration'[2].

The whole Psalm is a celebration of our King Messiah for 'He shall reign forever and ever' (Rev. 11:15).

---

[1] B.W. Newton, *The Acknowledgement of God by Earthly Governments*.

[2] *Testimony of the Reformed Presbyterian Church of Scotland* (1932).

Day 355   Psalm 145:8-13

The glory of his kingdom

This is an 'alphabetical' Psalm with each successive line starting with the next letter of the Hebrew alphabet[1]. In verses 8-10 the psalmist dwells upon the mercy and longsuffering of God. This was particularly shown when Israel came out of Egypt - compare v8 with Exod. 34:6 and Numb. 14:18. Today's portion leads from that to the glory of the LORD's everlasting kingdom, in verses 11-13.

This kingdom of God is not yet seen in its manifested fullness and glory. It is viewed by those who have David's eye of faith. Then, away with all the kings of the earth, petty dictators, emperors, and princes! Let them flee to the dens and the rocks of the mountains! Let them even now kiss the Son lest he be angry (Rev. 6:15-17; Ps. 2:12). Do you not long with all your heart for such a manifest rule of God?

Let us humbly submit ourselves to our great King. Let us 'seek first the kingdom of God' (Matt. 6:33) and proclaim his kingdom (Mark 1:15) to all.

---

[1] The Psalm lacks the letter "n" which would fall between v13 and v14. The Septuagint, and virtually all the ancient versions (which have no alphabetical structure) add the lines at this point "Faithful is the LORD in all his words, and holy in all his works" (compare v17). This is present in the Dead Sea Scrolls in Hebrew (11QPs[a]) and begins with the "missing" letter. The lines have been included in the NIV, ESV, and other modern versions. However, note that Psalms 25 and 34 are apparently 'imperfect' acrostics by design.

Day 356   Psalm 145:14-21

Merciful in all his works

The remaining verses of this Psalm are a mine of rich promises. They offer encouragement to those in need, by speaking of the tender succour and kind mercy of the LORD. Dear reader, will you not ponder on your needs and ask the LORD to fulfil his word for you? The Comforter who inspired these words is speaking here, and is ready to supply your needs. Here is your 'letter from the King' – 'The LORD is nigh unto all them that call upon him, to all that call upon him in truth' (v18). Will not your 'eyes wait upon him' (v15 AV) until he gives 'in due season'.

Some of the words in this short passage go well beyond the current state of affairs in this world. We cannot yet say that the LORD *'satisfies the desire* of every living thing' (AV v.16)[1]. The same Hebrew word ('satisfies', 'fill the need') is used in Ps. 147:14 speaking of Israel's millennial days, when 'he makes peace in your borders, and *fills you* with the finest of the wheat'. Nevertheless, even in our days, the goodness of the LORD is abundantly manifest, as Paul could say in Acts 14:17.

We have to wait for 'all flesh to bless his holy name for ever and ever', but will you not join with David now? 'My mouth shall speak the praise of the LORD' (v21).

---

[1] It does not merely say that he provides "enough to satisfy" (Scottish Metrical Psalter). However, perhaps the verse is better translated 'as pleases you, you fill the need of every living thing'.

Day 357   Psalm 146
Praise, as long as I live

In the opening verses of this Hallelujah Psalm[1], the writer resolves that in whatever state of mental or physical weakness – 'while I live' – he will praise the LORD. John Wesley's sentiment is in the same spirit, 'Happy if with my latest breath, I may but gasp his name'. Even 'while I have any being' says the psalmist, I will sing praises. We need to stir ourselves up to praise God. The chief end of man is 'to glorify God and to enjoy him forever'[2]. This is not a passive thing, but a glorious labour that blends our voices with those of celestial beings who constantly cry 'Holy! Holy! Holy!'

The psalmist praises 'he who made heaven, and earth, and sea, and all that is in them' (v6; Rev. 5:13; 10:6). With such a king, who would want to 'put their trust in princes' (v3)!

The Psalm rises in a crescendo from its beginning to its end. In verses 6-9 the psalmist declares line after line the kindness of the LORD. Finally, the last verse declares that 'the LORD shall be king for ever and ever' (v10; Rev. 15:3; 17:14; 19:16).

Let us take up the song, for it will be our sweet delight through endless ages to come.

---

[1] The opening words "Praise the LORD" are, of course, "Hallelujah" in the original.

[2] *Westminster Shorter Catechism*, Question 1.

Day 358   Psalm 147:1-6

Bound up wounds and numbered stars

This Psalm witnesses throughout to a time of blessing for the people and land of Israel – even to the very grass, birds, and animals that are found there. Unless we charge the writer – and the Holy Spirit - with exaggeration and poetic licence, they speak of a time that has not yet been seen in that troubled land. The opening verses make plain that the context is the time when the LORD shall build up Jerusalem, and gather together the outcasts of Israel (compare Ps. 102:16).

As Psalm 146, this Psalm links the loving care of God our Father with his infinite power. Thus, we have the remarkable phrases together 'He heals the broken-in-heart, and binds up their wounds' (v.3); then, 'He counts the number of the stars' (v.4). Surely, this is the wonder of our God, and of our Gospel. There is nothing too hard for our God and, if we are in Christ, we are the chosen objects of his tender mercies.

The Heidelberg Catechism brings together the Lord's infinite knowledge and power with his kind personal care; 'He [my Faithful Saviour] preserves me in such a way that, without the will of my Heavenly Father, not a hair can fall from my head'.

Again, we say, 'If God be for us, who shall be against us?'

Day 359   Psalm 147:7-11

Delighting and pleasing God

The opening verse of this Psalm can be translated 'Praise the LORD because it is good to sing-psalms!' In the same way, verse 7 continues 'sing-psalms on the harp to our God!'

We are given a litany of reasons why we should sing praise in verses 7-9. Do we moan about an 'overcast, grey day'; or do we praise him, 'who covers the heavens with cloud'? Would we be stirred up to praise God for making grass to grow upon the mountains (v8)? And yet, why not?

Is it your desire to please God today? We are told what pleases him in verses 10 and 11. The reference of verse 10 is probably to cavalry and infantry, but we agree with the thought of Joseph Caryl, the puritan, that God does not delight in a man's legs … or his brain, or his tongue! – 'All the beauties and rarities both of persons and things are dull and flat, yea wearisome to God, in comparison of a gracious, honest, humble soul'.[1]

'The LORD takes pleasure in those who fear him, in those who hope in his mercy' (v11). This is the marriage of fear and hope. The one leads us to avoid sin, and the other stirs us up to follow righteousness. Our fear should not degenerate into legal bondage, but should be sweetened by hope; and our hope should not be sentimental, but sobered by fear.

---

[1] Quoted by C.H. Spurgeon, *The Treasury of David*.

Day 360   Psalm 147:12-20

Praise your God, O Zion

This passage forms a separate Psalm in the Old Greek version.

Jerusalem is described as a place of safety and peace (as v2), filled with the finest of the wheat. The land is the object of his singular care, for it is 'the holy land' (Zech. 2:12). Ice, snow, winds, and waters are all given at God's word (v15-18). Yet his word is particularly shown and revealed to Israel, as it will be when 'out of Zion shall go forth the law, and the word of the LORD from Jerusalem' (v19, 20 and Isa. 2:3, 4). Such a day has never yet been seen, although long awaited.

Verse 20 may seem strange. 'He has not dealt thus with any nation, and as for his judgments they [the nations] have not known them: Praise the LORD!' God's sovereign predestination should be accepted without question and made the subject of our worship. It declares God to be 'the fearsome, blameless, and just Judge and Avenger of sin.'[1].

God's distinguishing and electing grace is unconditional, despite our depravity and failure. The believer, as Israel, is effectually called into fellowship with God, and will be brought through trials to the blessing he has promised. Should we not marvel at his amazing grace to us, just as to wayward Israel?

---

[1] Canons of the Synod of Dort, Chapter 1, Article 15. Quoted from C.W.H. Griffiths, *Chosen – Called – Kept*. See Rom. 9:20; 11:33-36; Matt. 20:15.

Day 361   Psalm 148:1-6

Praise in the highest heaven

The psalmist here calls upon all creation, released from its groan and the bondage of corruption (Rom. 8:18-23), to join a chorus of praise. Heaven and earth, animate and inanimate, man and beast, are called to do their part in the praise of such a great and mighty God.

In this portion the heavens are called to worship and bring praise to God. Astronomy and space exploration have given us the knowledge of planetary systems beyond our solar system, vast nebulae, infinite myriads of stars beyond the imaginings of the psalmist, yet we still have a pigmy perception of the vast army of angelic beings ('all his angels', 'all his host') who surround the throne of God.

'Praise him in the heights' (v1), in the very 'heaven of heavens' (v4). So, at Christ's incarnation the angels called for there to be 'Glory to God in the highest!' (Luke 2:14). At Jesus's 'triumphal entry' to Jerusalem the very stones nearly cried out 'Hosanna in the highest!' (Luke 19:38-40). The wisdom of God is now made known in 'heavenly places' (Eph. 3:10). Christ is now exalted 'far above all' (Eph. 1:20, 21; 4:10). When the kingdom of our God at last comes, the heavens will again be called upon to rejoice (Rev. 12:10-12).

May we be privileged to hear that vast symphony of praise that the psalmist here calls forth, and to join in its song.

Day 362   Psalm 148:7-14

Praise from all the earth

In the first half of the Psalm, the heavenly creation was called to worship God. Here things of earth must add their voice. Surely here are 'the times of refreshing from the presence of the LORD', and 'the times of the restitution of all things' (Acts 3:19-21). All creation sings and declares the majesty and power of God.

All opposition, all pretended rivalry, is here put down. 'His name alone is excellent' and is lifted up on high (v13). We are reminded of the name of Jesus (Phil. 2:9-11). There is indeed 'No other name under heaven, given among men, by which we must be saved' (Acts 4:12). And what does the 'name' of God mean, but the expression of all that he is? And is not Christ 'the brightness of his glory, and the express image of his person' (Heb. 1:3)?

O what a marvel that his people are also exalted, and that he calls them <u>his</u> '*ḥasîdim*' (v14. AV 'saints') – those who are his beloved, and demonstrators of his *ḥesed* – covenant love. As Girdlestone notes[1], 'It is a remarkable fact that the word "chasid" [*ḥasîd*], when applied to man, has usually a possessive pronoun affixed to it'.

Are you one of his saints, in the New Testament sense? Can your voice be silent before such a God?

---

[1] R.B. Girdlestone, *Synonyms of the Old Testament*. See AV margin at Psalm 145:17.

Day 363   Psalm 149:1-4

The beauty of salvation

We have here the repeated themes of these closing Psalms. Here again is the 'new song'. Here too is the LORD taking pleasure in his people.

Matthew Henry's comments on verse 3 are worth quoting at length here 'They who from hence urge the use of music [accompaniment] in religious worship, must by the same rule introduce dancing, for they went together, as in David's dancing before the ark, and Judg. 21:21. But whereas many Scriptures keep up singing as a Gospel-ordinance, none provide for the keeping up of music and dancing; the Gospel canon for psalmody is to sing with the spirit and with the understanding'.

The picture given is of a joyful worshipping congregation - the sons of Zion rejoicing in their King. We must again assert the context of this worship. It is plainly of Israel restored and triumphant.

An interesting word occurs in verse 4, 'He shall beautify the meek with salvation'. Redeemed Israel is 'beautified'. The beauty was evident in the House of the LORD restored by Ezra and Nehemiah (Ezra 7:27). It is characteristic of the time of millennial blessing (Isa. 55:5; 60:7, 9, 13); and is applied to the head-covering of the priests (Exod. 28:2, 40). The Greek equivalent word may be translated 'glorify' (see Rom. 8:30).

Day 364   Psalm 149:5-9

To perform the judgment written in his Word

These verses have reference to the subduing of the nations, as Messiah will do when he returns (Psalm 2). His people are seen here executing 'the judgment written' (v9). This is a persistent theme in prophecy[1]. It confirms the context of this Psalm.

Wrong interpretation of such texts as verses 7 and 8 inspired the folly of the Church of Rome in its Crusade ventures, and countless other travesties throughout Church history. On the other hand the 'spiritualising' of such Scriptures evacuates them of any real meaning, and reduces them to little more than an allegory.

The joyfulness of God's people is here – 'singing aloud (or, for joy) upon their beds' (v5). It is in startling contrast to the night-time sorrow of God's people elsewhere in the Psalms (e.g. Ps. 6:6).

We work and witness in a day largely characterised by disappointment and failure of the people of God. O for such an experience of God that we cannot sleep or even be silent upon our beds for joy, when he visits us, commissions us for service, and grants us success. Let us be confident that he will do all that he has promised in the Scriptures, and so let us praise him.

---

[1] For example, Isaiah 49:22,23; 60:3ff; Joel 3:12ff. We are told that, when the Lord Jesus returns in Judgment, his saints will participate in his work – Jude 14,15; Rev. 19: 11-21. B.W. Newton comments "It will be an honour to take part in the destruction of Antichrist"!

Day 365   Psalm 150
The Great Hallelujah

This doxology of praise concludes the Psalms, and it is rightly known as 'The Great Hallelujah'. This 'Book of Praises' began with a short Psalm extolling the qualities of the Perfect Man, just as Genesis introduces Adam in the Garden of Eden. It concludes in the Sanctuary, with praise from the whole of creation. The response to its call to praise is found in Rev. 5:13 and Rev. 19:6, 7. Thus we have in the Psalms Genesis to Revelation.

Dear reader, the measure of our praise should be the measure of our God. May we answer the exhortation of Heb. 13:15, 'Let us offer up a sacrifice of praise to God continually, that is, the fruit of our lips giving thanks to his name'.

For John Brown, completing his notes on the Psalms[1] was just the beginning. 'Dare not, my soul, to finish thy notes, and to conclude the book, without commencing an heartiness in the work. Awake then my inward powers, let me even here, begin my high hallelujahs and hosannas to HIM who loved me and gave himself for me'.

Let us sing the words of this Psalm, given by the Holy Spirit for our praise. 'Let everything that has breath praise the LORD'. Yes, and one day everything will! Praise the LORD.

---

[1] *The Psalms of David in Metre with notes* John Brown of Haddington.

APPENDICES

APPENDIX 1

THE EXCELLENCE OF THE PSALMS

The Psalms were the universal song book of the Church from New Testament times until the 18th century. They were almost the only material used in sung worship by Celtic Christians or Nestorians, by Orthodox or Catholic. For example, the Orthodox Catechism of Philaret declares of the Book of Psalms 'It is the perfect manual of prayer and praise, and on that account is in continual use in the Divine Service of the Church'.

The Reformation revived the use of the Psalter for the common people to sing. During those times innumerable humble Christians found comfort singing the words of the Psalms on their way to martyrdom, when they exchanged them for 'the new song' in glory.

In France, to be a Psalm-singer was the same as to be a Protestant. The singing had such a profound effect on those who stood by that the persecutors of the French Huguenots did all in their power to silence the martyrs and to prevent them from singing a Psalm before they were burnt at the stake.

The uniqueness of the Book of Psalms rests in its ability to reflect all the affections and feelings of the heart of man and to bring them to God.

Martin Luther wrote

You may rightly call the Psalter a Bible in miniature, in which all things set forth more at length in the rest of the Scriptures are collected into a beautiful manual of wonderful and attractive brevity. From the Psalms you may learn not the works of the saints only, but the words, the utterances, the groans, the conversations, which they used in the presence of God, in temptation and in consolation; so that, though they are dead, in the Psalms they live and speak. The Psalms exhibit the mind of the saints, the working of their thoughts, and their most secret feelings.[1]

John Calvin wrote

This Book I familiarly call 'an anatomy of all parts of the soul'; for no-one will find in himself a single feeling of which the image is not reflected in this mirror. There the Holy Spirit has represented to the life all the griefs, sorrows, fears, doubts, hopes, cares, anxieties, in short, all the stormy emotions by which men's minds are often agitated[2].

Dr John Gill wrote

The subject matter of the book is exceeding great and excellent; many of the Psalms respect the Person, offices, and grace of Christ; his sufferings and death, resurrection, ascension, and session at the right hand of God; and so are exceeding suitable to the Gospel dispensation. The whole book is a rich mine of grace and evangelical truths, and a large fund of spiritual experience; and is abundantly suited to every case, state, and condition that the Church of Christ, or particular believers, are in at any time.[3]

Charles Haddon Spurgeon wrote, as he completed his seven volume commentary

---

[1] Martin Luther, *Works* (Volume 3).
[2] Calvin, Preface to his *Commentary on the Psalms*.
[3] Dr John Gill, *Commentary on the Whole Bible*.

A tinge of sadness is on my spirit as I quit 'The Treasury of David', never to find on this earth a richer storehouse, though the whole palace of revelation is open to me. Blessed have been the days spent in meditating, mourning, hoping, believing, and exulting with David! Can I hope to spend hours more joyous on this side of the golden gate? The book of Psalms instructs us in the use of wings as well as words: it sets us both mounting and singing. Often have I ceased my commenting upon the text that I might rise with the Psalm and gaze upon visions of God.

In these busy days, it would be greatly to the profit of Christian men if they were more familiar with the Book of Psalms, in which they would find a complete armoury for life's battles, and a perfect supply for life's needs. Here we have both delight and usefulness, consolation, and instruction. For every condition there is a Psalm, suitable and elevating. The Book supplies the babe in grace with penitent cries, and the perfected saint with triumphant songs. Its breadth of experience stretches from the jaws of hell to the gate of heaven. He who is acquainted with the marches of the Psalm-country knows that the land floweth with milk and honey, and he delights to travel therein[1].

Stewart Perowne's major critical commentary states

No single book of Scripture, not even of the New Testament, has, perhaps, ever taken such hold on the heart of Christendom. None, if we may dare judge, unless it be the Gospels, has had so large an influence in moulding the affections, sustaining the hopes,

---

[1] C H Spurgeon, *The Treasury of David*.

purifying the faith of believers. With its words, rather than with their own, they have come before God. In these they have uttered their desires, their fears, their confessions, their aspirations, their sorrows, their joys, their thanksgivings. By these their devotion has been kindled and their hearts comforted. The Psalter has been in the truest sense, the Prayer-book of both Jews and Christians'[1]

Adolph Saphir, the great Hebrew Christian expositor of the nineteenth century wrote

In the Psalms we learn the mind of Messiah in his union with his people. Hence the Psalter is the incomparable manual and hymn-book of the saints[2].

B.W. Newton, the expositor of unfulfilled prophecy wrote

Among the prophets no one so fully as David delineated the bitterness of the sufferings of the Messiah of Israel. Isaiah more clearly declared the reason of Christ's sufferings, and revealed why 'He was led as a lamb to the slaughter', but no one so fully as David describes the character and intensity of his agony ... On the other hand, where do we find more clear and amplified descriptions of his coming reign in glory?[3]

John Brown of Haddington wrote

Indited under the influence of Him, to whom all hearts are known, and all events foreknown, they suit

---

[1] J.J. Stewart Perowne, *The Psalms* (chapter on the use of the Psalter).

[2] Adolph Saphir, *On the Book of Hebrews* Volume 1, p197.

[3] B.W. Newton, *David, King of Israel*, p126.

mankind in all situations, grateful as the manna which descended from above, and which conformed itself to every palate. The fairest productions of human wit, after a few perusals, like gathered flowers, wither in our hands and lose their fragrancy; but these unfading plants of paradise, become, as we are accustomed to them, still more and more beautiful; their bloom appears to be daily heightened; fresh odours are emitted, and new sweets extracted from them. He who has once tasted their excellencies, will desire to taste them again; and he who tastes them oftenest, will relish them best.[1]

---

[1] John Brown of Haddington, *The Psalms of David in Metre with Notes.*

APPENDIX 2

THE SUBJECT OF THE PSALMS

1. **The Psalms speak of Christ** – the Lord Jesus explained them of himself when he appeared to his disciples (Luke 24:44). The Lord Jesus is 'the one person in whom these breathings, these praises, these desires, these hopes, these deep feelings found their only true and full realisation'.[1]

In particular, they speak of:

a. His communion with the Father. The New Testament shows many of the Psalms to be his prayers (Acts 2:25-31). No other Scriptures take us closer to the heart of Christ.

b. His sufferings. The Gospels describe his outward trials and sufferings, the Psalms frequently reveal these and his inner thoughts and grief (Psalm 22 is a prime example).

c. His glory. Time and again the Psalms lead us on to his exaltation and triumphant Kingdom (For example, Psalm 72).

It follows from this that the Psalms speak of:

2. **Salvation and deliverance**. Luther especially loved what he called 'Paul's Psalms' – Psalms that are full of the Gospel of salvation by grace alone. But all the Psalms speak of the LORD's saving work.

---

[1] Horatius Bonar, *Christ and His Church in the Book of Psalms* (speaking of the early Church's view of the Book of Psalms). The use of the Psalms in Hebrews 1:9-12 demonstrates this.

3. **The loving-kindness of God.** The Hebrew word *ḥeṣed* is used 250 times in the Old Testament. It is used 127 times in the Book of Psalms. It is the great word used to describe God's steadfast covenant love, his grace, favour, and mercy. Ps. 144:2 even says 'God is love' (*ḥeṣed*) (compare 1 John 4:16).

4. **The vindication of God's justice.** The Book of Psalms is a theodicy. It continually pleads for the LORD to judge, to see, to come down, to punish. The cry 'How long?' goes up again and again. The so-called 'Imprecatory Psalms' are a part of this instruction. They principally look on to a future point when the day of God's wrath will finally come upon those who oppose Christ and his Church. How the persecuted Church needs this assurance today![1]

---

[1] See Appendix 5.

APPENDIX 3

THE CHARACTER OF THE BOOK OF PSALMS

It is the Book of Praises – *'Tehilim'* in Hebrew. Deep and mournful notes may at times be heard, but they make up the harmony, and the book rises to its final exultation in Psalm 150.

The Hebrew verb *zamar* is used again and again, urging us sing to praise to God. It gives us the word *Mizmor* – a Psalm. Praise and Psalm singing are inseparable.

It is a Book of Prayers – the psalmist constantly turns to God in all his circumstances. He most naturally and intimately addresses his God as a familiar friend even as he looks up amazed at 'the heavens, the work of your fingers' (Psalm 8). As well as providing words for us, the Book frequently gives valuable patterns for our prayer. Here is the answer to the disciples' prayer (Luke 11:1). Its prayers are frequently marked by repentance for sin. This is particularly so in the 'Penitential Psalms' – 6,32,38,51,102,130 and 143.

It is a Book of Prophecy. David was a prophet (Acts 2:30. Compare Ps. 137:8, 9 with Isa. 13:16 and Jer. 50:15 and 36). As well as predicting the sufferings of Christ the Psalms often unfold the circumstances of yet unfulfilled prophecy – they often give commentary on events predicted elsewhere in Scripture. They show the working of the enemies of God, and particularly *the* Adversary, Satan, and in the last times, Antichrist. The future and prophetic nature of many of the Psalms is proved by the frequent description of the complete deliverance of Israel.

APPENDIX 4

FOR WHOM ARE THE PSALMS GIVEN?

We believe that we must guard against two errors

- of those who reject the Psalms as Jewish and unfit for Christian worship.

- of those who claim the Psalms for Christian use by excluding Israel - transferring to the Christian Church all references to Israel, Zion, or Jerusalem.

1. **It is the Book of Praise for the Church in all ages.** There is only one authorised and inspired Book of Praise in the Bible. The Apostles did not give us a New Testament equivalent. It is our conviction that this Book was intended for permanent use by God's people. Dispensationalism old and new seeks to discard the Psalms. The desire 'to make my author to speak like a Christian'[1] denigrates the inspiration of the Holy Spirit. The Psalms express the thoughts and longings of the 'man after God's own heart' (1 Sam. 13:14; Acts 13:22), who could say 'the Spirit of the LORD spoke by me and his word was on my tongue' (2 Sam. 23:2).

2. **It is a Book for Israel.** The Psalms refer to Israel and Jerusalem. The Gentile Church must not steal all the blessings and leave all the curses to the literal Israel. It is important to start with the natural and literal meaning of 'the hill of Zion' and other such expressions. We may apply such Scriptures. The

---

[1] Isaac Watts, *The Psalms of David imitated in the Language of the New Testament*. Preface, 1719.

Gentile Church has been grafted in among them and partakes of Israel's blessings (Rom. 11:17) - 'We are blessed with faithful Abraham' (Gal. 3:9). However, we must not confuse the present time of rejection of Christ by Israel with his coming triumphant reign, in which Israel has a central part.

APPENDIX 5

SO-CALLED 'IMPRECATORY PSALMS'

Some Psalms have earnest prayers for vengeance upon enemies, or exalt over their destruction. People have labelled these 'imprecatory Psalms'. Many, including Isaac Watts, have deemed them unworthy to be sung by 'sincere Christians'.

All the Psalms are in words given by the Holy Spirit, and we must not regard them as contrary to, or inferior to, the Gospel. It is rather our understanding of 'the Gospel' that has been infected with sentimentality. Today's evangelicalism is often so man-centred that, whilst emphasising the goodness and kindness of God, it denies his of his 'severity' (of which Rom. 11:22, Rev. 19 are an example)

We believe that all of the Psalms may, and indeed, should be sung by God's people. We reject those who would act as a censor of the words of the Holy Spirit. In singing the Psalms we pray the Lord's Prayer – 'your Kingdom come, your will be done, on earth as it is in heaven'.

We have shown in our notes that the desire for the punishment of the wicked expressed in the Psalms may in every case be linked to words of prophecy foretelling the doom of such wicked people. Furthermore, we may also note that the speaker (inspired by the Holy Spirit) often gives words that we may directly associate with the Lord Jesus Christ himself.

We fear that there is something fundamentally wrong with an 'evangelicalism' that baulks at the words of Scripture as though 'progressive revelation' had made them obsolete.

The words of C.H. Spurgeon on Ps. 129:4-5 are apt.

'Sooner or later a righteous God will interpose, and when he does so, his action will be most effectual; he does not unfasten, but cuts asunder, the harness which the ungodly use in their labour of hate. Never has God used a nation to chastise his Israel without destroying that nation when the chastisement has come to a close: he hates those who hurt his people, even though he permits their hate to triumph for a while for his own purpose. If any man would have his harness cut, let him begin to plough one of the Lord's fields with the plough of persecution. The shortest way to ruin is to meddle with a saint: the divine warning is, "He that toucheth you toucheth the apple of his eye"'.

"Let them all be confounded and turned back that hate Zion" (v5). And so say we right heartily, for so it shall be. If this be an imprecation, let it stand; for our heart says "Amen" to it. It is but justice that those who hate, harass, and hurt the good should be brought to naught. Those who confound right and wrong ought to be confounded, and those who turn back from God ought to be turned back. Loyal subjects wish ill to those who plot against their king.

'Confound their politics

Frustrate their knavish tricks'

is but a proper wish, and contains with it no trace of personal ill-will. We desire their welfare as men, their downfall as traitors. Let their conspiracies be confounded, their policies be turned back. How can we wish prosperity to those who would destroy that which is dearest to our hearts? This present age is so flippant that, if a man loves the Saviour, he is styled a fanatic, and if he hates the powers of evil, he is named a bigot. As for ourselves, despite all objectors, we join heartily in this commination; and would revive in our heart the old practice of Ebal and Gerizim, where those were blessed who bless God, and those were cursed who make themselves a curse to the righteous'[1].

From the earliest days of the Church, the entire Book of the Psalms, without any Psalms removed, was sung right through every week, or every month (as in the Book of Common Prayer). It was the custom of the Church in Scotland to sing the Book through consecutively Sunday by Sunday, without any omissions. We need to beware of the sin of King Jehoiakim, who sought to remove inspired words that he did not like (Jer. 36).

---

[1] C.H. Spurgeon, *The Treasury of* David.

APPENDIX 6

THE STRUCTURE OF
THE BOOK OF PSALMS

There is a danger of losing the big picture in reading or singing a short passage each day. The reader of these notes is therefore encouraged to think on the wider context as he or she works through the Psalms.

We should not look for a rigid structure in the Book of Psalms. Matthew Henry wrote, 'There is no connection (or very seldom) between one Psalm and another, nor any reason discernible for the placing of them in the order wherein we here find them'.[1]

We can however give some outline. The book has a unity and completeness. It is not a disjointed scrapbook of inspired songs.

The Hebrew Text is divided into five 'books'. These may have been separate collections brought together at various times and for various purposes. Some, following Jewish tradition, see these 'books' as reflecting the 5 books of the Pentateuch[2].

There is evidence of correspondence between the ancient Jewish 3-year cycle of Sabbath Torah readings *(seder)* and Psalms, as if the arrangement of the Psalms was designed to accompany this Sabbath worship[3].

---

[1] Matthew Henry, *Commentary* (Preface to the Psalms).

[2] E.W. Bullinger's *Companion Bible* makes an elaborate attempt to demonstrate this.

[3] Norman Snaith's *Hymns of the Temple* claims the start of the first 4 books of the Pentateuch in the lectionary corresponds to Psalms 1, 43, 73, 90. Psalm 23 coincides fittingly coincides

However, we must exercise caution. Bishop Horne wrote, 'The Hebrews have distributed them into five books, but for what reason, or upon what authority, we know not'. The 'books' themselves also have sub-sections or mini-collections.

Each 'book' ends with a doxology, Amens or Hallelujahs.

Book 1 = 1 - 41. Just over half of these Psalms are ascribed to David in their titles and they mainly use the name 'JEHOVAH' or 'LORD' when speaking of God.

Book 2 = 42 – 72. In this 'book' the name 'LORD' is used infrequently and 'God' is used instead. It begins with a section of 8 Psalms produced by 'the sons of Korah' (42-49).

Book 3 = 73 – 89. This is a shorter section. It includes a sub-section of Psalms by Asaph (73-83), most of which are a history series. There are also more Psalms by the 'sons of Korah' and others.

Book 4 = 90 – 106. This short 'book' has Psalms that seem to be associated with public worship. Few have titles. More than a third of this 'book', including 95—100, are about Messiah's Kingdom. The covenant name, JEHOVAH, or LORD, is mainly used for God.

Book 5 = 107-150. This last 'book' contains sub-sections – the Hallel (113-118) which is used by the Jews in their Passover services; The unique Psalm 119 with its 22 parts; The Songs of Ascent (120-134) probably used in pilgrim journeys up to Jerusalem, but having strong prophetic undertones; Five Hallelujah Psalms (beginning and ending with 'Hallelujah' – Praise

with Gen. 28:8-22.

the Lord) conclude the book of Psalms.

The 5 'books' are not arranged randomly. The first and the last Psalms plainly fit their place well. The other Psalms are mostly threaded together. Psalms with a similar thought or subject often link from the beginning of one to the start of the next. There is also some grouping of the Psalms by their titles, e.g. 'maschils' (Psalms 42-45).

Nine of the Psalms have an alphabetical structure (9, 10, 25, 34, 37, 111, 112, 119, and 145): the first letter of the first word of successive verses is in the sequence of the Hebrew alphabet.

The titles of the Psalms are accepted by the Jews as part of the text, and their verse numbering starts at the title. The titles are extremely ancient. The meaning and purpose of many of the Hebrew words in them has been lost in the mists of time. Even the Old Greek Version (produced more than 200 years BC) often just transliterates, or gives improbable translations of their meaning.

APPENDIX 7

PSALM 119

Psalm 119 has a unique alphabetical structure. There are 22 letters in the Hebrew alphabet. The eight lines in each of its 22 sections begin with the same letter of the Hebrew alphabet.

We have noted that in alphabetical Psalms there is often limited connection between each verse. They rarely follow a theme, and it is best to see such Psalms as a string of pearls, and to consider each verse separately.

However, Psalm 119 does have a theme – the 'word', or 'law', of the LORD. In singing through the whole Psalm it is important to take from each verse a lesson on devotedness to the LORD rather than looking for development of thought or a new subject.

The opening three verses can be seen as an introduction, or preface, to the Psalm.

C.H. Spurgeon described the Psalm as like a kaleidoscope or waves of a sea. What you see is the same truth, but always placed in a new light and new connections. It gives many turns to its one thought. Failing to take time to consider these various turns has led critics to dismiss the Psalm as little more than a word game or pious repetition.

Psalm 119 is a response to the instruction of Deuteronomy 6:1-9. The psalmist seeks to make God's law – all that he requires of us – a guide to every part of his life. Obeying God is the psalmist's governing principle for life. Although the Pharisees and Orthodox Jews developed this to a rigid code of commands and prohibitions, it is clear that this was not the thought of the psalmist. He desired a spiritual obedience, rather than a mechanical observance of rules. It is remarkable that there is no reference to sacrifice or the ceremonial law in the Psalm. The writer shows devotion and a close personal relationship with God. He often speaks directly to God in the words of the Psalm.

As the reader of this book uses this Psalm over 22 days, it is hoped that the following comments will be helpful in continuing to benefit from its fulness.

1. What God requires of us is expressed in almost every verse of the Psalm by means of such words as 'commandment' 'precept', 'way', 'path', 'testimony', 'word', 'saying', 'law'. It is profitable study to find these words in each verse.[1]

2. It has been suggested that the Psalm is like a journal, with thoughts written at different stages and at different times in the writer's life. Consider each part in the light of your own life experience

3. The verses of the Psalm are a mingling of three elements – testimony, prayer, and praise. It is helpful to note these as one works through the Psalm.

4. Charles Bridges[2] shows the likeness of the Psalmist's expressions to the experience, yearnings

---

[1] There are further notes on these 'law words' of the Psalm in C.W.H. Griffiths, *Every Psalm for Easy Singing Expanded Edition,* Appendix 2.

[2] Rev. Charles Bridges: *Psalm 119: As Illustrative of the Character and Exercises of Christian Experience.*

and faithfulness of Paul: insight into the extent and spirituality of the law of God (v.96 and Rom. 7:9); his continual conflict with indwelling sin (v.113, 163 and Rom. 7:14); awakening in him a spirit of wrestling prayer (v.25, 28 and Rom. 7:24); confidence in the God of his salvation (v.114, 176 and Rom. 7:25). Throughout his 475 page book Bridges demonstrates that the Psalm is a mirror of Christian experience from which we can greatly profit.

APPENDIX 8

'HOW SHALL WE SING
THE LORD'S SONG?'

It is plain from Scripture that the Psalms are intended to be sung by God's people in worship. We must therefore ask 'How?' Here is some practical advice.

1. We must understand the meaning of the passage of Scripture that we sing. (Ps 47:7; 1 Cor. 14:15).

2. Unless we sing complete Psalms, we must understand the theme or structure of each Psalm and use sections that provide a rounded and complete part.

3. The version that we sing must be written in intelligible English.

4. The version sung should be an accurate translation of the Hebrew. A loose paraphrase misses the whole point of singing words the Holy Spirit has given.

5. We must interpret and apply the Psalm correctly.

6. We should sing at a speed that allows us to reflect on, and understand, what we are singing.

7. The music should serve the words, rather than the music dominating the words. The tune is the carriage that conveys the Psalm. The Psalm should travel comfortably in it.

8. The music should not become an object of wonder or excitement. Our worship is essentially 'the fruit of our lips, giving thanks to his name' (Heb. 13:15). It is the 'word' which edifies, not the music (Col.

3:16), and we are to 'speak' our songs (Eph. 5:19). It is good if we can sing without having to concentrate upon the tune, and perhaps not even noticing it.

Lining out

The practice of 'lining out' could be considered when singing the Psalms with small children or with those unable to read. The person leading the worship reads or sings each line, which is then sung by the group together. This is slow, but allows reflection upon the words. This was once used extensively in Scottish and North American Presbyterian Churches. A modified form continues in the Gaelic services of Scottish Presbyterian Churches. Lining out (although not by that name) is still used by the Eastern Orthodox Churches. The practice is an ancient one.

APPENDIX 9

RESOURCES FOR PSALM SINGING

Some will have familiar friends that they will want to use in singing the Psalms, such as the old Scottish Metrical Psalter. Others will be looking for help in beginning what will be for them a new experience.

A companion book to this *Help* has been produced, *Every Psalm for Easy Singing*. It is divided into the same 365 portions as this book. See the advertisement at the end of this book.

The following notes describe the resources for singing the Psalms in English. We have excluded books that do not include all the Psalms or all the verses, and 'versions' that wander far from the Biblical text.[1]

I have tried to be clear and candid. I have no desire to offend by criticism of versions that have been the source of personal encouragement and blessing to the readers of this book.

1. ***The Scottish Metrical Psalter 1650*** is the 'Authorised Version' of Psalters. It has done good service to the Church and has stood the test of time for more than 350 years. It maintains simplicity of form and can be readily sung to familiar tunes.

   It provides all of the Psalms in Common Metre, with additional versions of 13 in alternative metres. The advantage of this is that, with a very small repertoire of tunes (even one!) it is possible to sing

---

[1] On this basis we have excluded the 1912 Psalter of the United Presbyterian Church.

through every Psalm. It was the version used by the Scottish Covenanters during their times of persecution. Christians all over the world continue to use this version.

Although it is faithful to the meaning of the Hebrew text, the lines often appear to be back to front to achieve metre and rhyme, and therefore the meaning is not immediately clear. The language is archaic and, quite apart from the old personal pronouns ('thou', 'thee', etc.) it has words that are unused today. 'Sith' (=since) and chuse (=choose) are each used 10 times. 'Froward thou kyth'st unto the froward wight' Ps. 18:26 (the stubborn one will find you hostile too). It also uses current words in an archaic sense – 'passengers' Ps. 80:12 for 'those who pass by'. The metre requires the pronunciation of –ed (as in some older hymns) unless otherwise indicated. Psalms 18:26 and 104:10-15 will illustrate some of the difficulties of language and metre, and 119:24 the embellishment of translation.

All the Psalms can be sung to familiar tunes such as 'Amazing Grace' (a.k.a. 'New Britain'); Crimond ('The Lord's my Shepherd'), O God Our Help in Ages Past (a.k.a. St. Anne),

The Free Church of Scotland (Continuing) has produced CD resources to teach the part-singing of the tunes of the Scottish Metrical Psalter.

There are a number of online resources available providing all the major tunes and the text of the Scottish Metrical Psalter.

2. A *Revised Version of the Scottish Psalter*
    produced in 1879 by the Presbyterian Church in
    Ireland[1].   The Committee that selected and
    arranged this was drawn from the PCI, the Church
    of Scotland, the Free Church of Scotland, and the
    United Presbyterian Church.   Its aim was 'to
    remove the blemishes which mar to some extent
    that admirable version'.   The changes were
    relatively minor and 'very tenderly dealt with' the
    old version.   However, it intermingled with the
    Scottish Psalter additional alternative Psalms of
    very varied quality.   It was the last attempt to
    update the Scottish Metrical Psalter, and met with a
    mixed reception.   Millar Patrick referred to it as
    'irritating tinkering' with the traditional Psalter.[2]

3. *The Psalms in Metre, Scottish Metrical Version
    with Tunes, Supplement, and Additional
    Versions* was used by the Reformed Presbyterian
    Church of Ireland from 1979.   In addition to the
    Scottish Metrical Psalter, its supplement has 85
    alternative versions drawn from the PCI revised
    Psalter, and the Psalter of the Reformed
    Presbyterian Church of North America.   It has a
    supplement of 47 tunes (including Cwm Rhondda,
    I need Thee every hour, etc).

Modern Psalters

The words of the following Psalm books are generally

---

[1] *The Psalter: A Revised Edition of the Scottish Metrical Version
of the Psalms with Additional Psalm Versions.* It was
reprinted as late as the 1960s and is available as a print on
demand book.

[2] Millar Patrick, *Four Centuries of Scottish Psalmody.*

in contemporary English. They also increase the number of different metres, and generally demonstrate enthusiasm for new tunes. They therefore do not work so well for those without the ability to read music.

4. ***The Book of Psalms for Singing*** was produced by the Reformed Presbyterian Church of North America in 1973. It was a thoroughgoing revision of earlier Psalters used by the RPCNA. It divided the Psalms into shorter sections (1A, 1B etc.), using more than 60 metres, some of them drawn from popular hymn tunes, and tied each Psalm to a tune. A slimmed down edition of this (***The Book of Psalms translated for Singing***, 1994) is in use by the Presbyterian Church in America (PCA) and suggests hymn tunes well-known in the PCA. This edition does not give alternative versions.

5. The Free Church of Scotland published ***Sing Psalms*** in 2003, giving new versions of all the Psalms. It sought to widen the number of metres used and introduced new tunes. The version sought to be faithful to the names of God in the Psalms and used LORD with capital letters for the Hebrew 'Yahweh' or 'JEHOVAH'. 'Every effort has been made to set out in verse what is found in the original text'.

6. The Reformed Presbyterian Church of Ireland produced ***The Psalms for Singing*** in 2004, which provided revised and new metrical versions. It also sought to widen the number of metres used. It treats with care the Divine names of the original, rather than choosing 'the LORD' or 'God' simply to fit the metre as in the old Scottish Metrical Version. It retained some of the best-known Psalms of the

old version. It specifically chose to use the New
International Version, the New American Standard
Version and existing psalters as its main resources
in English rather than working from scratch from
the Hebrew.

7. ***The Complete Book of Psalms for Singing*** was
produced for the Presbyterian Church of Eastern
Australia in 1991. 'The translation is a rendering in
international English, with reasonably natural
word-flow, rhymed in about 50% of cases'. It uses
about 40 different metres and gives a tune to each
Psalm.

8. ***The Book of Psalms for Worship*** was produced
by the Reformed Presbyterian Church of North
America in 2009. It is a thoroughgoing modern
language version that eliminates archaic words
apart from 3 Psalms retained from the Scottish
Metrical Psalter. It seeks to preserve the use of
'LORD' throughout when the Hebrew 'Yahweh' is
used for God. It divides the Psalms into sections,
each headed with a New Testament verse. We do
not fully see the point of this, and it gives the
Psalter the feel of a hymnbook. Indeed, one
Baptist publication reviewed it, referring to it as a
hymnbook throughout! As with other modern
versions it seeks to multiply the tunes (more than
80) and musical settings.

Crown and Covenant Publications have an online
tune resource for *The Book of Psalms for Singing* and
The Book of Psalms for Worship.

9. ***The Genevan Psalter***, produced at the
encouragement of Calvin, was completed in 1562.
Psalms were tied to specific tunes (100 metres and

123 tunes). Translations have been made into many languages, retaining the Genevan tunes. The tunes are unfamiliar to Christians brought up on hymns, or the Scottish Metrical Psalter. The tunes that have been brought across into hymnbooks have generally been mangled in the process. For those familiar with the Genevan Psalter, the Canadian and American Reformed Churches produce the **Anglo-Genevan Psalter** using the traditional tunes in their *Book of Praise*[1]. This was first published in 1984 and was later subject to a complete revision. The language is often quaint, and occasionally appears to be a translation from the Dutch, rather than from the original Hebrew. The most recent edition, which includes liturgical material and the Three Forms of Unity, is the 2014 *Book of Praise*.

Chanting

The use of chanting enables the original words and word order to be kept. This uses a simple repeated tune to which the words are fitted. Chanting is not a skill that many evangelicals possess these days. It can be an uphill struggle when done alone. It focuses the singer's mind on the words, but it could be questioned whether this meets the desire for 'spiritual songs' that can be sung with joy. The simple 'Anglican chant' focuses upon the words, matching the natural speech-rhythm of the words to a short piece of metrical music. More complex systems such as Gelineau Psalmody attempt to represent the rhythmic pattern of

---

[1] *Book of Praise: Anglo Genevan Psalter*, Premier Printing and Publishing, Manitoba.

the Hebrew, as set out in stanzas of different lengths.

The traditional version for chanting is the **Prayer Book Version (1662)**. The beauty and rhythm of its English is excellent. In its text it is imperfect. It is based on Coverdale's Bible (1539)[1], which at times follows the Latin Vulgate and the Greek Septuagint. Priory Records produced the complete Book of Psalms in the Prayer Book Version in Anglican chant on a set of 10 CDs. The quality is mixed. Where there is organ accompaniment it often drowns out the singing. The Church of Scotland published the Psalms in the **Authorised Version** pointed for chanting in 1929 toghether with the Scottish Metrical Psalter and hymns. It has chants allocated to each Psalm.

---

[1] Coverdale "allowed himself considerable freedom in dealing with the shape of the original sentences", (Westcott).

APPENDIX 10

FAMILY WORSHIP

This book is not a guide to personal or family worship. However, we hope that the following brief notes and suggestions will be useful in highlighting some basic principles and in signposting helpful resources.

1. Family worship is a means of grace, for the Lord is present wherever two or three are gathered in his name.

2. For children, it shows adults in worship on a daily basis and gives the regular and natural opportunity to engage every family member on spiritual matters.

3. In making family worship a priority over other activities in the home, it demonstrates the principle that 'man shall not live by bread alone, but by every word that comes forth from the mouth of God'.

'Family worship' should not just be something done for the children before they go to bed. It should indeed be 'family' worship, where adults and children worship together. There is no substitute for the head of the family adapting, explaining, and applying what is said in family worship.

The worship of the Church should be governed by 'the regulative principle'. The same principle must logically also apply to family and personal worship. The passage in Ephesians that instructs us how we should sing (Eph. 5:19) is followed by verses that are concerned with the ordering of Christian families.

'The regulative principle' may be defined as follows:

The acceptable way of worshipping the true God is instituted by himself, and so limited by his own revealed will, that he may not be worshipped according to the imaginations and devices of men, or the suggestions of Satan, under any visible representation, or in any other way not prescribed in holy Scripture.[1]

We are not to make an image of God in any way, nor to worship him in any other manner than he has commanded in his Word.[2]

At the same time as the Westminster Confession and Longer and Shorter Catechisms were being prepared, the General Assembly of Church of Scotland produced *The Directory for Family Worship* (1647), 'for piety and uniformity in secret and private worship, and mutual edification'. The James Begg Society has published a very helpful commentary and study guide on this, entitled *Returning to the Family Altar*.[3] We strongly recommend it. It asks and answers fifteen key questions, including, 'why and how is family worship to be maintained?'; 'what preparation is necessary for family worship?'; 'what are the basic elements of family worship?'

A further short consideration of the subject is produced by Reformation Heritage Books in its 'Family Guidance' series[4]. It considers: (1) Theological

---

[1] *Westminster Confession* on the Second Commandment.

[2] *Heidelberg Catechism*, Answer 96.

[3] Douglas W. Cronin, *Returning to the Family Altar: A Commentary and Study Guide on the 'Directory for Family Worship adopted by the General Assembly of the Church of Scotland in 1647'*. ISBN 0-9539241-8-1.

[4] Joel. R. Beeke, *Family Worship*. ISBN 978-1-60178-058-4.

Foundations of Family Worship. (2) The Duty of Family Worship. (3) Implementing Family Worship. (4) Objections against Family Worship. (5) Motivations for Family Worship. It includes the *Directory for Family Worship.*

A larger resource is *The Family Worship Book[1]*. It includes *The Directory for Family Worship*, Catechisms, a Bible reading scheme and other helpful suggestions and advice. It also includes a Family Psalter/Hymnal that has 68 Psalms and Psalm portions and 60 hymns. It nevertheless concludes with the statement 'a revival of Psalm-singing is one of the great needs of our day'.

'Family' worship should not begin when children are first added to the home, it should commence with marriage (or even as a part of marriage preparation!). It should not cease when children leave home. It is a lifelong privilege and responsibility. It should be a focal point of family reunions. Peter instructs us on husband - wife relations (1 Peter 3:1-7). Dr John Gill comments on v7 ('that your prayers be not hindered'); 'From hence we may observe, that family prayer is a duty incumbent on professors of religion, and great care should be taken that it be not neglected and hindered'.

All guides to family worship that we have seen assume that husband and wife are 'equally yoked' and there is an acceptance of the need for family worship. Where the headship of the man is not followed in this by the wife, or where the man does not have the capacity to lead because of his spiritual state, true family worship

---

[1] Terry L. Johnson (Ed.) *The Family Worship Book: A Resource Book for Family Devotions.* ISBN 1-85792-401-0.

becomes all but impossible. The oversight of the Church should constantly teach and reinforce the necessity of family worship, and support families accordingly in whatever way possible[1]. Family worship is an integral part of the worship of the Church and should be recognised as such.

We urge all our Christian readers to engage in regular family worship. Douglas Conin notes that some families may feel awkward about introducing Psalm singing into their family worship. His advice is 'the first step in overcoming a sense of uneasiness about singing together is simply to do it'!

[1] *The Second Helvetic Confession* (Chapter 29:2) urges 'Let lawful judgements and holy judges be established in the Church, who may maintain *(tuenantur)* marriages, and may repress all dishonesty and shamefulness, and before whom controversies in matrimony may be decided and settled'.

APPENDIX 11

THE PSALMS IN CONGREGATIONAL WORSHIP

The purpose of this book is to give help and encouragement to singing the Psalms daily at a personal or family level. It is beyond its scope to discuss Psalm singing in congregational worship.

We would encourage readers to carefully consider the case for using the Psalms in congregational worship.

Readers may find the following publications helpful:

- *Sing the Lord's Song. Biblical Psalms in Worship* by John W. Keddie. Crown and Covenant Publications. 74 pages

- *The Singing of Psalms in the Worship of God* by G.I. Williamson. The Covenanter Bookshop, Northern Ireland, 31 pages.

- *The Psalms in Christian Worship* by Rowland Ward. Presbyterian Church of Eastern Australia. 140 pages

- *God's Hymnbook for the Christian Church* by Malcolm Watts. The James Begg Society. 63 pages

- *The Songs of Zion* by Michael Bushell. Crown and Covenant Publications. 217 pages.

- *The Singing of Psalms the Duty of Christians under the New Testament* by Thomas Ford. The Presbyterian Standard, Issue 63/64.

SUPPLEMENT

THINKING POINTS

THINKING POINTS

These are open questions and suggestions intended to form the basis of discussion in a family or small group, or for personal study. They give an opportunity to 'search the Scriptures' on various topics. The object is to encourage the habit of Bible Study and close attention to the words of each Psalm.

If used for family worship, some preparation may be needed by the head of the family.

1. Why is Psalm 1 such a good introduction to The Psalms?

2. What are the 'cords' or 'chains' that governments of this world do not like? (2:3).

3. What does it mean to 'kiss the Son'? (2:12).

4. What does 'salvation is of the LORD' mean? (3:8). See also Jonah 2:9.

5. How can we sleep 'peacefully' (3:5; 4:8) when everything seems against us?

6. When does God hear your voice in the morning? (5:3).

7. Do we pray against the evil plans of wicked people? (5:10).

8. How do we know when God is 'rebuking' us? (6:1).

9. How (from the New Testament) do we know that our prayers will be received and accepted? (6:9).

10. When did you last do something nice to your enemies? (7:4).

11. We will hurt ourselves by doing wicked things (7:15, 16). What does the word the Lord Jesus spoke to Paul mean (Acts 26:14)?

12. What does God 'visiting us' mean? (8:4).

13. How do we go into *our* refuge in *our* time of need? (9:9).

14. Find examples in the Bible of wicked people who were caught in their own trap. (9:15).

15. Why does God sometimes seem to be far off from us? (10:1).

16. What does God raising his hand mean? (10:12, Deut. 32:39-43).

17. What can the righteous <u>do</u> when moral, religious, and doctrinal foundations are destroyed? (11:3).

18. How do *we* treat the Bible, and the words of Scripture? (12:6).

19. Do you pray this sort of prayer? What can you learn about prayer from this Psalm of David?

20. Why is an atheist foolish? (14:1).

21. What does it mean to abide, sojourn, or dwell with God? (15:1).

22. We are sinners and failures. Why are we called 'holy ones' (saints) and 'excellent'? (16:3).

23. Read Acts 2:14-33, which quotes this portion.

24. Does the LORD ever *visit* you at night? (17:3). (The word is used in Gen. 21:1 and 50:24).

25. Where else is death spoken of as falling asleep, and resurrection as waking up? (17:15).

26. What is meant by the 'cords of death and Sheol'? (18:4, 5). (See Psalms 88:3-8, 5-17, and 116:3).

27. These are the last words of David (2 Sam. 23:1). What were the last words of 'the rich man' (Luke 12:16-21); Stephen (Acts 6:56, 60); the Lord Jesus (John 19:30). What will your last words be?

28. 18:16 says 'he sent down from on high – took hold of me'. Compare Ps. 40:2, 3. Read Westminster Confession X.1 and/or Canons of Dort Heads 3-4 Article 11 on effectual calling.

29. 18:26 speaks of 'rewards'. After we are justified and our sin covered, our imperfect obedience becomes rewardable. Read 1 Cor. 3:11-15.

30. What does 'your gentleness has made me great' mean? (18:35). In what ways is God gentle with us?

31. Read of our victorious Saviour in Rev. 19:11-19.

417

32. Rom. 15:9 puts the words of v49 in the mouth of Christ, saying he would give thanks and praise (literally, 'sing Psalms') 'among the nations'. Read Rom. 15:8-13.

33. Spend some time this week where the heavens can be seen, and think about God's greatness.

34. What are 'presumptuous sins'? (19:13). Think of an example.

35. What does 'setting up your banners' mean? (20:5). See Exod. 17:15; Song 6:10, Isa. 59:19.

36. This portion may be read as the Covenant of Redemption between God the Father and Christ ('the king'). Read of the glory promised to Christ in this covenant in John 17:1-12.

37. Unless we have obtained peace by the blood of Christ's cross (Col. 1:20), we are numbered among the LORD's enemies. Read Eph. 2:1-10.

38. Why did the Father forsake the Lord Jesus on the Cross? (22:1).

39. Read the account of Christ's death in Matt 27:35-50.

40. Christ was and is 'truly human, like us in all respects, apart from sin'. Consider how the description of his sufferings in this portion confirms his humanity.

41. We are Christ's brothers and sisters, and share his victory and glory. Read Hebrews 2.

42. Read the words of the Good Shepherd in John 10.

43. Consider Jesus washing his disciples' feet and the cleansing that he gives to us. 24:4 and John 13:3-11.

44. If you had to face death like Margaret Wilson, which Psalm would you sing?

45. From today's portion, what sort of people does God guide and teach?

46. 25:18. 'Forgive' here means 'to bear away'. Are you, like Bunyan's pilgrim, bearing your own sins (Lev. 5:17), or has the Lord Jesus borne them away from you (John 1:29, 1 Pet. 2:24)?

47. 'Compass God's altar' (26:6) by reading Mark 15.

48. God's glory dwelt in the Temple (26:8). What promises of God's presence do we have when we meet together?

49. Are you afraid of the dark? (27:1).

50. 27:11. Read the parts of *Pilgrim's Progress* that speak of 'by-path meadow'.

51. Where is your 'speaking place' with God? (28:2).

52. In what ways is the LORD's voice like thunder?

53. Why is night time often a time of sorrow? (30:5). What can we learn from this?

54. What does it mean to be 'content' in every phase of your life? Phil. 4:11, 12.

55. Consider the way you pray compared with the example in v1-5.

56. What does God 'vindicating' mean? Why is it important that God does this?

57. What is 'the goodness' God has in store for us?

58. What does it mean to 'wait on the LORD'? (31:24).

59. What is meant by 'transgression', 'sin', 'iniquity', and 'deceit' (32:1, 2).

60. Consider the use of a 'bridle and bit' (32:9) in God's dealings with a believer.

61. Do instruments have a place in the worship of God under the New Covenant?

62. What does it mean to 'fear God'? (33:8).

63. Can you think of examples of 33:16 in the Bible?

64. What does it mean to 'trust in his holy name'? (33:21).

65. Relate the events of this Psalm's title (1 Sam. 21:10-15) to the words of this Psalm.

66. Where else can we read about angels protecting God's people? (34:7).

67. What is the significance of not a bone being broken? (34:20). Exod. 12:46; John 19:46.

68. What is chaff and what is winnowing? (35:5; 1:4). What did John the Baptist mean when he spoke about Jesus? (Matt. 3:12).

69. Are we ungrateful to those who have helped us? (35:12-16).

70. What, where and when is 'The Great Congregation'? (35:18).

71. God 'delights in our well-being' (35:27). What does this mean?

72. Do we really 'hate' what God says is wrong? (36:4).

73. What does it mean to be under the shadow of the LORD's wings? (36:7).

74. What does it mean to 'cast' or 'roll' something on the LORD? (37:5). CAN you give an example?

75. What does 'meekness' mean? (37:11).

76. Have you ever borrowed and not given back? (37:21). What should you do about it now?

77. What does the Bible say about beggars? (37:25). Can you name a beggar in the Bible?

78. Compare 37:31 with Psalm 37:23; 26:1 and 73:2.

79. Where else in Scripture are people spoken of as being like trees?

80. God 'chastises' in anger, and 'chastens' in love. How can we tell the difference?

81. Do we control our tongues? Compare 38:13, 14 with Isa 53:7; 1 Pet. 2:23; and Jas. 3:1-12.

82. David pleads with God not to be distant from him (38:21; 22:1, 2, 11, 19). Do we experience God's closeness in our daily lives?

83. Compare 39:4 and 5 with Ps 90:9 and 10.

84. What does the Bible say about moths? (39:11).

85. The LORD delivered David (40:2). Has he ever saved you from that sort of situation?

86. Find out about the four sacrifices of 40:6. Why did God

420

'not desire' them?

87. Compare the ending of the Psalm from its beginning. What do you learn from this?

88. Are we considerate for the needs of the poor and the weak? Give an example of how we should do this.

89. What evidence is there that the Lord Jesus treated Judas as a friend? (41:9).

90. When did you last know a time of 'intimate fellowship with God'? (42:1, 2).

91. If people asked if your God is real, what answer would you give?

92. Suggest practical ways to avoid being 'cast down' (43:5).

93. Read about a time when God delivered his Church.

94. What does it mean to be false to God's covenant? (44:17).

95. Consider and contrast Paul's use of 44:22 in Rom. 8:31-39.

96. In what ways are we 'fellows' of the Lord Jesus? (45:7).

97. Consider other verses like 45:10 and 11 that speak of marriage or discipleship.

98. How many names are given to God in this Psalm? What do they mean?

99. What other Scriptures speak of God being 'enthroned'? (47:8).

100. How many names are given to Jerusalem in this portion?

101. What was in the inner parts of the Temple? (48:9).

102. What do you want to tell your children about what God has done in your lifetime? (48:13).

103. Read Luke 12:13-34. Compare today's portion with the words of the Lord Jesus.

104. Find and read the poem *Ozymandias*. What does it and this Psalm say about human greatness?

105. Find out more about the LORD's 'shekinah glory' (50:2).

106. What other references are there to sacrifices of praise or thanksgiving? (50:14).

107. In what sense do we as Christians 'take God's covenant into our mouths'? (50:16).

108. Read about the death of Lady Jane Grey (Foxe's Book of Martyrs).

109. What is hyssop? Where else is it mentioned in the Bible?

110. What is 'a broken and a contrite heart'? (51:17).

111. In what way(s) is David like an olive tree? (52:8).

112. Read Romans 3:10-23, which quotes 53:1.

113. What does 'save me by your name' mean? (54:1).

114. 55:4 refers to 'the terrors of death'. Compare Ps. 23:4; Luke 1:79 and Rom. 8:35-39.

115. Read Numb. 16:1-35.

116. Compare 55:22 with Ps. 37:5.

117. Consider what 56:3 and 4 say about overcoming fear.

118. What comfort does it give us that the LORD 'keeps count' of our wandering and keeps our tears 'in his bottle'?

119. Compare 57:1 with Matt. 23:37.

120. What do you think David means by telling different things to wake up?

121. Can you think of other places in the Bible where wicked people are called 'snakes'? (58:4, 5). What does that comparison teach us?

122. 'Shall not the Judge of all the earth do right' (58:11 and Gen. 18:25). Consider these verses in connection with Rom. 9:14-24.

123. Where else in the Bible do we read of God laughing? (59:8).

124. We read about wild dogs in a city (59:14, 15) in 1 Kgs. 21:23. Who did they eat?

125. Compare 60:1 with Rom. 11.

126. What does 'Judah is my sceptre' (or 'lawgiver') mean? (60:7). See Gen. 49:10 and Numb. 24:17.

127. There are three 'forevers' in today's portion. What are

they?

128. How much time do we spend quietly 'waiting upon God'? (62:1 and 5).

129. How much respect should we give someone because of their status? Compare 62:4, 9 with Acts 24:10, 11 and Jas. 2:1-9.

130. Where is 'the wilderness of Judea'? (63:1). What is it like?

131. What does it mean to 'vow' or to 'swear'? (63:11). Compare Deut. 6:13; Isa. 45:23; Phil. 2:10.

132. How many times does the psalmist speak of the *secretive* actions of wicked men in this portion?

133. David knew a lot about archery (64:3, 4, 7). Can you think of any story where David used a bow and arrow?

134. The word the AV translates 'purge' in 65:3 means 'to cover' or 'to make atonement'. What is 'atonement'?

135. The 'God's river' is mentioned in 65:9. Read about the river Ezekiel describes (Ezek. 47:1-12).

136. Can you think of other places in Scripture where people are invited to 'come and see'? (66:5).

137. Find out how silver was refined (66:10). What spiritual lessons does this teach us?

138. Compare the testimony of the psalmist (66:16, 17) with that of the demoniac – Mark 5:1-21. If you can, read Christmas Evans sermon on Mark 5, where he describes his return to his family.

139. Compare this Psalm with the Levitical blessing of Numb. 6:24-26.

140. Look up other references to smoke and wax (e.g. Psalms 37:20 and 97:5; Hos. 13:3; Mic. 1:4).

141. Where else is rain (68:9) described as a blessing in Scripture?

142. Paul applies 68:18 to Christ's gifts to the Church. What gifts are listed in Eph. 4:7-13?

143. Cush will one day eagerly seek after God (68:31). Where

is Cush?

144. Read about Jesus prayer in Gethsemane (Matt. 26:36-46), thinking about the words of this Psalm.

145. Think about the 'zeal' of the Lord Jesus (69:9). Read John 2:13-17.

146. Today's portion and Heb. 5:7-9 are remarkable verses. Should we not all the Lord to teach us obedience through suffering?

147. Judas is spoken about here (69:25, Acts 1:20). Did he hear the Lord's warning to all of us in Matt. 7:20-23?

148. How often do you praise God's name with a song? (69:30).

149. Notice the urgency of 70:1 and 5. How earnest and urgent are we in our prayers? Read Luke 18:1-8.

150. Consider how awful abortion is in the light of v6 and Jer. 1:4-6.

151. What does the psalmist want to do in the future, especially in old age? What do you want to do then?

152. Compare the psalmist's state in the earlier verses with his state in these verses.

153. Compare the justice and peace of Solomon's reign with that of Christ the 'Greater than Solomon' (Matt. 12:42).

154. Compare yesterday and today's portion with Isa. 42:1-17.

155. Their blood shall be precious (72:14). Consider Gen. 4:10, 11; Ps. 116:15; and Rev. 6:9-11.

156. What does 'Amen' mean? (72:20). See 2 Cor. 1:20, Rev. 3:14; 22:20.

157. What does it mean to have a pure or clean heart? (73:1).

158. How does 73:15 provide a defence against temptations to sin?

159. Can we say 73:25 truthfully with the psalmist?

160. Compare 74:3, 4 with prophecies of Antichrist in Matt. 24:15; 2 Thess. 2:4; and Rev. 13:14, 15.

161. What is meant by 'our signs'? (74:9). Consider Matt.

16:1-3; 24:32, 33; 1 Pet. 1:19, 20.

162. God is in control of every change that affects us. Consider Eccles. 3:1-8.

163. In our prayers today let us 'remind God' (74:18,25) of the challenges we and our family face.

164. What does Asaph mean by 'your name is near'? (75:1). See Deut. 4:7; Ps. 34:18.

165. What is meant by the cup of wine in 75:8? See Ps. 11:6; Rev. 14:9, 10; 16:19.

166. Compare what happened to the Midianites in Jdgs. 7:18-25 with 76:5.

167. Do you fear God? How would 'the fear of God' affect the way we live? Consider Mal. 2:5, 6.

168. Do you know someone who is having 'a day of trouble'? (77:2; 20:1). Pray for them today.

169. Think of one thing that God did 'of old' in the Scriptures (77:11) that will help you when you feel abandoned by the LORD.

170. Do you give respect to your pastor or minister as one whom God has given to lead his Church? (77:20; Acts 20:28).

171. What does this portion teach about the duty of parents toward their children? Read also Deut. 6:1-9.

172. Can you think of others in the Bible who 'turned back' (78:9) from service and obedience?

173. The things spoken of here were given as examples to us (1 Cor. 10:1-13). What can we learn from them?

174. How many times has God turned his anger away from you in the last week? (78:38).

175. 'Remember' ways in which God has intervened in your life in the last month?

176. What is meant by 'a deceitful bow'? (78:57) (see also Hos. 7:16).

177. What sort of worship pleases God? (78:58-60). Read

Westminster Confession XXI.1, and/or Shorter Catechism Q.50, and/or Heidelberg Catechism Q. 96.

178. David had to shepherd the flock before he shepherded Israel (78:71, 72). Compare 1 Tim. 3:4,5.

179. Using this passage pray for today's persecuted Church.

180. How do the things that are described in this portion affect 'the glory of God's name'? (79:9).

181. God hears our sighs and groans (79:11). Read and think about Exod. 2:23-25; 3:7-10.

182. What is taught by the LORD 'dwelling between the cherubim'? (80:1, Exod. 25:21, 22). Compare this with Ezek. 43:1-9.

183. Pray for the conversion of the Jewish people (80:7).

184. Find other passages where Israel is called a vine or a vineyard.

185. Christ is here referred to as 'the man of your right hand'. What ways is this true, and what is meant by this. (see Matthew Henry's commentary).

186. How are we to regard the Feast days of Israel? Does God command feast days for the Church? (81:3, 4).

187. What does the command to open our mouth for God to fill it mean? (81:10).

188. Compare 81:12 with Rom. 1:18-32.

189. Read and consider Rom.13:1-7 in connection with this portion.

190. 82:8 is not praying for the Last Judgment (Rev. 20:11-15). What is it praying for?

191. Consider Psalm 2 in connection with 83:4, 5.

192. Look up the events to which Asaph refers.

193. Spend some time thinking about the picture language Asaph uses in 83:13-15.

194. We do not have a Temple or a holy building. How can we follow the example of the writer in 84:1-4, 10?

195. What names of God are used in this Psalm? Do we use

God's different names when we speak to him?

196. In what ways has God been 'favourable to our land'? Thank him in prayer.

197. What is meant by mercy and truth meeting, and righteousness and peace kissing? (85:10).

198. Are you saved? Are you backslidden? Call to God in the words of 86:5-7, 15-17.

199. How many superlatives (full, lowest, evermore, etc) can you find in this Psalm?

200. What is a token? (86:17). God will not always give a token, but it is not wrong to ask (see Jgs. 5:17; 6:36-40).

201. Read Isa. 56:1-8; Zech. 8:20-23 regarding all nations finding their blessing in Zion.

202. Consider the solitude and loneliness of the Lord Jesus in Gethsemane, his trial, and death, in the light of 88:8, 18.

203. What will be forgotten about us when we die and what will be remembered? (88:12).

204. Anyone, young or old, may be close to death (88:15). Read the warning in Luke 12:16-21.

205. One day every believer will fulfil 89:1. Read Rev. 5:8-14.

206. 'A holy awe must fall upon us in all our approaches to God' (Matthew Henry on 89:7). Is it so in our Church services?

207. The word 'joyful sound' (AV 89:15) is translated 'loud shout' in Ezra 3. Read about it in Ezra 3:10-13.

208. 89:20. Jesus is our King, Prophet and Priest. All three were anointed in the Old Testament (2 Sam. 2:4; 1 Kgs. 19:16; Exod. 28:41). What does this mean for us?

209. Why does God chasten us? (89:30-32). Read Heb. 12:5-11.

210. Read the prophecy of Israel's apostasy and God's wrath on them. Deut. 32:15-43.

211. Compare Ethan's 'bearing in his bosom' (89:50) with Paul's feelings towards Israel (Rom. 9:1-3; 10:1).

212. Consider the infinity and eternity of God (90:2). See also 2 Pet. 3:8, Job 11:7-10 (Westminster Shorter Catechism Q4 / Belgic Confession 1).

213. Do you have sins you think are secret? (90:8). Read the warning of Luke 12:1-3.

214. Do you desire to show 'the beauty of the LORD' (90:17), or are good looks more important to you? Read 1 Tim. 2:9,10 and 1 Pet. 3:1-5).

215. Live today/tomorrow as someone 'under the shadow of the Almighty' (v1). What does this mean?

216. Consider how the ministry of angels affects you – 91:11; 2 Kgs. 6:16, 17; Heb. 1:13, 14.

217. This Psalm is headed 'A Psalm. A Song for the Sabbath Day'. How do you keep the weekly Sabbath of rest and worship?

218. Worldly people are 'brutish' (92:6). In what sense are they like cattle/brute-beasts?

219. Are you 'planted' and 'flourishing' in the house of the LORD? (92:13).

220. Where is the clothing of the Lord Jesus described in the Bible? (93:1). What can we learn from this?

221. What does it mean that God is 'a GOD of vengeances'? (94:1).

222. Consider the theory of evolution in the light of 94:9.

223. What other people in the Bible lost all human help? e.g. 2 Tim. 4:14-18.

224. Why do you think the early Church began its services with this Psalm?

225. Read Heb. 3:1-4:7 where this Psalm is quoted.

226. Do we tell others God's salvation daily? (96:2). If not, why not? See also Mark 6:15; Acts 8:4.

227. What would the heavens, the earth, the sea, the field, and the trees look like if they rejoiced? (96:11, 12).

228. Is your country ruled on the basis of 'righteousness and

justice'? (97:2).

229. What are 'images' and 'idols'? (97:7). Read Heidelberg Catechism Q.96-98, and/or Shorter Catechism Q.49-52.

230. The Scripture commands us to sing (98:1) many times. How could you learn to sing God's praises better?

231. How many different sounds are dedicated to God's praise in this portion?

232. Find out what the cherubim (99:1) symbolise. See Gen. 3:24; Exod. 25:10-22; Ezek. 10; Rev. 4:6-11.

233. Can you find examples of Samuel's prayers? (99:6)

234. How do you enter your place of worship? (100:4).

235. Could this be 'the President's Psalm', or 'the Prime Minister's Psalm' in a democracy?

236. Why is speedy justice and punishment a good thing? (101:8).

237. Explain the comparisons of 102:3, 4.

238. Do you praise or blame other people for what happens to you? See 102:10.

239. Compare 102:16 with Isa. 60:1-3 and Matt. 24:30, 31).

240. God has given us a written revelation. Why is this important? Compare 102:18 with Rom. 15:4 and 2 Tim. 3:15-17.

241. God is unchangeable. Why is this important for our trust in him? See 102:27, Mal. 3:6, Jas. 1:7.

242. Consider each of the 'alls' of this portion.

243. What does the LORD do for those who are 'oppressed'? (103:6). What does 'oppressed' mean? See also Acts 10:38).

244. What does 'keeping God's covenant' mean? (103:18).

245. How do we bless the LORD 'with our soul'? (103:22).

246. How do angels differ from us? (104:4).

247. Where does God promise that he will not flood the earth again? (104:9).

248. Should we complain about rainy days? (104:13).

249. What does God's provision for all living things teach us? See Matt. 6:25-34.

250. God made day and night to order men's lives (Gen. 1:14-19). Do you have a good daily routine?

251. Playful Leviathan (104:26) is a mysterious creature. What can you find out about it?

252. Do you 'sing to God' (104:33) at home, or just when you go to Church?

253. What does 'glorying in God's holy name' mean? (105:3).

254. How long is a 'generation'? (105:8). Consider Numb. 32:13.

255. Read about Joseph in Gen. 50:14-21.

256. Which plagues are not mentioned in this portion?

257. What was God's 'holy word' to Abraham? (105:42).

258. What does it mean to be 'chosen' by God? (106:5). Read Westminster Confession III and/or Canons of the Synod of Dort I.6-8.

259. What does 'nevertheless' (106:8 AV) mean?

260. Read Numb. 16:1-35 for the background to this portion.

261. Compare Phineas (son of Eleazar) with the Lord Jesus Christ.

262. Why was it wrong for Israel to share the land with the Canaanites?

263. Compare the endings of the five 'Books' of the Psalms - 41:13; 72:18-20; 89:52; 106:48; 150:1-6.

264. How do you get from a v4 situation to a v7 situation?

265. Who in the Bible was released from captivity by God?

266. How does a word from God (or the Word of God) heal us? (107:20).

267. Read Paul's experience at sea in Acts 27:9-44.

268. Try to find out more about the Hebrew word *ḥeṣed*, translated 'loving-kindness', 'steadfast love', and 'mercy'

(107:43).

269. Do you wake early enough to meet with God before you go to work or school? (108:2).

270. Read and consider Isa. 11:10-16 in connection with today's portion.

271. Write down a problem you face, and decide on times when you will pray about it. 109:4. See Paul's example in 2 Cor. 12:7-9.

272. Compare the experience of wicked Judas (109:6, 7) with Joshua the High Priest (Zech. 3:1-7).

273. Read Rev. 19:11-21 in connection with this portion.

274. What does the LORD 'standing at the right hand of the poor' mean? (109:31).

275. Read how the Lord Jesus used this Psalm in 22:41-46.

276. Read about Melchizedek in Gen. 14:14-24 and Heb. 6:20 - 7:28.

277. The Jewish festivals caused the LORD's 'wonderful works' to be remembered (111:4). How do we remember his 'wonderful works'?

278. Have you begun to be wise? (111:10).

279. Will we be wealthy if we keep God's commandments? (112:3). If not, what does this mean?

280. Read Job 1:1 – 2:10; 42:10 in connection with this portion.

281. How do we 'serve' the LORD? 113:1. See Rom. 6:15-23.

282. What does 114:4 refer to? See Exod. 19:18 and Ps. 68:8.

283. Berkhof's *Systematic Theology* quotes 115:3 three times. Why is it an important verse? See too 135:6.

284. In what ways is the LORD our shield? (115:9-11).

285. Does 115:16 say anything about space exploration?

286. How can we be 'at rest' (116:7) in a stressful world?

287. What does Paul mean when he quotes 116:10 in 2 Cor. 4:13?

288. What are or were your 'bonds' or 'chains'? (116:16). Has the LORD freed you from them?

289. David Baron translates 117:2 'his grace has prevailed over us'. Is this your experience? Read Eph. 2:4-10.

290. Are we fearful of what other people may do to us? See verse 6. Read Matt. 10:28 and Rom. 8:31-39.

291. Read v9. Who are our 'princes' (AV) today?

292. What are the gates that are spoken of in 118:19, 20?

293. What is a 'head corner stone'? (118:22). Why is it important in a building? How does this relate to the Lord Jesus?

294. How many different words are used in this portion for God's rules that we must follow?

295. Consider the sinful pressures on young people (119:9) and the example of Daniel (Dan. 1:8-20; 3:12-18).

296. 119:19. Consider Abraham's life and ours. Read Heb. 11:8-16, 12:1.

297. What does 'enlarging the heart' (119:32) mean? See also 2 Cor. 6:11-13. What was Paul saying to the Corinthians?

298. Consider 'enduring to the end' (119:33) and the perseverance of believers John 10:27-29. Read Westminster Confession XVII and/or Heidelberg Catechism Q1.

299. Who in the Bible, or Christian history, has had to speak before kings? (119:46).

300. Consider starting a diary of your walk with God so that you may 'keep in mind' and 'remember' what the LORD has done for you.

301. What is your circle of friends like? (119:63).

302. Have you had trials? (119:67, 71). How could you use your experience to help others (2 Cor. 1:3-7)?

303. Our body is God's workmanship (119:73). What are the implications of this regarding a person's gender? Read Gen. 1:27; Ps. 139:14-16.

304. 119:84. How many years do you have left in your life if you live to 70 [90]? How many days?

305. All things are God's servants (119:91). What does Paul say about 'all things' in Rom. 8:31?

306. Find out what the Bible says about honey, and what it symbolises. 119:103.

307. Find out about the 'The Solemn League and Covenant' and the Scottish Covenanters. 119:106.

308. What is dross? (119:119). What does this verse mean when it speaks of the fate of wicked people?

309. Read Nehemiah 1. Make 119:126 a prayer for the country where you live.

310. How do you react when wicked people break God's laws? (119:136). Think about Lot (2 Peter 2:6-8).

311. It is good to store up God's word in our heart so that we do not forget it (119:139,141). Could you start learning some verses of the Bible by heart?

312. Do you try to 'pray in your head', or do you speak to God when you pray? (v149).

313. 119:154 says 'plead my cause'. What is the Lord Jesus doing for us now? Read Heb. 7:22-28.

314. How many times do you praise God every day? (119:164).

315. 119:176. Read Luke 15:1-7.

316. Our words can be dangerous things (120:2-4). Read Jas. 3:1-12 and consider Isa. 6:5-7 with it.

317. 121:1. Do you look up or down when you pray? See John 11:41, 17:1; Ps. 123:1 and Ezra 9:6, Luke 18:13. See also Ps. 141:8.

318. Do you 'pray for the peace of Jerusalem'? (122:6). We have a responsibility towards the Jewish people. Read Rom. 11:15, 23.

319. 123:2 refers to faithful and attentive slaves. What is the Bible's attitude towards slavery? See Lev. 25:39-46; Eph. 6:5-9

320. Use the words of this Psalm to thank God for a past deliverance you have had.

321. 125:3 is a promise. What does it mean?

322. What is meant by 'sowing in tears' and 'reaping in joy'? (126:5).

323. You might not build a house (127:1), but put something you hope to do in these words; 'except the LORD does XXX, all my efforts are in vain'.

324. What does the picture language of 128:3 mean?

325. How do we greet our fellow Christians when we meet them? 129:8; Ruth 2:4; Rom. 16:3-16.

326. Have you ever been 'waiting for the dawn'? (130:6). How did you feel when it happened?

327. Compare the words of David in this portion with the lesson Baruch had to learn? Jer. 45:1-5.

328. 132:2. David made a promise to God. Have you ever done that? Have you kept your promise? Read Acts 5:1-11.

329. In 132:16 God makes a promise. What clothing has been promised to us now and in heaven? Read Isa. 61:3,10, and Rev. 3:4,5; 19:14.

330. How can our family have the unity spoken of here?

331. Why do some people lift their hands when they praise God or pray? (134:2). See Psalms 28:2, 141:2, 143:6, and 1 Tim. 2:8.

332. Why did God choose Israel? (135:4). Read Deut. 7:6-8. Rom. 9:1-13.

333. Why did God give the holy land to Israel? Read Ps. 44:1-3; Zech. 2:11, 12.

334. 135:21 speaks of the LORD dwelling at Jerusalem. Read how he will one day dwell with his elect forever Rev. 21:1-4.

335. Apart from this Psalm 'his mercy is forever' is used sixteen other times in Scripture. How many of these can you find? [The AV translates it differently in Ps. 100:5].

336. 136:16. How does God lead us today?

337. 136:25. Why should we pray 'Give us this day our daily bread'?

338. What things can we learn about singing in worship from 137:3,4?

339. Why is Jesus called 'the King of kings'? (138:4).

340. What is meant by 'God's right hand'? (138:7).

341. What words have been 'on your tongue' today? (139:4).

342. Read how Jonah tried to run away from God. Jonah 1 and 2.

343. God's thoughts are more than the sand at the seaside (139:17, 18). Try counting how many grains of sand are needed to fill an egg cup!

344. Are you brave enough to pray David's prayer in 139:23, 24? See also Ps. 19:12.

345. Read Paul's use of this Psalm in Rom. 3:9-23. What is Paul saying about sin?

346. Think of ways in which evil 'hunts' very bad people. 140:11. See also Numb. 32:23 and Prov. 13:21.

347. 141:2. In what ways is incense like prayer?

348. 141:5. Why was Nathan's reproof so effective in bringing David to repentance? Read 2 Sam. 12:1-15.

349. David prayed to get out of prison so he could praise God (142:7). In the New Testament, who praised God in prison, and who praised God when they got out?

350. How are we 'justified' before God? Compare 143:2b with Gal. 3:10-14.

351. How does God teach us to do his will? (143:10).

352. Our warfare with Satan requires strength and skill 144:1. Read Eph. 6:10 and 1 Sam. 17:37-40. Ask the Lord teach you to be a great warrior for him.

353. In what sense are the LORD's people 'happy'? (144:15).

354. How do we 'meditate'? Ps. 145:5 (AV 'speak of' – the same word as in Ps. 119:15, 23, 48, 78).

355. When will all the LORD's works give thanks to him? (145:10).

356. What is it to 'call upon God in truth'? (145:18). Read John 4:19-24.

357. 146:4. One day you will die and all your thoughts and plans in this world will end. What do you want to leave behind for people to remember you by?

358. 147:3. Read Isa. 1:5,6, and the story of the Good Samaritan in Luke 10:29-37. This is what the Lord does for us sinners.

359. Consider God's care for all his creation … and you. 147:9. Read Matt. 6:24-34.

360. Consider the LORD's electing love to Israel. Read Rom. 9.

361. Consider this portion in connection with God's unchangeable purposes in election. Read Jer. 31:35, 36 and 33:24-26.

362. What does 'a people near him' (148:14) mean? Read Deut. 4:5-9 and Eph. 2:11-22.

363. Where is dancing referred to in the New Testament? Is it found in connection with worship there?

364. We have a two-edged sword now (149:6; Heb. 4:12). The Lord Jesus has one too (Rev. 1:16, 2:12). Beware of Satan's two-edged sword (Prov. 5:1-14).

365. Read Rev 5. Hallelujah!

ADVERTISMENT
Other books by Pearl Publications

Every Psalm for Easy Singing:
Verse Only Edition

This is a new translation of the Psalms to enable the entire book of Psalms to be sung. It uses a single metre throughout, so individuals and families can easily sing without requiring musical ability.

This edition simply has the verses for singing and suggested tunes. It is arranged in the same daily portions as the *Help for using the Psalms in Personal and Family Worship*, which enables the singing of the complete Book of Psalms in a year.

250 pages

Every Psalm for Easy Singing: A translation for singing arranged in daily portions. Verse Only Edition

    Paperback: ISBN 978-1-901397-06-2

    Hardback: ISBN 978-1-901397-07-9

    E Book: ISBN 978-1-901397-08-6

Every Psalm for Easy Singing:
Expanded Study Edition

This expanded edition in larger format has extensive footnotes and appendices. The extra materials explain translation issues and show the basis of the decisions made in translating, as well giving exegetical comments. For example, it shows how we have carefully distinguished Hebrew words in the translation, such as the different words used for man and for God.

It shows how, in the preparation of this translation for singing, constant reference was made to Reformation and post-Reformation translations such as the Geneva Bible, the Authorised Version, the Welsh Bible, the Dutch States Bible (*Statenvertaling*), and Calvin's translation.

It uses the same 365 portions as *A Help for using the Psalms in Personal and Family Worship*. It is an aid to serious Bible Study, and will assist anyone who leads group or family worship working through the Psalms.

410 pages

Every Psalm for Easy Singing: A translation for singing arranged in daily portions. Expanded Study Edition

Paperback: ISBN 978-1-901397-09-3

Hardback: ISBN 978-1-901397-10-9

E Book: ISBN 978-1-901397-11-6

Chosen – Called – Kept:

The Conclusions of the Synod of Dort translated and arranged for prayerful reflection and study

In 1619 all the Reformed Churches of Europe met to discuss the great subject of 'How God saves'. That gathering was the Synod of Dort. Its decisions were unanimous. Chosen-Called-Kept is a new and very accessible translation of its conclusions. Its imaginative typesetting is designed to encourage regular and prayerful reflection on these great truths. It is not an edited version or a paraphrase. It is particularly useful for the catechising of children and young people.

First published in September 2022.

100 pages

Chosen – Called – Kept.   The Conclusions of the Synod of Dort translated and arranged for prayerful reflection and study

Paperback: ISBN 978-1-901397-01-7

Hardback: ISBN   978-1-901397-02-4

PEARL PUBLICATIONS BOOKS are available online on Amazon (and Takealot in South Africa) and from bookshops via wholesale distributors. Ebooks are available from a range of outlets. Enquiries are invited for direct bulk sales to Bookshops, Churches and Colleges.

Pearl Publications is working on a not for profit basis and any proposals to make our books available more widely and at a cheaper price would be very welcome.

Printed in Great Britain
by Amazon

22256861R00248